BRUSSELS

Cities of the Imagination

Cities OF THE IMAGINATION

BRUSSELS

A *cultural and literary history*

André de Vries

Signal Books
Oxford

First published in 2002 by
Signal Books Limited
36 Minster Road
Oxford
OX4 1LY
www.signalbooks.co.uk

Reprinted and updated, 2008

A catalogue record for this book is available from the British Library

ISBN 978-1-904955-47-4

Drawings by Nicki Averill

Cover Design: Baseline Arts
Production: Devdan Sen
Cover Images: Franky De Meyer/istock; Belgian Tourist Office; BITC O. van de
Kerckhove, Brussels International

Printed in India

Contents

Foreword

Brussels is increasingly visible on the world map, its profile growing ever higher. But its familiarity conceals a distinct literary deficit. The city is not associated, to say the very least, with an evocative sense of the imaginary. If someone strolling on the banks of the Seine or the Thames is constantly reminded of books they have read, if one cannot cross the Pont Mirabeau without Apollinaire's verses coming to mind, if the streets of London inevitably evoke pages from Dickens just as St. Petersburg's solstice nights recall Dostoevsky, nothing comparable, at first sight, happens in Brussels. Here is a city, it seems, untouched by literature.

It is all the more regrettable that while so much is written about Brussels, none of this is to celebrate its poetic wealth, the legends that fill its streets, the myths that have taken form here. Manneken Pis was born from a fragment of history but is the hero of no tale, not even of a farce. The Atomium was not inspired by a science fiction novel. The prestige of a city is mirrored in the fictional characters with which it is associated. Sherlock Holmes is not only the most celebrated of detectives, but is also the Londoner *par excellence*. Can one walk in the gardens of the Tuileries without Marius, the turbulent hero of *Les Misérables*, springing to life? And, in the Marais district, how can one not hear the clashing swords of Dumas' musketeers? Oddly enough, Brussels has none of this aura. This is all the more strange since well-known authors such as Victor Hugo or Dumas himself have stayed here without using the city as a backdrop for their novels. During the time of his exile in Brussels, which lasted about a thousand days, Hugo was able to store away a great many "choses vues" that he sometimes consigned to his notebooks, even illustrating them with drawings, but his imagination did not build on these observations to endow them with the magic that fiction alone can confer. Classical literature only provides Brussels with two important appearances as the background for dramatic or fictional events. One is Charlotte Brontë's *Villette*, where it would be difficult to exaggerate how much the author bears witness to the ambivalent status of a city both modest and already destined to an international vocation. The other is *Egmont* by Goethe, a play that dramatizes an immensely significant episode from the sixteenth-century Reformation in the Low Countries. Here the fundamental question is whether nations can remain autonomous within a greater entity. In an age of gradual European integration, this theme is as pertinent as it ever was. And the fact that this tragedy was set in the context of Brussels testifies to the extraordinary and visionary intuition of its author.

There is a reason for this apparent literary neglect. Writers in Belgium do not define themselves in terms of any geographical belonging, but feel themselves to be part of wider cultural contexts. Those who write in French take France as their point of reference, while those who write in Dutch or its Flemish variant situate themselves in an even more complex psychological space, of which Brussels is in any case not the centre. It was decreed not long ago that Brussels was to be the capital of Flanders. The measure is no doubt a strategic one, with understandable objectives, but it has little meaning in the real world.

This lack of focus on Brussels means that those who use the French of Molière or the Dutch of Vondel are hardly motivated to use the city as a setting. Or rather, they were not in the past. The French speakers among them sometimes went as far as to move the action of novels written with Brussels in mind to some Parisian *arrondissement*. The pressure exerted by their Left Bank publishers probably had something to do with it... In this connection, one cannot fail to notice the remarkable indifference shown by Georges Simenon towards the Belgian capital: in the course of hundreds of novels he practically never refers to the place. A typical *Liégeois* reflex? In Liège people tend not to make too much of the Brabantine capital, whose dominance of Belgian life is considered an usurpation. But it is unlikely that this form of *Liégeois* chauvinism actually influenced the creator of Maigret. Quite simply, Brussels never fired his imagination. Paris was the pole of attraction from his adolescence, and at the age of twenty-five he was already a king there.

For a long time only those poets and storytellers who were profoundly smitten with the city would speak of Brussels. Whether Flemish in origin, Walloon or homegrown, these were the real *Brusseleers*, those who loved its distinctive language and wanted to give it literary status. Such was the case with the *revuistes*, who wrote satirical sketches for the many café-theatres, creating the tradition that spawned the masterpiece of local dialect theatre, *Le Mariage de Mademoiselle Beulemans*. This, too, was the aim of Roger Kervyn de Marcke ten Driessche, an aesthetic-looking aristocrat who invented the character of Pitje Schramouille in the 1930s. Pitje, the archetypal Brussels street urchin, is the hero of many spicy tales, written in a subtly stylized *Bruxellois* dialect, a small marvel of popular poetry that has recently won an enthusiastic new audience. Pitje, cousin to Woltje, the folkloric marionette of the Royal Théâtre Toone, is also equally related to those two jokers Quick et Flupke, dreamt up by Hergé, the father of Tintin.

But the real lovers of Brussels are not only humorists. Just as painters planted their easels in the various *quartiers* (Rik Wouters or Paul Delvaux, both residents of Boitsfort, are the best-known examples), certain poets have found inspiration along the city's streets. This has given us the *Bruxellois* elegies of Odilon-Jean Périer in French, or of Jan van Nijlen in Dutch. They have both succeeded in rendering a sort of melancholy that suits this collection of villages hidden away in valleys or clinging to hillsides. Assembled together they form a patchwork city whose diverse charms make a tour of Brussels a kind of strange odyssey through an urban archipelago with all its varied temptations.

In the last twenty years the climate has changed. Brussels no longer just interests its native writers, more of whom are locating their novels here. They are also happy to find that the city they inhabit is becoming less and less anonymous, that it attracts growing numbers of curious visitors, and yet that its streets, squares, lakes and parks have not yet become clichés worn out by novelists, filmmakers, and singers. Novelists such as Pierre Mertens, Jean-Baptiste Baronian and Jacqueline Harpman take delight in this virgin territory. Among the younger generation, such as Jean-Luc Outers, Alain Berenboom and Xavier Hanotte (the most "British" of Belgian writers) Brussels is no longer taboo. Indeed, there even seems to be a literary movement towards the city; Dutch writers come to settle here and proclaim themselves more *Bruxellois* than the locals. The French are not far behind. Since the high-speed Thalys train has reduced the distance between Brussels and Paris to the point where one hardly has time to finish the newspaper, the French have discovered that the maligned capital of Europe has an active and intense cultural life, whose literary importance continues to grow.

André de Vries has traced the path of this slow but sure process of literary emergence over time. His in-depth exploration has the great merit of returning to the city's origins while keeping in mind the living present. His book takes the wider view, considering a city that for a long time lived only on the margins of literature, but which could in the new century become one of its centres.

Jacques De Decker
Brussels 2002

Acknowledgements

It is a pleasure to thank all those who helped in the writing of this book. Christel Mertens and Jean-Pierre Glibert were instrumental in urging me to take on this project. My father, Dr. Isidoor de Vries, took a keen interest in this book but did not live to see its completion.

My task would have been a great deal more difficult without the kind hospitality of the Centre d'Études Tibétaines in Brussels, who housed me while I carried out my researches. My discussions with Sophie de Meyrac and Ani Péma helped me better to understand Brussels identity. Carlo Luyckx and Peter Burnett also gave me the benefit of their extensive knowledge of Brussels.

I am especially grateful to the staff of the Koninklijke Bibliotheek in Brussels for their patient assistance in helping to locate obscure works on Brussels; also to the Brussels Tourist Office and the Sint-Lukas Archief for help in finding illustrations.

M. Jacques De Decker of the Belgian Académie de Langue et de Littérature Françaises kindly agreed to write the foreword to this work at very short notice.

Finally, I would like to thank my publisher for keeping me to the straight and narrow path and ensuring that a readable text emerged from the mass of material that I had accumulated. My thanks also to Nicki Averill for her fine illustrations.

For the second edition I would like to thank Erik Sauwen for his timely assistance, Martine Van Goubergen and Liutauras Kazakevicius for their hospitality in Brussels, as well as Geert van Istendael, Robin D'Hooghe, Anton Stevens, Filip Demeyer and Derek Blyth for their comments. Also special thanks to Bernadette Hillaert for her driving and Sergei Mouraviev for beer sampling.

André de Vries
Brussels and Oxford, May 2008

Introduction

"Sire, there are no Belgians."

Jules Destrée, in an open letter to King Albert I, 1912

There was once an American film called *If This is Tuesday it Must be Belgium*. To know anything at all about Belgium is a matter of pride to some foreigners, even though what they know is usually that the French- and Dutch-speakers don't get on with each other. Some may make a vague connection between the fictitious Tintin and Hercule Poirot and this country that is somewhere on the way to somewhere else. Those who worry about British sovereignty expect that they will soon be ruled by "Brussels" and their legal system obliterated. Those in the know will tell you that this is the home of the world's best beer and French fries/chips, and chocolate into the bargain, which confirms that this is the capital of a nation of gluttons. After all, Brussels are what you eat with your roast beef.

Anyone who knows their European history will be aware that Belgium is not only a close neighbour of England in the geographical sense, but also one of its oldest trading partners. Indeed, there has been a two-way flow of people and ideas since the Belgae tribe invaded England and Ireland some 2,300 years ago. Julius Caesar suffered a major defeat at the hands of one of their leaders, Ambiorix, in 58 BC. In the Middle Ages the Counts of Flanders and Dukes of Brabant were a match for any great European power, but for many centuries the Belgians have been victims of foreign invasions and have had little taste for military conquest (aside from the colonization of the Congo). Belgium's history of occupations (see below), is a key to understanding the Belgians and their steadfast dislike of all forms of authority.

BEYOND STEREOTYPES

A window cleaner goes into a bookstore. The bookseller is trying to fill in her annual tax return. He suggests various things not to declare, and certain false expenses she can claim. Soon she has a list of suggestions. She goes to make some coffee. The window-cleaner takes a tape-recorder and a camera out of his bag and photographs the evidence; he is revealed as an *agent provocateur* from the tax office. The shopkeeper comes back and says,

"You know, my friend next door could do with your help as well."

The television sketch from the 1970s by the Brussels humourist Stéphane Steeman exemplifies the Belgian obsession with tax evasion, and their view of the state—an alien intrusion into everyday life. In the early Middle Ages there was no Belgian state, rather a collection of towns that had to be persuaded to work together. The different towns did not mind being vassals of the French or the Holy Roman Empire. They wanted their rulers to respect their "rights"—which meant the right to run their businesses as they pleased and not to pay too much tax—rather than worrying too much about sovereignty. When, after 500 years of foreign domination, the Belgians finally won their independence in 1830, they created a state that was, by the standards of the time, relatively decentralized, but based on the premise that the language of the majority, Dutch (also known as Flemish), would eventually be eliminated, an absurd idea that is now threatening the existence of the Belgian state. Since the 1960s the Belgian state has been gradually federalized to satisfy the aspirations of the three language communities: the Dutch-speakers, the French-speakers and the Germanophones. The ordinary Belgian can now identify with their new region, while the *Bruxellois* (or inhabitant of Brussels) identifies most strongly of all with his or her language community.

Ask Belgians about their national identity and they often say: "We are a small country," because there is no easy answer to this question. Belgium was born out of an opera performance in 1830 (see below), but without any common programme that could bind its people together. The strong individualist or "particularist" streak (as it is often called) in the Belgian psyche, or rather the proliferation of local identities, has led to vagueness about collective identity. Thus the Antwerp art critic and poet Paul van Ostaijen writing in 1925:

> When God created the world he gave men free will, and the Walloons and Flemish freedom. That purely negative formula is the only thing that unites us. It is the kernel of Belgium. In inverse proportion to our desire for liberty, everything speculative is foreign to us... We are very happy to define ourselves by our desire to escape all definition, without attaching any importance to indefiniteness itself.

The theme is picked up again by the Brussels writer Jean Muno in his *His-*

toire exécrable d'un héros brabançon (Execrable Tale of a Brabantine Hero, 1982), where he remarks: "Belgium is so Chinese these days it's best to be as indefinite as possible."

Non-identity became a popular theme with some French-speaking writers once it appeared that the unitary Belgian state was about to disappear, but people on the ground feel more that they have a dual identity. Rather than considering themselves simply "Belgian", the French speakers are now Belgian and something else (not very clearly defined), while the Flemish are certainly Flemish and perhaps Belgian as well. Clichés about the other community in the media are accepted without much reflection. Dutch travel companies a few years ago coined the term "Burgundian" to define Belgium as different from the Calvinist Netherlands, and this has been taken over by the Flemish, at least, to signify that aspect of the Belgians which distinguishes them from neighbouring countries, which is taken to mean hedonism and lack of restraint. The term "Belgitude" has also become widely used to define what makes Belgium different from other countries, with connotations of pragmatism, flexibility and nonchalance when dealing with apparently insoluble problems, such as trying to govern Belgium. Belgitude also implies preferring ad hoc solutions to problems and acting first and thinking later, which echoes a common perception that the Belgians are disorganized and dislike hierarchical management structures. The Flemish and *Bruxellois* also talk about their country as being "a good place to live," and the Dutch certainly agree, as they are moving in large numbers south of the border.

Wars and foreign occupations have given Belgians an overwhelming desire for a quiet, comfortable life. The most significant event by far in Belgium's history was the Counter-Reformation, when the Inquisition was let loose, followed by a mass exodus of most of the progressive elements in Belgian society, the so-called "Spanish lobotomy". Jean-Claude Dotru (quoted in Didier Pavy, *Les Belges*) believes that "our country has always been confronted with war and death. This explains why Belgian culture is drive-related (*pulsionnelle*) and playing with death is associated with pleasure." The playwright Michel de Ghelderode's whole œuvre revolves around the time of the Inquisition. Belgians have a strong liking for "horror" writing, as though they had a need to relive the atrocities they suffered under the Spanish and many later occupations. Another significant consequence of foreign occupations has been a feeling of solidarity and needing to be able to rely on others in one's community. The Belgian welfare state is one of the most generous in Europe.

The Catholic Church wielded immense power for hundreds of years, and its impact is still very evident. Everyone takes a position in relation to the Church: there are Catholic political parties, Catholic sickness funds and Catholic trade unions. There are even Catholic football leagues and amateur dramatic societies. Saints' name days are posted on the weather forecast on Brussels television, yet church attendance is lowest in the capital, with just five per cent of the population going to Sunday mass in 2008 (in Flanders it was eight per cent). Octave Mirbeau (author of *The Diary of a Chambermaid*) wrote about driving through Belgium in 1902:

> As soon as you enter Belgium, you are hit by the religious miasma which reigns here. Religious superstition is the sovereign master of the souls of the people, the countryside, the laws. On the roads, the tracks, in the villages, you encounter these figures of stubborn faith in their thousands, sombre and aggressive figures at prayer, just as they are depicted in the triptychs of the Flemish primitives. The centuries have passed them by, progress and science have passed them by, without softening their hard, dull edges. Belgium cannot eliminate the Spanish blood that flows in her veins.

Carnivals and religious processions are still an important part of local culture, a time to put aside awareness of the tragic nature of life, and in medieval times an outlet for the resentments of the populace against their rulers. There is also the Ommegang, a ritual procession that takes place around towns or villages whereby the people retake possession of their territory. Public ostentation has always made rulers popular in Brussels.

LATINS AND GERMANS
Brussels is about halfway between Paris and Amsterdam, both geographically and culturally. The opinion of the outside world of Brussels and the Belgians has been very much formed by the many French artists and writers of world stature who spent time here. The Marquis de Sade found the city "not very agreeable because of its location. You are always going up and down hills." Charles Baudelaire reviled the place in quite extravagant terms, a symptom of his increasing madness. Voltaire found it to be

the abode of obscurantism—"too many Flemish people"—but he wrote this at a time when 99 per cent of the population still spoke Flemish. The low cost of living in earlier times made Brussels a very attractive place for British aristocrats and other foreigners who wanted to maintain the style of life they were accustomed to, and they flocked here in great numbers after 1815.

Everyone agrees that the city offers remarkable hospitality to all who pass through. Lodovico Guicciardini, the most insightful observer of the Low Countries in his time, stated in *Descrizioni di tutti i Paesi Bassi* (1567): "The *Bruxellois* welcome strangers with great cordiality and sometimes even give their confidence too easily."

The French do not recognize the Belgians as Latins. They are too slow and heavy; they lack *esprit*, wit or spirit. One of the more astute French observers of Belgians, the Abbé de Pradt, one-time archbishop of Mechelen, wrote in 1820:

> They are devoted to the cult of habit, and a succession of equally peaceful days; calm is his joy; his life follows a straight line, his affections lack emotion, but do not judge him by the coolness and the awkwardness of his manners. His heart does not lack warmth, particularly for good works.

The French stereotype of the Belgians as slow-witted peasants is known through countless jokes. French writers often remark somewhat condescendingly that Belgians are "mystical" or "superstitious", less rational than intuitive.

At the risk of generalization one can safely say that Belgian literature favours descriptions of the sensory and the physical; ideas and philosophy are rarely at the forefront. It seems that Belgian writers prefer to keep their heads down and not take on the big issues, although lately the best-selling writer Amélie Nothomb has given Belgian French literature a whole new dimension (see p.100), but she spent her early life in Asia and did not come to live in Brussels until she was seventeen. Nothomb's writings display the kind of exaggeration, the love of the Baroque and fantastic that is typical of many Belgian writers who write in French. One can also credit Brussels French-speakers with developing their own version of surrealism in the 1920s, led by René Magritte, by carefully reproducing physical appearances while adding some odd twist, with the intention of subverting the solidity of perceptions.

It is important to understand that Belgians are not simply a hybrid of Latins and Germans. They tend towards a certain Germanic literalism, they are excessive rather than extreme (as Jacques Brel said). "You can never have too much of a good thing" could be their motto. Their peculiarly direct connection to physical reality and remarkable capacity for hard work could be a throwback to the Middle Ages, or it could be that they have never lost their connections to their peasant roots. Belgians have variously been accused of being positivists, cynical, materialistic and taciturn. Balzac remarked that the Belgians "have a calm conscience." They are not easily impressed by celebrity or given to extravagant praise, which at its worst manifests as contempt for anything that appears pretentious (i.e. high culture). It has even been suggested that Belgians are deliberate under-achievers, that they have developed a habit of decompensation, which seems to have started with the trauma of the revolt against the Spanish in the 1560s. The effect of so many foreign occupations has perhaps been an instinct to look for security in the home and family.

The Dutch-speakers, generally known as the Flemish, naturally share more in the Germanic cultural sphere, looking towards the Netherlands, the US and Britain for cultural affinities. The Flemish struggle for cultural and linguistic rights has given them a strong identity. The French-speakers, or Walloons, are oriented towards French culture, but their relationship with the French is uneasy. French-speakers in Belgium take very seriously the opinion of the French about their capacity to speak their own language. Belgians who write in French have great difficulty in being accepted in Belgium until they have received the approval of the French literary establishment. The *Bruxellois*, more specifically, are neither Flemish (in the sense of living in Flanders) nor Walloons, but Brabantine. In its other sense, the term Flemish is relevant to Brussels, in that it is historically within the Flemish language area.

BRUSSELS IDENTITY

The location of the city of Brussels, a mainly French-speaking island surrounded by Dutch-speaking territory, is the biggest hindrance to splitting the Belgian state, or attaching the French-speaking part to France, as some would like. Brussels is also an obvious place for the capital of Europe: its inhabitants are not nationalistic, and the local authorities are excessively accommodating towards the European Union. As far as the city's officials are concerned, being accommodating has in the past meant taking bribes, thus making it easy for multinational organizations to put up whatever buildings they want.

What kind of identity do *Bruxellois* claim to have? The local tourist office website stresses the spirit of *zwanze*, a sort of mockery or derision directed against oneself and everybody else, a self-deprecating trait perhaps engendered by too many foreign occupations. Yet the idea of Brussels identity is becoming less and less meaningful. The number of residents with foreign passports may be as many as 27 per cent in 2007 (many have acquired Belgian citizenship), giving rise to hybrid cultures and languages with little connection to Brussels' past. There is nevertheless a mainly French-speaking core of *Bruxellois* who could represent an indigenous population, but they themselves only adopted French quite recently, since Brussels was a Flemish-speaking city for most of its history.

Jean Muno's *Histoire exécrable d'un héros brabançon* was one of the first serious attempts to analyze Brussels' identity; up until then most writers were happy to rehash the theme of *zwanze*:

> We were intellectuals, we were not Flemings. Nor Walloons. Take note. Even an anarcho-syndicalist had the right to some sort of French origins. A Walloon, in effect, was soft, a bit faded, good-natured and folksy. People from small valleys. Their accent made people laugh, and their processions as well. The Fleming was austere, to be sure, but could be serious, and even intimidating. But a Walloon, never.
>
> In spite of appearances, we weren't Bruxellois either. If you were Bruxellois you spoke badly, or you were a liberal, or often both. We spoke correctly and we weren't liberal... In the end, we were a paradoxical pile of negations... Among all the negations that defined us, there was one affirmation that forcefully imposed itself on us: our fatherland was our beautiful language. Our mission was to learn it, to use it, to teach it in all its purity.

The French-speaking *Bruxellois* hold on to their language, but paradoxically they have to struggle to speak it as purely as possibly in order to define themselves as Francophones. The most despised French-speaker is the *fransquillon*, or *franskiljon* in Dutch, someone of Dutch-speaking background who denies their own culture and imitates French-speakers. The *fransquillon* is not much liked by the Walloons, the original French-speakers in the south of the country. The Walloon literary critic, René Andrianne, gave this harsh definition of the French-speaking *Bruxellois*: "An arrogant francophone [or] a Franco-Flemish bastard of indeterminate parentage" (in *Écrire la Belgique*, 1983).

It has been said that there are only between one and two hundred original *Bruxellois* families; everyone else has come from elsewhere. The city has a remarkable diversity of cultures: at the latest count there are 72 languages spoken in Brussels. On top of that, most Belgians living here have both Dutch- and French-speaking ancestors, and there are many who will tell you that their grandparents spoke Dutch but switched over to French. Another view is that of Roger Mols in his *Bruxelles et les Bruxellois* (1961):

> He is not difficult to approach, as he is simple, welcoming, hospitable, without haughtiness, and wears his heart on his sleeve. But that is just the approach, which doesn't even touch on his deeper identity. In fact, like every Brabanter, his temperament is closed and rather uncommunicative. Normally, he needs a special reason to engage in conversation with strangers... The very opposite of the southerner, he is made in the image of the house he inhabits: a house which is well locked, guarded, bolted, reserved, where he feels at home, a place he only shares with his family and which he only opens to his neighbours and friends.

To overcome their shyness, many Belgians join societies and clubs. These days there are not so many of these *chochetés*, as they were called. Modesty is also a key to Belgian identity. The *Bruxellois* (and Belgians in general) dislike pretentiousness and dispose of a rich vocabulary of insults reserved for *stoeffers* (braggarts) or *dikkeneks* (bigheads). A sharp-edged humour, the *zwanze*, has been a constant feature of *Bruxellois* culture. The working-class *Bruxellois* in the past cultivated the image of a *chârel* (tough guy), oddly enough derived from Emperor Charles V, rather than that of a *kiekefretter* (chicken-eater), their traditional nickname. The locals like to call themselves *ketjes* (from *kereltje* in Dutch), meaning "little boy" or in the (distorted) French version, *een ketche van de strotche* (street urchin).

The term *zinneke* is also very popular, signifying a mongrel dog only fit to be drowned in the Zinneke, a small tributary of the River Senne. To celebrate its increasingly mixed identity, Brussels holds the annual Zinnekeparade in May.

A History of Occupations
"Everyone is welcome in Belgium, as long as they leave their guns at home."

When Caesar arrived, he called the Belgians "the bravest of the Gauls". But while they have shown their courage in facing powerful oppressors, the Belgians have not been inclined to attack other countries since the early Middle Ages. The dukes of Brabant fought wars to control the trade route to Cologne, but in most respects Belgians abhor violence and try to settle their internal differences peacefully. Lengthy foreign occupations have also made the Belgians adept at compromise in order to get along with whoever is running the country, but this has also exacted a heavy price in terms of diminished self-esteem. While the natives may be naturally rebellious, their country can boast one of the lowest crime rates in Europe, and this is most likely attributable to a strong sense of solidarity, a desire for peace and quiet, family values and an excellent education system, not to speak of the influence of the Catholic Church.

Foreign occupiers have come and gone; some became popular and others were hated. The first historically well-known ruler was Charles, Duke of Lorraine, a grandson of Charlemagne, who established his castle on an island in between branches of the River Senne some time around 979 AD. The first real dynasty of rulers, the dukes of Brabant, were originally counts of Louvain, who gradually moved their capital to Brussels in the fourteenth century. The city's success as a centre of commerce and cloth manufacture made her a power to be reckoned with, but did not attract foreign invaders. Brabant included what is now Antwerp and the province of Limburg to the north-east. A war in 1357 with the Count of Flanders cost the dukes of Brabant Antwerp and Mechelen.

Antoine of Burgundy, the grandson of the last Duchess of Brabant and a younger son of the Duke of Burgundy, took power in 1406 with the support of the *Bruxellois*. His successors enjoyed considerable popularity, and restored the city's economy. Charles the Bold, who came to the throne in 1467, lost the Duchy of Burgundy to the French. His daughter, Marie of Burgundy, was pushed aside, and the Spanish Habsburgs came onto the scene in 1482, in the shape of Philip the Handsome, married to the Spanish queen Jeanne the Mad; their son, Charles V (1500-55) became the ruler of the world's greatest empire. The troubles of the Reformation began under Charles' rule, and worsened under his son, King Philip II of Spain, who sent in the Duke of Alva to deal with the heretics taking charge of the city. After a period of Calvinist control (1581-85), the Belgians had to accept Spanish domination, while the Netherlands declared independence.

The restoration of Spanish rule began well, with the regime of Albert and Isabella from 1598 to 1633, but Brussels, and Belgium, could not help but be caught up in the decline of the Spanish Empire and its increasingly ineffectual rulers. Isabella, the daughter of Philip II, encouraged more religious orders to set up in the city; the Catholic faith duly took on its southern European air that has been commented on by so many writers.

The period of stagnation under the Spanish ended with the War of the Spanish Succession (1700-14), a war to prevent the crowns of France and Spain being united. Belgium came under the Austrian Habsburgs, with the romantic figure of Prince Eugene of Savoy as governor-general. The long rule of Maria Theresa (from 1740 to 1780) restored some of Brussels' glory as a centre for the royal court, but her successor, Joseph II (ruled 1780-90) stirred up intense hostility with his drive for drastic reform of the Belgian state institutions in the name of "enlightened despotism". While nobody had imagined that the Belgians were interested in running their own affairs, the example of the American Revolution inspired them to declare a United States of Belgium in 1790. The independent state lasted for a short time, but was then invaded by the French Revolutionary armies and incorporated into France in 1794. The French period was an unhappy one for Brussels. The French stole or vandalized everything that they could lay their hands on, and imposed conscription on the population.

From 1814 to 1830, Brussels was under the Dutch King William I. Though admired for his commercial sense, his attempt to impose the Dutch language on the whole of Belgium and his anti-Catholic stance made the marriage impossible. The revolution of 1830, started in a Brussels opera house, finally led to independence. The first King of Belgium, Leopold I, a German Protestant who was casting about for an available throne, successfully defended Belgium's territorial integrity during the first difficult years of independence. His rule, from 1831 to 1865, saw the industrial revolution take off, with help from the British.

Brussels was now the centre of a modern industrialized state with a liberal constitution. The second half of the nineteenth century saw a huge influx of immigrants from within and outside Belgium. The megalomaniac building projects of King Leopold II (ruled 1865-1909) divided the city's people and left scars that can still be seen today. With the acquisition of the Congo, Belgium also became a colonial power. The miserable condition of the proletariat led to much unrest, although mostly in the industrialized south and east of the country, rather than in the capital. Leopold II's successor, Albert I, refused to bow to the German Kaiser Wilhelm II's demand to allow his armies to march through Belgium to attack France. The Belgians, under their soldier king, fought bravely, and won the respect of the international community.

At the end of the First World War, the language question became a pressing issue. Brussels was officially declared a bilingual city in 1932, and French and Dutch received equal status throughout the country from 1935. Plans for federalization were also in the air, but they came to an abrupt halt with the onset of the Second World War. The Belgian King Leopold III chose not to leave the country when the Germans invaded in May 1940 and thus discredited the monarchy. There was widespread collaboration, as well as heroic resistance. The Germans attempted to use the conflict between Dutch-speakers and French-speakers to their advantage, and thus compromised the cause of the Dutch-speakers down to the present day.

Belgium quickly recovered from the occupation, and benefited from an immense amount of American investment in the post-war years. Leopold III was, however, forced to abdicate after a referendum gave him insufficient support in the French-speaking area. His son, Baudouin, became king in 1950 and restored the standing of the monarchy. As a fervent Catholic, he was generally respected for his integrity. As he had no children, his brother Albert II became king on his death in 1993.

Brussels became first the seat of the European Common Market in 1956 and then the headquarters of NATO from 1966. The concentration of some 1,500 international organizations in Brussels has made it *the* city of meetings and conferences. The capital's architectural heritage has, on the other hand, been damaged by reckless building programmess from the

1950s onwards. Brussels' original inhabitants are more and more leaving for the suburbs, while their place is taken by immigrants from Morocco, Turkey and Eastern Europe. In the future the number of "foreigners," i.e. those of non-Belgian ancestry, will increase, while the indigenous population moves out to the suburbs. The realization of the apocalyptic vision of a city completely taken over by the European Union may not be that far off.

The Changing Shape of the City

Brussels has long been called the "city shaped like a heart," or La Pentagone, on account of the five-sided shape of the second set of city walls, or *seconde enceinte*, which stood from 1384 until 1810. They took some twenty years to remove, the inner ring road or *la petite ceinture* taking their place. The only remnant is the Porte de Hal, at the southern end, which was rebuilt in 1868 to look like a proper Gothic city gate. The original was more a rectangular slab. The heart of the city has had several bypass operations, and some radical surgery at its centre, to clear the traffic thromboses from its arteries, as they like to say. The worst operation by far was the link between the North and South rail stations, which took from 1910 to 1951 to complete and razed whole areas of the city in one of the legacies of Leopold II's rage for colossal public works. The logic of linking the two stations seems self-evident, but the damage has been tremendous. There was another trauma in the 1970s when the metro was being built. For safety reasons the work was done by excavating the boulevards and then covering them up again. The fact that the River Senne, which flows under the boulevards, had to be circumvented made the whole operation exceptionally difficult.

Before the *seconde enceinte* there was the *première enceinte*, an oval-shaped fortification from the twelfth century enclosing St. Géry, the cathedral of St. Gudule, the original Coudenberg Palace on the Place Royale, and the Steenpoort (stiil more or less standing) at the beginning of the Rue Haute. In medieval times, the area enclosed by the *seconde enceinte* was effectively Brussels. The city was surrounded by farmland. Even within the walls there were fields, as a precaution against having to withstand a long siege.

Radical changes to the shape of the city only started from the 1840s, when the area around the Avenue Louise was parcelled out to property developers. The Quartier Léopold, on the other side of the Boulevard du Régent, was also under construction, as was the Faubourg de Laeken around the new Gare du Nord, and the Faubourg de Schaerbeek north of the Jardin Botanique. With the industrial revolution most factories set up on the west side of the city, in St.-Gilles, Anderlecht, and Molenbeek-St.-Jean. These days industry has moved more to the north to Vilvoorde and the area around the international airport of Zaventem. The outlying *communes*, such as Uccle, the Woluwes, and Watermael-Boitsfort still retained some of their rural appearance until the Second World War.

The tendency for reckless demolition was already well established during Leopold II's reign. The French, under Maréchal de Villeroy, had already set a precedent for wanton destruction by bombarding the city in 1695. There is barely one building still standing from before 1695, with the exception of some churches and the Town Hall. On the other hand, the onslaught was convenient in that it allowed the city to clear away a lot of narrow medieval streets.

In the 1960s the city gained a bad reputation for crass redevelopment, such that the word *bruxellisation* entered the French language. The situation these days is a little better; more buildings have preservation orders, and there is not quite the same haste to tear inconvenient old buildings down. Destruction has given way to *façadisme*, which represents some kind of progress. There are still battles going on to preserve residential areas, such as around the Gare du Midi, where many buildings have been allowed to deteriorate by developers who see the chance to put up new office blocks near the station. A large area around the European Union area in the Quartier Léopold has also turned into a wasteland, waiting for more steel and glass palaces to appear.

While in the past Brussels could absorb neighbouring municipalities, the Flemish political establishment has vetoed any expansion beyond the present limits, otherwise it might join up with French-speaking Wallonia and could thus (theoretically) be absorbed into France, if Wallonia ever seceded from Belgium. As it is, the city will always be surrounded by (nominally) Dutch-speaking territory, regardless of what language is spoken to the south of the city.

ADMINISTRATIVE STRUCTURE

The basic institutions of the Belgian state have recently undergone a period of reform, which may not be ended yet. The process of federalization has its roots in the differing aspirations of the Flemish, or Dutch-speaking, and the Walloon, or French-speaking regions. The demands of the Dutch-speakers relate to language and culture, and they go as far as wanting to declare an entirely independent Flemish state. The French-speakers, including both the Walloons and most of the population of Brussels, are mainly concerned to prevent the complete break-up of the unitary state, and to be able to determine their own economic policy, which in effect means continuing to receive subsidies from Flanders. In the post-war environment, the Dutch-speaking area became increasingly wealthy, while Wallonia has become the Belgian rustbelt. The Dutch-speakers not only outnumber French-speakers by six to four, but they also hold overwhelming economic power.

The structures of the state are mind-bogglingly complex, with six levels of government: federal state, Regions, Communities, provinces, *arrondissements* and *communes*. The federalization process began with the creation of cultural councils or "communities" in the 1960s under pressure from the Dutch-speakers, to allow the language communities more control over education, culture, and other matters where language was an important factor (so-called "personalizable" matters). This led to the creation of Community Assemblies in 1970. There then came the Regions, whose boundaries were decided in 1980. In the case of the Dutch-speakers, the situation was simple: the Regions and Communities were the same, so there was only one parliament. For the French-speakers matters were less easy; the French-speaking members of the Brussels Parliament do not sit in the Walloon Regional Parliament, but they are members of the French-speaking Community Assembly. There is also a German-speaking community in the east of Belgium, with their own Community Council. The 62,000 Germanophones belong to the Walloon Region, as they are too few to merit their own region.

The case of Brussels itself was far more difficult. The decision on how to share out power in an equitable way between French- and Dutch-speakers was not resolved until 1988. The question of where Brussels' borders were to lie first had to be settled; it was agreed that Brussels could not expand beyond nineteen *communes*, even if the *communes* around the city had a French-speaking majority. The nineteen *communes* of the Brussels Agglomeration comprise central Brussels, Ixelles, Etterbeek, Schaerbeek, Anderlecht, Jette, St. Josse-ten-Noode, St.-Gilles, Koekelberg, Molenbeek-St.-Jean, Forest, Uccle, Watermael-Boitsfort, Woluwe-St.-Pierre, Woluwe-St.-Lambert, Evere, Ganshoren, Berchem-St.-Agathe, and Auderghem. The Agglomeration is, at least officially, surrounded by Dutch-speaking territory. Around the city there are six *communes à facilités*, municipalities with "protected" French-speaking minorities: Kraainem, Drogenbos, Linkebeek, Rhode-Saint-Genèse, Wemmel, and Wezembeek-Oppem. The difficulty is that these municipalities now appear to have French-speaking majorities (language censuses are not allowed), as more foreigners and French-speakers move out to the suburbs. Here French-speakers come up against the Flemish neo-fascist Vlaams Belang in the municipal government, and sometimes Flemish extremists take direct action by defacing French signs in Flemish areas or disrupting meetings.

The Brussels government reflects the system in the other two Regions; there is a Parliament, and there are two Community Assemblies, dealing with education, employment, tourism, health and some other matters, one each for the French- and Dutch-speakers. The two Community Assemblies also meet together as the Assemblée Réunie de la Commission Communautaire Commune. The agreement on the nature of the federal system of government, the St. Michael's Accord, was signed in 1992, on the name day of St. Michael. Because of the devolution of power to the Regions and Communities, the upper house of the Belgian parliament, the Senate, was reduced in size to seventy-one seats. Ten members of each Community Assembly are co-opted to the Senate. The lower house remains the same with 150 seats.

Within Brussels, and on the level of local communes, there are questions about who is responsible for funding basic services. About half of the members of the Brussels Parliament are also municipal councillors (the same proportion as the rest of Belgium), so that they have a dual role in the government of the city. Out of the total eighty-nine seats on offer in 2004, seventy-two went to French-speakers, and seventeen to Dutch-speakers. Brussels politics was dominated in the 1960s and 1970s by the

Front Démocratique des Francophones (FDF), a party specifically set up to defend the interests of French-speakers in the capital. The FDF has formed an alliance with the French-speaking liberals to form the Mouvement Réformateur (MR). These days no one party dominates in Parliament.

The federalization of the country is unfinished business. Following general elections in June 2007, it took nine months to form a new government on account of the unrealistic demands of Brussels French speakers. The new government under the Flemish Christian Democrat Yves Leterme is not likely to last for long. Although Belgium may not split up immediately, it seems to be only a matter of time before Dutch-speaking Flanders in the north and French-speaking Wallonia in the south go their separate ways. The main stumbling block is the status of Brussels, which is rather incongruously the capital of Flanders, although it is not in Flanders. While they may not be able to incorporate Brussels into Flanders, Flemish institutions are successfully buying up as many buildings as possible in the capital, thus making it impossible for Brussels ever to become part of Wallonia. The Brussels government, on the contrary, seeks to solve its problems by expanding Brussels to incorporate French-speaking areas of Flanders, an equally impossible demand.

Note: The inhabitants of Brussels are *Bruxellois* in French, *Brusseleers* in Brussels Flemish, *Brusseleirs* in Brussels French and *Brusselaars* in Dutch.

BRUSSELS

0   yards   500
0   metres   500

N

AV. DU PORT
Q. DE WILLEBROEK
CHAUSSÉE D'ANVERS
R. DU PROGRÈS
RUE
GARE DU NORD
DE BRABANT
RUE ROYALE

BD DE LA LIGNE
BOULEVARD BAUDOUIN
BOULEVARD D'ANVERS
AV. DU BOULEVARD
BOULEVARD DU JARDIN BOTANIQUE

PARC

JARDIN
BOTANIQUE

BD. BISSCHOFSHEIM

AV. DE L'ASTRONOMIE
CHAUSS. DE LOUVAIN

CHAUSSÉE DE GAND
RUE DE FLANDRE
RUE DE LAEKEN
BD. EMILE JACQMAIN
BD. ADOLPHE MAX
RUE NEUVE

RUE DE LIGNE
BD DE NIEUPORT
BOULEVARD BARTHÉLÉMY
RUE DE FLANDRE
RUE ANTOINE DANSAERT

ST.
CATHERINE

RUE ROYALE

RUE DU CONGRÈS

CH. DE NINOVE
BD. DE L'ABATTOIR
THEATRE D.
L. MONNAIE

BD. DE BERLAIMONT
ST. MICHEL

STADE CH.
VAN DER
PUTTEN

CHAUSSÉE DE MONS
R. D'ANDERLECHT
RUE VAN ARTEVELDE
BOULEVARD DU MIDI

BOURSE

GRAND
PLACE

RUE DE LA LOI
RUE DE LA LOI

PARC DE
BRUXELLES

AVENUE DES ARTS
RUE BELLIARD

GARE
CENTRALE

ST.
ANTOINE
BD. M. LEMONNIER
AV. DE STALINGRAD
RUE DU MIDI
BD. DE L'EMPEREUR

PL. DES PALAIS

PALAIS
DU ROI

DU REGENT

BOULEVARD POINCARÉ
BOULEVARD

RUE BLAES
RUE HAUTE
RUE DE LA RÉGENCE

BOULEVARD
AV. MARNIX

RUE DU TRONE

QUARTIER
LEOPOLD

R. DE FIENNES
BD. JAMAR

AVENUE DE LA MIDI
PORTE DE HAL

RUE BLAES

PARC
D'EGMONT

PORTE DE
NAMUR

CHAUSSÉE

DE

WAVRE

GARE
DU MIDI
AVENUE FONSNY

PALAIS
DE JUSTICE

HOPITAL
ST PIERRE

BOULEVARD DE WATERLOO
AV. DE LA TOISON D'OR

CHAUSSÉE D'IXELLES

AV. HENRI JASPAR

AVENUE
LOUISE

✚ Church
▽ Park/Gardens
━ Railway

Chapter One

ÎLE ST. GÉRY: A SWAMP AND AN INVISIBLE RIVER

"I would like to meet the water-nymph of the Senne. She must resemble a coal merchant, with her face all black."

Charles Baudelaire

The early history of Brussels is obscure. While the remains of some half-dozen Roman villas have been unearthed around the city, it lay well outside the main area of Roman settlement in Belgium. Almost surrounding present-day Brussels were the borders of the vast Silva Carbonaria or "charcoal forest", whose plentiful reserves of iron ore and fuel encouraged the large-scale production of weapons for export, even in prehistoric times. The Belgae in southern England were importing swords from their cousins on the other side of the Channel long before records began; Belgium still has something of an arms industry centered near Liège.

All that remains of the Silva Carbonaria now is the Forêt de Soignes, the only surviving remnant of the forests that covered Gaul before the Romans came. Where Brussels now lies, by contrast, was a bleak area of marshlands, criss-crossed by tributaries of the River Senne, its frequent flooding and changes of direction making settlement difficult. On the eastern side of the town, fast-flowing tributaries had carved out steep hills, such as the Coudenberg. To the west it descended more slowly, depositing a rich silt.

The inhabitants of Belgium in pre-Roman times were not only Celts, who had moved here in the second millennium BC, but also Germanic tribes from the north and east, who had been expanding into the area for more than a century before Julius Caesar and his legions arrived in 59 BC. The idea that Belgium was somehow a unitary nation of Celts when the Romans arrived was popular with French-speaking historians such as Henri Pirenne in the nineteenth century, as one could then make a simple equation of Celts with French-speakers. Yet this is disproved by the evidence of place-names, among other things.

Once pacified, Gallia Belgica served as a frontier region between the Rhine and the more important provinces of Gaul itself. The Romans mainly settled in the southeast around the imperial highways running from Bavay in northern France through Tongeren to Maastricht and Cologne, and between Arlon and Trier. The north and west of the country were apparently too marshy to be of much agricultural value, but the southeast had textile and metal-working industries that were needed to equip the legions.

After three centuries of Pax Romana, Gallia Belgica found itself again under threat from Germanic invasions. In AD 255 a coalition of tribes we know as the Franks mounted their first invasion of Roman territory. In time the Romans were obliged to allow them to settle on the margins of Belgium on condition that they provided soldiers to defend the Empire. From 350 the Franks started to move into the more valuable areas of Gallia Belgica, and from there into France itself. Waves of invaders, Huns, Vandals, and others, passed through Belgium as the Roman Empire went through its death throes. The Franks continued to take advantage of the general anarchy; the first dynasty of Frankish kings, the Merovingians, began with Clodion in 431 in Tournai.

It is by no means certain when the Franks first appeared in the Brussels region. The evidence of burial sites suggests that they were present from the early fifth century. On the basis of place-names one can conclude that both Frankish (the ancestor of Dutch) and late Latin were equally in use in southern Brabant (now called Brabant Wallon), while in the rest of the country the linguistic boundary was more clearly defined.

The history of Brussels up until 1020 is found in texts that were written long after the events they describe. While there may be some truth in them, guidebooks to Brussels tend to take them far too literally. The earliest mention of the city, if one can call it that, is of a visit by a bishop to a place called Brosella in 697, in a text written down around 1025. Tradition states that a church dedicated to St. Michael, patron saint of Brussels, was erected on the right bank of the Senne in the ninth century, but this is undoubtedly a fabrication. The first church was more likely that of St. John, built in the hamlet of Brosella in Molenbeek. A sister church dedicated to St. Géry was then constructed around 1000 on an island formed by the Senne, on the site of what is now the Place St. Géry on the other side of the Boulevard Anspach from the Bourse. Tradition states that this church was connected to a *castrum* or fortification built in 979 by Charles, Duke of Lorraine, a descendant of Charlemagne, who had no territory of his own to rule over. It was for this reason that Brussels celebrated its 1000th anniversary in 1979. The date is rather arbitrary, as the first explicit mention of the *castrum* dates from the end of the fifteenth century.

A House in a Marsh

In the tenth century Brussels was called Bruocsella—a dwelling (*sella*) in a marsh (*bruoc*)—and the River Senne the Braina or Brakena. Braina derives from Braka, meaning brackish, and is still found in such place-names as Braine l'Alleud, Braine-le-Comte, and so on. The River Braka gave its name to the province of Bracbant, meaning the jurisdiction of the Braka. The name Senne appears to derive from the Celtic *senna* or *sunnia*, meaning slow-moving waters; evidently it also gave its name to the Soignes forest.

At some point the Franks decided that Brussels would be a useful staging post for goods transiting by road as well as by river, if the Senne could be brought under control and the surrounding marshlands drained. The area benefited from exceptionally good drinking water, filtered through the sandy clay known as *zavel*. The Senne, some sixty miles long, rises in Hainaut in southern Belgium, flows into the Rupel and thence into the Scheldt and the North Sea. The first reliable mention of Brosella as a *portus* dates from c.1020, so one can deduce that there were already merchants established here, where the Senne became a navigable waterway. Lambert I, Count of Louvain, became the ruler of Brussels in 1005, by virtue of being Charles of Lorraine's brother-in-law. Lambert saw the city as sufficiently important to establish a mint. A later successor, Lambert II (r.1041-62), built a new castle on the Coudenberg ("cold hill"), where the Place Royale is now situated, well away from the insalubrious Senne.

The first fortifications around Brussels were wooden palisades on an earth rampart, which surrounded the Île St. Géry and went as far as the Grand-Place. Once Lambert II had started building his new fort on the Coudenberg in 1047, a more substantial city wall was needed. The walls, known as the *première enceinte*, took around 80 years to construct. Two and a half miles long, they were punctuated by forty towers and seven gates. Much of the wall was still in existence in the nineteenth century; there are plentiful photos of the old towers. These days all that can be seen are the Tour Noire, on the Place du Samedi bordering the Rue de Laeken; the Tour d'Angle or Tour Anneessens, on the Boulevard de l'Empereur; and a section running along the Rue de Villers.

The Île St. Géry, or Grande Île, is always regarded as the original centre of Brussels. The first fortification was a wooden palisade on a mound, from which the street called Borgwal (Fortress Bank) gets its name. The original Borgwal in the eleventh century was an impasse at right angles to the current street of that name. It can lay claim to being the city's oldest named street. By the following century there was a stone construction, the Oude Borght, a little to the north of where the church of the Riches Claires now stands, not on the island itself but on the opposite bank. The street now known as the Rue de la Grande Île was then Oude Borght Strate. The Halles de St. Géry stand on the spot of the first palisade. The limit of the first city wall was a postern gate, the Viquet du Lion, about where the Rue de l'Eclipse joins the Rue de la Grande Île.

These days the Halles de St. Géry is one of the places to go for the more fashionable locals and is a real success story as far as architectural restoration goes. Dating from 1881 and originally used as a food market, the ground floor offers a cafeteria with jazz and world music concerts, the first floor an exhibition space.

The Île itself is not a very obvious tourist attraction. Lady Sydney Morgan, in *Princess or the Beguine* (1835), which was first meant to be a history of Belgium, and then became a novel, has the following little cameo:

> " Comment! monsieur," he said; "you do not know the Isle de St. Géry and the Borgval? Sacrement!"
>
> "I am a stranger," said the old gentleman. "Well, monsieur, you are now on the site of the ancient citadel, where stood the chateau or first fortress of Brussels, occupied by the Emperor Otho the Second, in the tenth century. All that remains of that old bulwark is a ruin within that old brewery there, before you."
>
> "An ancient site, indeed!" said Sir Frederick, perceiving he had fallen in with an original.

RUE DE LAEKEN AND THE BÉGUINES

The Rue de Laeken has been here since the origins of the city as the starting point for the road to Mechelen and Antwerp. The entire area between the Rue de Laeken and the Quai au Bois à Brûler was known as Le Béguinage during medieval times. The word *béguine* derives from Lambert le Bègue (Lambert the Stammerer), a wealthy but uneducated priest of Liège. Displeased with the debauched clergy, Lambert built a church dedicated to St. Christopher in 1179, with small houses around it for young women who wished to renounce marriage and live a virtuous life in peace. Naturally he stirred up opposition from the Church authorities, who sent him to see Pope Gregory VII in the hope that he would be declared mad. To everyone's surprise the pope encouraged him in his works, but Lambert died soon afterwards anyway.

The institution of *béguinages* arose to accommodate the large numbers of people who wished to follow a religious life of poverty, mendicancy and preaching, but who could not gain entry to a religious order, or simply wanted to satisfy their religious urges without having to take formal vows. The male equivalents, the Beghards, were wandering beggars. Some said they were the most devout Christians of their age; they embarrassed the priesthood by their piety. In the late thirteenth century they came increasingly under attack for their unconventional ideas, and in 1317 the pope issued edicts against them.

The *béguinages* fulfilled a useful purpose; young women could remain there until they decided to marry, as long as they remained chaste and obeyed the instructions of their superior, the Grande Dame. By 1400 there were about 1,000 of them in Brussels alone. They became a wealthy order, as can be seen from their church, St. Jean-Baptiste-au-Béguinage. The order declined after the religious troubles of the Reformation. When the French took over in 1794, they turned the *béguinages* into almshouses for elderly women. The present Hospice Pacheco (named after the last Spanish governor-general of the Netherlands by his wife, who left funds for its building) continues the same function as a home for the elderly poor.

Further up the Rue de Laeken at no.146 is the Koninklijke Vlaamse Schouwburg, the Royal Flemish Theatre, opened in 1887. The building is a converted customs depot, in Flemish Renaissance style, and was recently renovated. In earlier times it was the Simpelhuys or madhouse. The KVS is at the heart of Flemish culture in the capital, even if performances are not necessarily only in Dutch. Every year many foreign writers and performers are guests. The theatre also has a permanent contemporary dance company and choreographer in residence.

The area at the far end of the Rue de Laeken still has some of its former commercial atmosphere. As Lady Sydney Morgan observed:

> Still lower down in the town, near the Porte de Laecken, the neighborhood of the canal presented its usual commercial groups, the Wapping of Brussels; and everywhere the manufactories of lace, of thread, of woollen cloths, of silk hosiery, of hats, of calicoes and muslins, and of the thousand other articles of use or luxury which support the multitudinous population of the city, were teeming with life and movement, as in the height of the fashionable season: such branches of industry know no vacation, and continue their wonted hum of activity in the absence, as in the presence, of their fancied protectors.

CHESS AND HAUTE COUTURE

To the south of the Bassin St. Cathérine, from the Porte de Flandre to the Place de la Bourse, runs the Rue Antoine Dansaert. The street has emerged as the place to see the best in Belgian haute couture, which has built up an excellent reputation in the last decades, mostly around the Antwerp school of design. On the same street, at no.6, is L'Archiduc, one of the most popular jazz clubs in Brussels. At 7 Rue des Chartreux, which joins the Place du Jardin aux Fleurs and the Rue Antoine Dansaert, stands one of Brussels' most attractive and popular cafés, the Greenwich Tavern, the name stemming from the English beers that were traditionally served there. It is famous as a chess café; the painter René Magritte, who loved chess, was a *habitué*. Players await opponents in a fabulous Louis XVI décor, the walls turned yellow by the ages of cigarette smoke. The game of chess was popular with many of the Brussels Surrealists. Paul Nougé, the poet who gave titles to some of Magritte's paintings, wrote a *Notes sur les échecs* (Notes on Chess, 1965) and imaginatively tried to find links between chess and Surrealism:

> In chess, the most difficult thing to be won, if not the most essential, is liberty. It only exists at the extremes. Because of lack of attention or ignorance one finds it with the beginner. It reappears with masters. It dis-

appears in the middle underneath a mediocre technique, automatism and clichés.

Close to the Place St. Géry is the birthplace of another major figure in Brussels Surrealism, E.L.T. Mesens (1903-71), at 36 Rue de la Grande Île. There is a plaque with the legend "Sans dieu sans maître sans droits" ("No God, no master, no rights"). Mesens started out as a musician, and then became a collagist and writer. He moved to London in 1939 and worked to promote Surrealism in England.

The River Senne
The River Senne (or Zenne in Dutch) is in many ways Brussels' *raison d'être*, so it is ironic that almost no one actually sees it. The river originates at Naast in Hainaut, and flows for about 60 miles northwards where it joins the Dyle downstream of Mechelen. It has four main tributaries, the Maelbeek, the Molenbeek, the Pede and the Geleytsbeek.

Brussels grew up at the point where the Senne was no longer naviga-ble and goods had to be unloaded onto horses. The small islands in the river at this point—the Île St. Géry and the Petite Île—could be easily de-fended. Later, numerous water mills and ponds lined the river, which could be used for fishing as well as navigation. In 1434 the river was deepened and straightened to make it easier for ships to pass. The creation of the Canal de Willebroeck in 1531 took away some of its function as an artery of commerce. After the Canal de Willebroeck was linked with the Canal de Charleroi in 1832 the river was no longer needed at all for transport-ing goods and could be covered up.

The Senne, where one could fish in the Middle Ages, became more and more of a slow-moving sewer with industrialization. The dyers, tanners and brewers all poured their effluent into the long-suffering stream. The result was periodic epidemics of cholera and other diseases, which steadily worsened as more and more houses were built right on the banks of the river. Thousands of people made their living up until the *voûtement* or cov-ering-up by collecting "nightsoil" and other rubbish deposited on the banks. A cholera epidemic in May 1866 killed 3,467 people out of a total Brussels population of 190,000. There was a grim music hall refrain at the time:

See the Senne and die.
Die of pleasure?
No, die of typhus or cholera.

The young and energetic mayor of Brussels, Jules Anspach, determined that the noxious waters had to be covered up, but he still met with opposition from the city's engineers. A Belgian Public Works Company was set up the following year, with British money, to start the works. Unfortunately, a company director, one Frederick Doulton MP, tried to swindle the city out of 2,500,000 francs by submitting inflated invoices and then pocketing the difference through a middleman. The case was tried in Britain, but it inevitably meant that the city had to take on the cost of the whole project. The British had in any case only been engaged to deal with the redirection of the Senne itself, and no provision had been made for the 40,000 people who were made homeless; most of them moved out of the town centre.

The plans of the engineer Léon Suys envisaged boulevards thirty metres wide; in the event they are twenty-eight metres wide. The Senne had to be straightened and widened, and escape channels constructed to allow for peak rainfall. The new buildings that went up along the Boulevards Lemonnier, Anspach and Adolphe Max were meant to be hotels and apartments for the wealthy, with shops and cafés at street level. The authorities wanted to create boulevards on the model of Baron Haussman's urban renovation in Paris, but they did not take into consideration the possibility that the city's wealthier residents might prefer to live outside the city centre.

John Lothrop Motley, an American diplomat and historian, has left a graphic description of the pestilential stream as it was in 1853 in his *History of the Dutch Republic* :

If you come out of [the Grand-Place] you may go either up or down; if you go down you will find yourself in the very nastiest and most dismal complications of lanes and culs de sac possible, a dark entanglement of gin shops, beer houses and hovels, through which charming valley dribbles the river Senne (whence I suppose is derived Senna)—the most nauseous little river in the world, which receives all the outpourings of all

the drains and houses, and is then converted into beer for the inhabitants—all the way, breweries being directly upon its edge.

In earlier times, it had been a vital waterway with numerous ingeniously constructed bridges. John Evelyn observed in 1641: "I was pleased with certain small engines by which a girl or boy was able to draw up or let downe, greate bridges, which in divers parts of the City crossed the channell, for the benefit of passengers."

Many writers have commented that Brussels is sadly in need of a river. The French make puns on the name. Thus Octave Mirbeau: "There was indeed once a river, a river which, in the spirit of imitation and to justify their Parisianism they called Senne, although they misspelt the name. But they hid it under the ground and covered it up a long time ago." Charles Baudelaire also had to have his say:

> "Look," said this jocular Belgian:
> (He was certainly no spirit of the waves)
> "The imitation of the Seine."
> "Yes," I told him, "*une Seine obscène.*"

The general condition of the Senne these days still merits the epithet *obscène*. Until recently, used water went into the Senne without any treatment, but there are now plans to try to restore some life to the river with new water treatment plants to separate effluent from rainwater. Since the *voûtement*, the river goes underground just south of the Gare du Midi, level with the Rue des Vétérinaires, to re-emerge at the Pont van Praet in Laeken, where it follows the Canal de Willebroeck in the direction of Mechelen.

The Musée des Égouts, or Sewer Museum, is well worth a visit, and one can go underground to see the Senne. It is located in what was once the Pavillon d'Octroi, by the Boulevard du Midi in Anderlecht. The underground river may not be accessible after heavy rainfall.

Chapter Two

THE GRAND-PLACE: THE RISE OF
BRUSSELS

"The world's richest theatre."

Jean Cocteau

The safety afforded by the first city walls gave the impetus for many more buildings to be constructed. The well-to-do put up *steenen*, fortified mansions made of stone, and although none of these remain, their name lives on in the streets called the Plattesteen and Cantersteen, and the Rue des Pierres. Ordinary houses were made of a wooden framework filled in with lath and plaster, with thatched roofs. Mindful of the threat of fires, from 1326 onwards the city fathers instituted laws against the use of wood and thatching without demolishing buildings that were there already. Evidently these laws had a considerable impact on the appearance of the city; the first representations of the city centre in the following century show only buildings made of brick with tiled roofs.

The counts of Louvain, or dukes of Brabant as they were from 1106, still ruled from Louvain. To look after their Brussels domains they appointed a *bailli* (bailiff), a *châtelain* (castle warden) and an *amman* (administrator). From 1100 Brussels thrived as a centre of commerce. Wool imported from England provided the raw materials for the new cloth industry. Godefroid III (r.1142-90), Duke of Brabant, concluded an alliance with England. In the following century artisans at the mint were sent to England to lend their expertise in the manufacture of coinage. The custom of the Joyeuse Entrée (Joyful Entry) also dates from this time, under which the new ruler promised to uphold the rights of the city's residents before being welcomed into the city. The custom is still followed to this day.

Rapid commercial expansion and an increasing population required more sophisticated forms of city government. From 1138 one reads of échevins (magistrates) being appointed by the dukes of Brabant; they were charged with trying law-breakers, anyone giving false measure or selling adulterated wine, and so on. The financial contribution that Brussels made during times of war led to the granting of the first charter or *keure* in 1229, which confirmed the liberty of the bourgeoisie. A further ordinance of 1235 determined that the duke of Brabant should appoint seven magistrates and thirteen jurors annually. Most public buildings at the time, including the city walls, were the private property of the duke; the notion of public property took a long time to establish itself.

The importance of Brussels grew over time. Henry III (r.1248-61) preferred to receive foreign dignitaries at the Coudenberg rather than in Louvain. Commerce was given a new impetus after the acquisition of the County of Limburg gave Brabant complete control of the trade route from Bruges to Cologne under John I "the Victorious" (r.1261-94). The new charter of 1292 gave *Bruxellois* even greater privileges. Customs duties now reverted to the city and the provision of military assistance was to be voluntary. Immigrants could enjoy the same privileges that they had in their country of origin. The all-powerful drapers' guild is mentioned for the first time in 1282. The cloth on which the fortune of Brussels was built, the *écarlate*, was of fine English wool. It was not always red, although it gave its name to the word "scarlet". The identification of Brussels with the colour red came a little later.

Under John II (r.1294-1312), Brussels gained jurisdiction over Schaerbeek, as well as St.-Josse-ten-Noode, part of Ixelles, and St.-Gilles. The area, known as the *franchise* of Brussels, had its own laws that gave greater protection to its citizens than those outside. His reign was marked by violent disputes between the patricians and the artisan classes. Brussels continued to prosper during the long reign of John III (1312-55); Louvain was still officially the capital of Brabant, but less favoured by the duke. John III left no male heirs, so his eldest daughter Jeanne took power, along with her much younger husband, Wenceslas. Duchess Jeanne soon found herself at war with her sister Marguerite, and brother-in-law, Count Louis de Male of Flanders, and suffered a crushing defeat in 1356, the so-called *Kwaed Woensdag* (Black Wednesday). Brussels was occupied by the Flemish for a short time.

The ease with which the Flemish had taken Brussels led the city authorities to build huge new walls, the *seconde enceinte*, which remained in place until the time of Napoleon. The project lasted from 1357 to 1383. The walls now enclosed 450 hectares, including farmland, to support the city in case of a siege. Out of the 48 towers, only the Porte de Hal now remains. The *seconde enceinte* gave Brussels its five-sided shape, or as some would have it, the shape of a heart. Before the city walls were even finished, the cloth industry went into a rapid decline. Rivalries within the guild of drapers led to mismanagement. Increasing amounts of inferior cloth or cloth re-labelled as Brussels cloth were being exported, and the French found other sources of supply. English wool, on which Brussels depended, became exorbitantly expensive. Although the city authorities tried to remedy the situation by taking over the cloth trade from 1385, there was little they could do.

THE FIRST BRUSSELS MARKET

During the eleventh century the Nedermerckt or lower market began to take shape near the present church of St. Nicolas, and then extended out to become the Groote Merct. What is now the Grand-Place was a marshy area that was first paved over in the twelfth century (the current street level is some four feet higher than it was then). The first permanent buildings appeared on a sandbank to the south and west of the square (the location of the Town Hall). The only one still occupied by the guild that built it is L'Arbre d'Or (The Golden Tree), at no.10, known as De Hille before 1695, and now usually referred to as La Maison des Brasseurs (The Brewers' House).

As one can see from the present-day street names, the medieval area around the Grand-Place was teeming with markets and traders' houses. The streets were paved over one by one, and an elaborate fountain erected in the centre. A new town hall, the Meertsteen, was inaugurated in 1302. The fact that the current Town Hall is not symmetrical is striking and gave rise to the legend that the architect (supposedly an Italian) killed himself when he realized his mistake. One may also notice that the entrance door is not precisely underneath the tower. For a time the people of Brussels were nicknamed *Breynloose Torenbauwers* (Brainless Builders of Towers) by the Flemish, who pointed out that the two towers on the cathedral of St. Gudule had never been finished either.

In 1517, the Italian Antonio de Beatis described the Town Hall:

> We saw the town hall with its massive tall tower facing a spacious square, paved, as is the general custom in these parts, with certain small stones

which create a very pleasing effect. This palace is so commodious that you could easily ride all over it on horseback. It contains thirty-six fountains, some of which rise to half the height of the tower. There is an especially fine fountain in the square and according to the burgomaster, there are 350 of them in the town as a whole.

John Evelyn, visiting in 1641, remarked: "The State house, neere the market-place, is for the carving in freestone a most laborious and finished piece, well worthy of observation. The flesh-shambles are also built of stone." "Flesh-shambles" refers to what was then the most substantial building in the square other than the Town Hall, the Brood en Vleeshuis (Bread and Meat House). It is now known as the Maison du Roi (no.41), and houses the city's Musée Communal.

The Grand-Place is remarkable for the harmony of its architecture, which it owes to the fact that most of the buildings had to be rebuilt after the French bombarded Brussels in 1695. Only the Town Hall, or rather its tower, which the French used to take aim, has survived.

The square was traditionally the market place of central Brussels. An early-morning fruit and vegetable market took place here every day until after the Second World War. Condemned criminals were exposed in the square until 1848. As recently as 1985 it was still possible to drive through, and trams ran through the square until the 1960s. These days the most famous market is the flower market on from Tuesday to Sunday (March-October). In winter there is sometimes ice-skating, but for most of the year the Grand-Place is kept clear for the vast numbers of tourists trying to get a view of the buildings. For four days during August every other year, the centre of the square is covered by the Flower Carpet (see cover), an advertisement for the Belgian horticulture industry.

The French novelist, Joris-Karl Huysmans (1848-1907), who lived for a while in the nearby Rue du Midi, has left a graphic description of the market in his *A la Grande Place de Bruxelles* (1874):

It was Sunday, the day of the flower market and the bird market. From eight in the morning the Grand-Place was bursting with people. On the left, near the buildings rising up in their multicoloured robes, emblazoned with emblems, at the foot of the Maison de la Louve, whose voluted gables jewelled with leaves and golden carved stone, cut through the white velvet

14

of the clouds, peasant women spread out under faded parasols bundles of greenery, baskets of flowers, sheaves of foliage, and frantically made their sales pitch with their scowling snouts, while the customers hemmed and hawed and refused their offers.

The daily fruit and vegetable market started and stopped early. Market gardeners, in particular from the Mechelen area, arrived at four in the morning. By eight the market was done. As there were few greengrocers outside the wealthier parts of the city, most people were obliged to come to the market to buy their vegetables.

The main square is used for great receptions. Every year, around the first Thursday in July, the Ommegang takes place, a procession in the centre of the city that recreates the Ommegang of 1549 when Charles V was present. Ommegangs take place in most Belgian towns once a year (see p.112), the Brussels version originating around 1350 as a thanksgiving for the end of the plague. There are also parades of giant figures up to thirty feet tall, held in Brussels and elsewhere.

HÔTEL DE VILLE

The Town Hall, the symbol of Brussels' prestige and wealth, was constructed in three parts. The left wing was completed in 1406 by Jacques van Thienen. In order to make the building more impressive, a right wing was put up between 1442 and 1455 by an architect whose name has not been preserved. There was already an ancient belfry in between the two, which had to be replaced as it was considered to be too small. Another architect, Jan van Ruysbroeck, the duke of Brabant's official architect (not to be confused with the great fourteenth-century mystic, John of Ruysbroeck), was given the task of erecting a huge tower, which starts off as a square and then takes on an octagonal shape once it reaches the level of the roof. In 1454 a fourteen-foot tall statue of St. Michael slaying the dragon was hoisted onto the pinnacle. The statue is of gilded brass, and was made by Martin van Rode. From time to time it is lowered to the ground for restoration. Because it is made of thin sheets of metal so as to be as light as possible, the features are surprisingly angular when one sees it close up. The tower itself is 376 feet, or 113 metres, high.

The construction of the Town Hall afforded the ideal opportunity for the sculptors of Brussels to show off their abilities. The carvings on the

capitals of the columns and the *culs de lampe* (ceiling pendants) show scenes of Brussels history, such as the legend of Herkenbald and the killing of Everard 't Serclaes (see p.39). A house that stood on the site of the Town Hall, the Scupstoel, or Ducking Stool, is commemorated in a *cul de lampe* of a particularly ingenious design. Another *cul de lampe* shows a woman confessing her sins to a priest while the devil whispers something in her ear. Above the entrance arch are statues of the respective patrons of the military: St. Michael of swordsmen, St. George of crossbowmen, St. Christopher of arquebusiers, and St. Sebastian of archers. The corner niches show Peace, Prudence, Justice, Force, Temperance and Law. A wrought-iron balcony over the entrance depicts the arms of Brabant, recalling that this was where the States of Brabant used to meet until 1789. The interior of the Hôtel de Ville is mostly nineteenth-century. Albrecht Dürer wrote in 1520 (in *Literary Remains of Albrecht Dürer*):

> At Brussels is a very splendid Townhall, large, and covered with beautiful carved stonework, and it has a noble, open tower. In the golden chamber in the Townhall at Brussels I saw the four paintings which the great Master Roger van der Weyden made.

The "golden chamber" that Dürer refers to was the meeting place for the highest administrative body of the city, La Loi. It is now used for marriage ceremonies. To remind the magistrates of their duties, there were paintings by Van der Weyden representing scenes of justice, subsequently destroyed in the bombardment of 1695. The pendant featuring one Herkenbald recalls a legend of an early city magistrate who was on his deathbed when he heard that his son had molested a woman. As his son approached to ask his pardon, Herkenbald got hold of him and cut his throat.

AROUND THE GRAND-PLACE

To begin with, the Grand-Place was a street rather than a square, called the Savel (meaning sand) which ran from the Rue de la Montagne to the Rue de l'Étuve. Houses went up in no particular order, and most of the original buildings were known by names such as "Hill" or "Mound" since they were built on sandy hillocks. Thus the building now known as In den Vos (The Fox) was first called De Berg; it served from 1129 as a hospice for

travelling merchants. The houses were initially all separated by small gardens to combat the spread of fire. From 1300 the city bought up the properties and had them rebuilt to prevent fire and disease from spreading, and to bring about some kind of architectural harmony. Following the revolution of 1421, when the guilds gained greater power and wealth, they built more and more in stone. All the buildings were rebuilt in a mixture of Italian and Flemish Renaissance style after the bombardment by the French in 1695.

The grandeur of the buildings demanded more than just house numbers, so they acquired ensigns and names. Yet they were expensive to maintain and tended to fall into disrepair. To add insult to injury, the French revolutionaries removed all symbols of the old régime in 1794 and threw much of the buildings' contents out of the windows. A law was only passed in 1852 ordering the preservation of the buildings. Burgomaster Charles Buls did most in 1883 by passing a law stipulating that the city would pay for the upkeep of the frontages of the buildings.

The Maison du Roi, directly facing the Town Hall, started out as the Broodhuys, or Bread Hall. Initially it was more a sort of barn with a roof on wooden pillars where the bakers set out their wares, hence its name. It was only later that bakers developed the habit of selling their goods from home. The building was then used as a law court by the dukes of Brabant, so it became known as the Maison Ducale. Charles V had his Royal Assizes built on the site between 1515 and 1525. The Counts Egmont and Hornes, the scapegoats for the Dutch King William the Silent in the wars of religion, were held in the Broodhuys before their execution in June 1568. It is said that a gangplank was built from the first floor onto the scaffold so that they would not be rescued by the mob. Charles de Coster describes the scene in *La Légende de Thyl Ulenspiegel* (1867):

> On a June day, clear and gentle, before the Hôtel de Ville, a scaffold was erected in the market place covered with black cloth and with two stakes nearby with steel points. On the scaffold were two black cushions and a small table on which was a silver cross. And on that scaffold the noble Counts Egmont and Hornes were put to death by the sword. And the king inherited their wealth…

When the French revolutionaries came, the Maison Ducale became the Maison du Peuple (Hall of the People). Quite logically, the building was renamed Maison du Roi (Hall of the King) when the Dutch took over. The present building dates from 1895 and was specifically designed in neo-Gothic style for the Musée Communal; it attempts to reproduce Charles V's version, but the restoration has not been entirely successful, and it looks somewhat out of place.

The American Thomas Jefferson Hogg visited an earlier version of the city's museum in August 1825: "The market before the Hotel de Ville was quite amazonian—a hundred women to one man. The museum, or picture gallery, has nothing but saints and saintesses: these, shown in Flemish pictures, are cruelly uninteresting." Today's city museum, housed in the Maison du Roi, is a great deal more interesting than the one that Hogg saw. It contains Brueghel the Elder's (1525-69) *Le Cortège de Noces*, which gives a good impression of what the villages surrounding Brussels looked like in his day. There are also some fine tapestries and retables, recalling two of the city's traditional arts. The first substantial tapestries date from the fifteenth century; they were hung up to keep out draughts, so they had a practical as well as decorative value. They were often woven in a series, to illustrate an entire legend. The basis of a tapestry is a woollen or linen horizontal warp on which a weft of wool, silk, gold thread or other material is woven to completely cover the warp. Several weavers could take a year to produce one tapestry. The weavers were given *cartons*, ready-made designs, to work from, which were placed behind the tapestry. The weaver's job was to reproduce the *carton*, working from the back of the tapestry so that none of the knots could be seen; the final product was a mirror image of the original design. Few *cartons* are preserved, as they were reused until they disintegrated.

Bernard van Orley (1488-1541) was the leading Brussels designer of his age, himself strongly influenced by Raphaël, whose designs for a series on the Acts of the Apostles, commissioned by Pope Leo X, were produced in the workshops of Pieter Van Aelst in Brussels between 1517 and 1521. The *cartons* are now in the Victoria and Albert Museum in London. Van Orley's first great work was the series *The Legend of Notre Dame du Sablon* (1516-18), one of which is displayed in the Musée Communal. After 1550 more mythological subjects appeared, and there was more of an emphasis on anatomically rounded forms. The final phase saw more scenes of nature and hunting, with flowers. The Musée Communal has one tapestry designed by Rubens (a total of four illustrate different developments).

Flemish weavers were very highly regarded and eventually most of them emigrated in search of religious freedom or better commercial opportunities. The Gobelins factory in Paris, for instance, was founded by descendants of Flemish tapestry workers. Owning tapestries, meanwhile, was a sign of great wealth and power. Philip II of Spain had a collection of some 700 Flemish tapestries which are now in Seville; he transported up to 500 of them with him on his tours around his empire. He also passed a law that only girls under the age of twelve could work on the tapestries, presumably to maintain their fine quality.

Retables were another Brussels specialty. These portable shrines illustrating scenes from the Bible were first placed behind side-altars, hence the name *retro tabulum*. Up until the fourteenth century, they were not placed behind the main altar, as they would have impeded the view of the congregation. Once it became the practice for no one to sit behind the altar, and for the officiating priests to stand in front of the altar, retables came into their own. The first retables were portable boxes that could be opened out to show scenes of the Nativity, and so on. As the art developed, three-dimensional scenes appeared inside a model of a Gothic church interior. The retables became so heavy that it was no longer possible to carry them around conveniently, so there was a return to two-dimensional representations. The production of retables required not only highly skilled wood carvers, but also gilders and painters. The retable industry in Brussels reached its high point around 1500; after this time Antwerp took over.

On a lighter note, the second floor of the museum houses one hundred of Manneken Pis' costumes (see p.34) out of the grand total of more than 800. There are also documents and models illustrating the history of the city.

EMBLEMS AND STATUES

The striking uniformity of the Grand-Place follows from the fact that most of it was reconstructed within a few years of the bombardment of 1695. The Maison des Boulangers (Bakers' House), also known as the Roi d'Espagne (nos.1-2), has a bust of St. Aubert, patron saint of bakers, on the first floor. The six ingredients of bread are represented by six statues on the balustrade: energy, agriculture, wind, fire, water and prudence. La Brouette (The Wheelbarrow, no.3) was traditionally the oil merchants' guildhall. The oil merchants had an important role in the city's economy in that they supplied the butter for greasing the wool to be made into fine cloth. Le Sac (no.4) is home to the furniture-makers and coopers. The emblem above the front door shows one worker holding a sack while another takes something out of it. La Louve (no.5) has a bas-relief with Romulus and Remus being suckled by a she-wolf (which gives the house its name). On the second story are Latin inscriptions; Truth holds an open book, while Falsehood hides behind a mask. Peace makes the doves coo, and Discord with a torch attracts the wolves. On top of this is a phoenix rising from the ashes, referring to the fact that La Louve burned down twice in the seventeenth century, and was rebuilt both times.

The boatmen had their guildhall at Le Cornet (The Horn, no.6) from 1434. Its luxuriant frontage is covered with nautical symbols. Next door is In den Vos (The Fox, no.7) the mercers' guildhall. L'Étoile (The Star, no.8) ceased to exist for a while, when it was knocked down in 1850 to make way for coaches. The building was restored in the 1890s over an arcade. Looking inside the arcade, you will see two commemorative plaques, one to Charles Buls, Brussels' campaigning burgomaster responsible for the restoration of L'Étoile, and the other to Everard 't Serclaes. On the right is the statue of the dying Everard 't Serclaes (1320-88), who was responsible for liberating Brussels from the Flemish occupiers from Ghent in 1356, by climbing over the city walls with a small band of soldiers. He was unlucky to be captured by the Flemish in 1388 and had his tongue cut out before being killed. It is a tradition to rub his arm for luck. Some French-speaking *Bruxellois* see him as a symbol of resistance to the current takeover of the city by the Flemish regional government; the more hard-line Dutch-speakers see his presence as a provocation.

Charles (or Karel) Buls—burgomaster from 1881 to 1899—worked tirelessly to encourage the uneducated Dutch-speaking workers of Brussels to better themselves by instituting evening classes, the *volkshogescholen*, and organizing workplace training. To begin with, the proletariat showed little interest in his initiatives and he had to go around working-class areas in person persuading people to join in. As a writer and artist (he was a trained goldsmith) he was sensitive to the destruction being wrought on Brussels' heritage by King Leopold II's mania for new building, and set up an association for the preservation of old houses and street names. A large-scale restoration program of the Grand-Place was undertaken during his tenure. He was also behind the founding of the Koninklijke Vlaamse Schouwburg (Royal Flemish Theatre) in 1887 on the Rue de Laeken, which reopened in 2006 after extensive modernization. His successor as mayor, Émile de Mot, did much to undo his work in the field of education, so it is ironic that they have a common monument at the junction of the Avenue Louise and the Boulevard Émile de Mot.

From 1720 Le Cygne (The Swan, no.9) became the butchers' guildhall. These days it houses an expensive restaurant. Karl Marx held meetings here of the German Workers' Union while he was composing the *Communist Manifesto* with Engels, and in 1885 the Parti Ouvrier Belge (Belgian Workers' Party) was founded in this building. La Maison des Brasseurs (Brewers' Guildhall, no.10), otherwise known as La Lampe d'Or is the only building in the Grand-Place still occupied by its original guild. The original statue of Charles of Lorraine on the roof was removed by the revolutionary French in 1794, as a royalist symbol. The current statue dates from 1854 and is by Joseph Jaquet. There is a museum inside, which is worth a visit, although the Cantillon brewery in Anderlecht is more interesting as a working brewery (see p.146).

The east side of the square is completely taken up by the House of the Dukes of Brabant, named after the busts on the pilaster covers. The right-hand end at no.13 houses a small chocolate museum. Belgium, and Brussels, is rightly famous for its chocolate. Although the Dutch are the biggest producers of chocolate, and the Swiss can claim the best milk chocolate, Belgian dark chocolate is unsurpassable.

THE SACRED ISLE AND VICTOR HUGO

The Grand-Place and the streets around it were dubbed the Îlot Sacré (sacred isle) by a journalist in the 1960s. The name has stuck and there is now a non-profit making organization, Îlot Sacré ASBL, dedicated to reining in some of the excesses of the tourist trade in the area. But commercial vulgarity is nothing new; even in 1815, the souvenirs on sale were in dubious taste. Robert Southey, a future British Poet Laureate, remarked rather primly:

> Brussels has been too much modernized, too much Frenchified in all respects. As a specimen of the leprous filthiness with which the French have infected these countries, I saw some toys in a shop window representing men with their loins ungirt, in the attitude of the Deus Cacaturiens, each with a piece of yellow metal, like a sham coin, inserted behind. The persons who exhibit such things as these for sale deserve the pillory or the whipping post—the very mob in England would not tolerate them. And where these are exposed, it may be easily guessed what sort of ware is to be found within. Indeed, I am told that such damnable abominations as were manufactured by the French prisoners during the war are always on sale here.

Victor Hugo (1802-85) had visited Brussels twice before when he decided to flee Paris in December 1851, after Napoleon III's coup d'état. Sooner or later he was bound to be arrested in France, and he needed a base from which to conduct his political campaign against Napoleon Bonaparte's nephew. Hugo arrived at the Gare du Midi dressed as a workman, with a false passport in the name of Jacques Lanvin; with a touch of irony, he claimed to be a printer. The authorities hoped that Hugo would be less noticeable with his false identity, but he was recognized wherever he went—to the Belgian public he was a hero—so he was given asylum under his real name. Charles Rogier, the Minister of the Interior, gave him some shirts; the poet André Van Hasselt supplied a sofa; and the mayor of Brussels, de Brouckère, who was almost a daily visitor, promised the protection of his police as well as sending him an armchair. He had been shocked to find that there was nothing to sit on when he first went to visit the great man.

The exiles' first port of call was the Hôtel La Porte Verte, in the Rue de la Violette. After a brief stay at 16 Grand-Place, the Hugos installed themselves in a two-room apartment above a tobacconist's at 26-27 Grand-Place, the house known as Le Pigeon (there is an inscription), once the painters' guildhall. Hugo's mistress, Juliette Drouet, followed the family, and rented an apartment in the Galerie des Princes. The tobacconist, Madame Sébert, was also French and shared Hugo's hatred of Louis Napoleon; she swore only to wear black as long as he was in power. On occasions, Hugo took his place behind the counter while waiting for his son Charles to return from his nocturnal ramblings early in the morning, even though he strongly disapproved of tobacco.

In *Les Contemplations* (1856), Hugo wrote:

I lived among the high Flemish gables
All the day, in the azure, over the smoking roofs,
I watched great drunken clouds flying...
Time's deaf thunder mixed with the noise around me,
From which the hours pass like dull sparks,
Imprinted the belfry of Brussels on my forehead.

Hugo had amazing stamina. He could write eighty pages in one morning, while Madame Sébert faithfully kept out unwanted visitors. His mistress copied out the results, and his publishers had to insert punctuation and capital letters as best they could. At lunchtime, he would go to a restaurant with friends in the Rue de la Fourche or the Rue des Éperonniers.

The poet was notoriously tight with money, and kept a careful note of all his expenses, including visits to prostitutes. As with all the well-known French writers, Hugo had long been a victim of Belgian printers selling pirated editions, or *contrefaçons*, of his works around Europe. On an earlier visit to Belgium in 1837 he had been amazed to find five pirated editions of his *Voix intérieures* and had written to his wife, with pride rather than with annoyance: "I have seen myself advertised everywhere in

Antwerp and Brussels, and printed in every possible format." By the time Hugo moved to Brussels, the era of *contrefaçons* was nearing its end. In August 1852 Léopold I signed the act which extended the law of copyright to Belgium, just before Hugo left for England.

Hugo's presence in Brussels led to tensions with the French authorities. The Belgian government made it clear to him that his forthcoming *Napoléon le Petit*, a strong attack on Napoleon III, could not be published while he was in the country. Hugo moved to Jersey and then to Guernsey, in the Channel Islands, leaving his wife and children behind, but continued to visit Brussels whenever he could. Alexandre Dumas *père* accompanied him to his ship in Antwerp. Hugo speaks of their farewells in *Les Contemplations*: "I haven't forgotten the Antwerp dockside, my friend/You standing on the quay, me on the bridge…"

Rue de la Tête d'Or and Rue Chair-et-Pain
The "golden head" refers to a legend recounted by Gérard de Nerval in *Les Fêtes de Hollande* (1852):

The architect of the town hall first had the misfortune to fail in his project. The left wing, which rested on soil that was not too solid, completely collapsed. They thought of ancient quarries and threw in cartloads of stones, but the more they filled it up, the deeper the hole became. In desperation, the architect finally felt obliged to sell his soul to the devil. From that moment the works advanced as easily as you could wish. The man died the day that the maytree was fixed to the ridgepole. It was only then that they learned his terrible secret. The Archbishop of Malines was called to bless the building, but, suddenly, they heard a terrible rumbling, and everything again disappeared into the abyss. It was then sprinkled with holy water. The workers, amply equipped with scapulars, bravely descended into the depths and found a huge bronze head with horns, which still had traces of gilding. According to some, it was an image of Jupiter Ammon, according to others, an authentic portrait of Satan. The same head was put onto the body of the devil which Saint Michael pierces with his lance, on the summit of the Town Hall.

One side of nearby Rue Chair-et-Pain still has some cafés and restaurants, as befits the name: Meat and Bread Street. The ever-ebullient Octave

Mirbeau visited a cabaret here in 1902.

> Need I say that the waiters are excellent; that they have their hearts on
> their sleeves? After all, it's not their fault that they're from Brussels... With
> their noisy friendliness, almost Marseillaise, they call themselves the
> Parisians of Brussels, or is it the Bruxellois of Paris?
>
> The Bruxellois, when they want to put themselves to some trouble,
> and show off their culture, and to show they are really from Brussels, only
> have two topics of conversation, art and Paris... Paris and art. Unfortu-
> nately, this evening, my hosts were particularly enamoured of art and of
> Paris, and particularly prolix.

Restaurant Culture
"An onion is round like a proverb." (Géo Norge)

Eating and drinking have a central place in Belgian life, national culture
in many ways being defined by restaurants and cafés. Belgians prefer a
simpler style of cuisine than the French, with more of an emphasis on
quantity rather than a lot of small courses. Camille Lemonnier coined the
term "active gluttony", in *La Vie Belge* (1905). Brussels has numerous excellent restaurants; wherever you eat, you can generally expect the food to
be of a high quality. The habit of overeating and then complaining about
the consequences is typical, but the English author who claimed in 1965
that "no day is complete without steak and chips" for the *Bruxellois* was not
quite correct. The locals are far more health-conscious these days. They
are more likely to have a blow-out one day and then eat very little the next.
Cooking habits have also changed. In the past everything had to be cooked
in butter or beef lard, while nowadays ordinary cooking oil is mostly in
use.

To the foreigner such an interest in food is not always easy to understand. The British traveler Henry Smithers in 1817 gave the following
opinion:

> The principal gratifications of the Flemish are of a sensual nature: of these,
> eating constitutes no small share; this in its very nature clogs the faculties
> of the mind and unfits it for the nobler gratifications and the liberal arts;
> consequently we find, that neither painting, which they once liberally pa-

tronized, nor philosophy, nor literature, receive any encouragement among them; they are however not destitute of benevolence when excited thereto by great occasions.

The richness of the Belgian soil gives ingredients their particular quality. The mud deposited around Brussels by the slow-moving River Senne was ideal for growing vegetables, giving rise to one of the city's first industries. The Abbey of St. Gertrude in Nivelles possesses a charter from the Holy Roman Emperor, Otto I, dated 966, giving it control over a *stadium* in Bruocsella by the River Braina, which has been generally interpreted as meaning a vegetable market.

The importance of vegetable-growing is illustrated by the charming legend of St. Veronus. At some point in the eleventh century a woman decides to keep working in her vegetable garden, although it is the Sabbath, a day of rest. To her consternation, the vegetables she has pulled up stick fast to her hands and are impossible to remove. So she is forced to do nothing the whole week long. But an appeal to St. Veronus frees her from her vegetables. The story illustrates the point that the locals are growing vegetables for profit by this time, even if it means working on a Sunday.

The medieval Brussels army made sure that they had everything they needed for a good meal. Jehan Froissart relates that, at the Battle of Bastweiler in 1370:

> the Bruxellois, some mounted on horses... had flagons and bottles of wine tied to their saddles, and amongst their provisions, salmon pâté, and trout and eels wrapped in pretty little serviettes, all of which greatly hindered them on horseback, so they could not give each other any assistance.

Not surprisingly, they lost. During the attack on the Castle of Gaasbeek in 1388 (following the murder of Everard 't Serclaes) the *Bruxellois* consumed so many chickens that they acquired the nickname of *kiekefretters* (chicken-guzzlers). It is also said that during the rebellion against the Dutch in 1830, both sides agreed that there should be no fighting during the lunch hour.

At some time in the twelfth century, Brussels sprouts (*sprotches* in Brussels) made their first appearance. In 1586 they were first described botanically and given the name *brassica capitata polycephalos*. These days they make do with *brassica oleracea gemmifera*. Some people believe that one should cut a sign of the cross in the base of the sprout so that it does not turn into a "weresprout".

Most foreigners associate Belgium not only with sprouts but with French fries. The story goes that American soldiers stationed in Belgium during the Second World War took a liking to the local *frites*, but did not realize that they were in Belgium, and so called them French fries. In the past they were fried in beef fat; their particular flavour comes from frying them twice (first at 325°F and then 375°F). According to leading *frite* expert Paul Ilegems, potatoes came to Belgium in 1680, and French fries arose when the locals had no small fish to fry and so used potatoes instead. The number of French fries stalls (*baraques à frites* or *fritkots* in Brussels French) on the pavements has greatly diminished along with the quality of the *frites*, while some communes actively discourage them. By general agreement the best *fritkots* are located on the Place Jourdan in Etterbeek and the Place Flagey in Ixelles, nowhere near the centre of town. Near the Grand-Place is the restaurant Fritland in the Rue Henri Maus. As well as *fritkots* there are even automated *frite* dispensers in a few places, catering for nocturnal cravings.

Another Brussels (and Belgian) speciality is raw ground beef bound with a raw egg, with some chopped onions and capers, known as *américain préparé*. On a piece of bread it is *broodje préparé*; on toast it becomes *toast cannibale*. In spite of mad cow disease and other health risks, this is still a popular item.

There are standard items of food one will not readily find outside Belgium. One is the *pistolet*, a bread roll with a gash in it, apparently named after a small coin called a *pistole*. (The word *pistolet* means "pistol" in standard French.) *Kramiek* or raisin bread is another indulgence. Bread is important for breakfast and tea-time, but is not essential with other meals.

Supermarkets have bread-slicing machines and special numbered bags for each kind of bread.

There are many traditional meat dishes specific to Belgium and Brussels. *Kip-kap* and *tête pressée* (literally "pressed head") are small pieces of offal and vegetables in a jelly. *Choezels* are a stew of offal. Very traditional is *bloempanch*, a white blood sausage. The fashion for horse-meat has not died out either. Smoked horse-meat, or *pièreju*, is one of the best items on the menu. A kind of horse-meat stew, *schep*, is the national dish of Vilvoorde. It has to be cooked extremely slowly with equal amounts of onions and meat. Horse steak is also popular.

On some streets you may still find stalls selling whelks or *caricoles*, a word which derives from the Spanish *caracoles*. Mussels and chips—*moules frites*—are a sort of national dish. The themed chain of restaurants, Léon de Bruxelles, started out selling *moules frites* in the Rue des Bouchers and has many branches in France.

RUE DES BOUCHERS

"Butchers Street" is something of a subject of shame to *Bruxellois*. What was once a street of decent restaurants and cozy cafés, where Victor Hugo would come to eat, has been turned into a Babel of eateries of dubious quality, with *racoleurs*, or whippers-in, harassing the passing tourists. It is entirely foreign to Belgium. Jacques De Decker was being charitable when he called it "an animated casbah". The only restaurant one could safely recommend is the Aux Armes de Bruxelles at no.13. The area around St. Cathérine on the other side of the Boulevard Anspach is the best place to go for genuine Brussels cuisine at a reasonable price.

The last café in the street, Le Bourgeoys, once jokingly called the town hall of the Îlot Sacré, closed its doors in 2001. Across the road, Jacques Brel used to eat at the Aux Armes de Bruxelles, near the cabaret where he made his debut appearances in Brussels, La Rose Noire, at 30 Petite Rue des Bouchers, virtually opposite the Toone puppet theatre. The Greek singer Georges Moustaki started his career at the same cabaret, in 1955, as a pianist. In 2000 he published a detective novel *Petite rue des Bouchers*. La Rose Noire was demolished in 1964.

The Rue des Bouchers was a much seedier area in the 1950s than it is today, a haunt of the gay community and other outsiders. In the 1860s, if one is to believe the French journalist Mario Aris, it was not a place to hang around after dark. In his guide to cafés doubling as brothels, *Bruxelles la nuit*, he mentions one café in this street, Le Café des Petits-Provençaux:

> The means by which one persuades the clients to go to the upstairs salons is charmingly simple.
> "Do you know the layout of the upper floors?" they ask their victim.
> "No."
> "Well, Olympia," says the madame, "Show the gentleman how the place is laid out."
> The victim goes upstairs.
> "What do you pay?" says Olympia as she puts her arm round his neck.
> "Whatever you want."
> There are rumours and shouts which have their echoes in the street itself. Judging by what the manager of this honourable establishment tells me, there is not even one night when someone doesn't have their throat cut a bit in this little street which they should call Butchery Street. You hear people cry "Murder," but you don't take any notice. The good bourgeois snuggle up in bed saying to themselves: "It's just our neighbours having fun." And if by chance the street remains calm one night, they say: "I didn't sleep well, no one got done in tonight."

The popular local Flemish singer Johan Verminnen sings of this street: "If you want to see Brussels live, and you don't have much money to give, then go and spend an evening in the Rue des Bouchers." A more general opinion is summed up by the curmudgeonly gay poet William Cliff:

> The Rue des Bouchers is disgusting
> The restaurants with their hateful glitter
> Past which bleating flocks look for a table
> Like animals in a stable exposing themselves to public view

THÉÂTRE TOONE: WOODEN PEOPLE WITH SOULS
The Impasse Schuddeveld, off the Petite Rue des Bouchers houses one of Brussels' great cultural institutions, the puppet-theatre Royal Théâtre Toone. The street name Schuddeveld evidently derives from "des Kuddeveld", meaning a field for cattle to graze, conveniently located between the

Butchers' Street, and the Hide Market. The puppet-theatre, or *Pouchenellenkelder* (from the French *polichinelle*—puppet— and the Dutch *kelder*—cellar) is strongly identified with the Marolles rather than with the city centre. It is said that when the chambers of rhetoric were banned by the Spanish from putting on plays, they literally went underground; the current Toone is in an attic. Each succeeding generation of puppet-master has taken on the name Toone (a deformation of Antoine) as a tribute to the first master of the current line. The current master is Nicolas Géal, or Toone VIII. The Toone theatre audiences are made up almost entirely of tourists.

The name Toone alludes to Antoine Genty (1804-90), who lived in the Rue de la Rasière in the Marolles. He ran his puppet theatre in various locations, ending up in the Impasse des Liserons, 369 Rue Haute. He was illiterate all his life and performed all his plays from memory. To find new story lines he had other people tell him the plots of well-known novels. The themes of the plays are varied. One can see a re-enactment of the Battle of Waterloo, *Faust*, *The Three Musketeers*, and so on; others are religious, in particular *La Passion*, written by Michel de Ghelderode, which is performed every Easter. Le Jeu de la Passion was a traditional piece in the Marolles, recalling the tale of Thomas Guys, who was condemned to death in 1440 for taking part in a revolt against the Duke of Burgundy. At the time criminals sentenced to death were spared if they could carry out the acts of Christ during the Passion. The puppet play died out in 1850, but de Ghelderode was able to find some old puppeteers to tell him the story, so that he could recreate it in French.

The languages used in the Toone performances can vary from one scene to another in the same play. The Brussels Flemish or "Vloms" is hard to follow even for Dutch-speakers. There are also performances in Brussels French and Brussels English.

The Toone Theatre almost died out in the 1960s, unable to compete with new forms of entertainment such as television. There was also the fact that few *Bruxellois* could understand the dialect. The current theatre opened in 1965 with its present owner, in a crumbling building constructed in 1696. When the future of the Toone Theatre was in doubt, Jean Cocteau wrote the following note to the owner: "To be sure, I am on your side. There are too many people with wooden souls not to save little wooden people with souls."

The "little wooden people" sometimes showed a bit too much life. At a performance in 1932 in front of the burgomaster Adolphe Max and other dignitaries, the puppet Woltje and his wife appeared unclothed and *in flagrante*. There were protests in the newspapers; unfortunately the performance has not been repeated. The offending parts are kept in storage in a matchbox.

Chapter Three

THE MANNEKEN PIS: BRUSSELS' OLDEST CITIZEN

"The municipality decided to join the useful with the natural…"
Alfred Jarry on Manneken Pis

MEDIEVAL CLASS STRUGGLE

The medieval history of Brussels was in many ways dominated by the struggle for supremacy between the patrician class and the artisans. The patrician class was made up of seven families, the *lignagers*. Since they risked their capital to finance the cloth trade, they expected to dominate the administration of the drapers' guild. The *échevins* or city magistrates, who were of the patrician class, nominated the administrators of the guild. The two *doyens* or masters of the guild could only come from the *lignager* families.

Following the victory of the Flemish textile workers over the French at the Battle of the Golden Spurs in 1302, the proletariat in Brussels rioted in 1303 and obtained the right to participate in the city's government. This brief period of democracy was short-lived. After a full-scale battle between the artisans and the duke's army, the situation was reversed. The workers could no longer organize meetings. They were not permitted to remain within the city walls after sundown, on pain of death and destitution of goods. On top of that, their leader was buried alive outside the city gates, just as a reminder.

There were both professional guilds, run by the ruling class, and guilds of artisans, the *métiers*. Guilds existed to promote a profession, for military and religious purposes, and to organize celebrations. As of 1421, there were some fifty guilds of artisans, organized into nine *nations*, each one under a patron saint: the textile workers under St. Lawrence, St. Christopher and St. Géry; the metal and construction workers under St. John and St. Nicholas; the leather-workers under St. Peter; and the food workers under Our Lady, St. Giles, and St. James.

The dukes of Brabant granted a more democratic form of city government from 1421. In the new system there were three councils. The first council, La Loi, made up of the duke's officers—the *amman* and his deputy—along with the seven city magistrates, and representatives of the guilds, was the executive power. The second council of retired magistrates and councillors could give their opinion on the laws proposed by La Loi. The third council, made up of representatives of the *nations*, the artisans, had only a limited role in passing laws. Laws could be passed by the first or second council, with the agreement of five of the *nations*, or by the first and second councils together, with only four of the *nations* in favour.

The system of guilds went into decline after 1500, as trade was conducted on a more international scale. Abolished by the French in 1794, guilds were revived in the twentieth century as clubs and to organize processions.

THE PALLADIUM OF BRUSSELS

On the corner of the Rue de l'Étuve and the Rue du Chêne (Oak Street) is Manneken Pis, often called "le plus vieux bourgeois de Bruxelles" (Brussels' oldest citizen). The little boy has been a symbol of liberty since no one knows when. The early references call him 't Meneke Pist, while the correct Brussels pronunciation is Menneke Pis. There is a reference to the Julianskensborre (Little Julian's Fountain) from 1377, which seems to refer to the little boy. The water was piped in from the Zavelpoel on the Sablon (now it comes from the usual water supply), down the Rue de Rollebeek and the Rue des Alexiens. The locals called him Juliaanske or Petit Julien (Little Julian) for many years. The name Manneken Pis is first mentioned in the city records in 1469. He was not unique, however: the town of Grammont claims to have had a similar statue from 1459. Several other cities have their own Manneken Pis, such as Colmar in France, and a wealthy Japanese has had a complete replica made of the fountain and set it up in Osaka.

Charles Baudelaire, the splenetic French poet, called him *le pisseur* and *le cracheur* (the pisser and spitter), further evidence of the crudity of the Belgians. Alexandre Dumas *père* felt that the infant Menneke represented "candour and independence". Even Robert Southey did not disapprove:

Of course I enquired for the Manneke, as the most notorious, if not the most famous piece of sculpture of modern times, and one which the populace value as if it were the Palladium of Brussels. The execution is so admirable that one can hardly forgive the artist for the design, and yet the figure is far too infantine and innocent to be deemed offensive. It might probably provoke the cognizance of a society for the suppression of vice; but for myself, certainly I should not indict it as contra bonos mores.

Earthy *Bruxellois* humour does not appeal to everyone: in 1997 the Pennsylvania Alcohol Control Board banned the sale of Manneken Pis White Ale, reasoning that "the label suggests lewd and indecent behaviour and the people of Pennsylvania should not be exposed to it."

The present statue dates from 1817. The first bronze, made after a stone original, was made by Jérôme Duquesnoy the Elder in 1619. In October 1817 it was stolen by an ex-convict by the name of Antoine Licas, who may have expected to get some ransom money for the infant. When the statue was recovered it was in several pieces and could not be repaired, so a new version was cast on the basis of the original. The miscreant was sentenced to be exposed in a cage in the Grand-Place, given eleven sentences of hard labour for life, and branded on the right shoulder with the letters T.P. (meaning *Travaux Forcés à Perpétuité*).

The precise origins of the statue have given rise to numerous stories. The most credible is that he was the son of a wealthy bourgeois, that he became lost, and when his parents found him on the corner of the Rue de l'Étuve and the Rue du Chêne he was doing what he does now. Other stories have him putting out a firecracker which was about to burn down the city, or claim that he was a five-year-old son of the duke of Brabant called Godefroi who managed to urinate for an entire hour while a procession was going by, the locals putting up the statue to commemorate what seemed to be a miracle. Victor Devogel in *Légendes Bruxelloises* manages to come up with five different stories to explain the incontinent toddler.

The custom of decking the little boy out in different uniforms goes back to the time of Governor-General Maximilian-Emmanuel of Bavaria, who donated blue Bavarian costumes to the Serment des Arquebusiers in 1698, and included one for the Menneke. In 1745 he was carried off by

British soldiers to Grammont. The *Bruxellois* went after them and got their symbol back with the help of the *Grammontois*. Two years later he was again removed by the French. When Louis XV heard of the abuses suffered by the Menneke, he made him a Chevalier of the Order of Saint Louis and ordered his garrison to salute every time they went by. On some festive occasions the little boy used to produce wine or beer for the populace, greatly adding to his popularity. In the early part of the twentieth century there was a great vogue for Manneke Pis postcards showing him urinating on the head of a passing German.

The Menneke had about 800 costumes at the last count, with 100 on display in the Musée Communal in the Grand-Place. The Musée Communal will supply the pattern of his costume to anyone who is interested, as making clothes for such a diminutive person is not that easy. Less known is Manneken Pis' older sister, Jeanneke Pis, who leads an almost forgotten existence at the end of the Impasse de la Fidelité, off the notorious Rue des Bouchers. The statue dates from 1985, and is supposed to symbolize Tenderness, Virtue and Admiration. Throwing a coin into the water will bring you good fortune, they say, but the custom has not really taken off.

VERLAINE AND *MES PRISONS*

The Hôtel Amigo, on Rue de l'Amigo, stands on the site of the former city prison. Its ancient appearance stems from the use of bricks from the Convent of the Visitandines. The Dutch name was Vrunte, *vroonte* being an enclosure in modern Dutch; supposedly the Spanish confused Vrunte with *vriendt* (friend) and translated it as Amigo. The street was Rue de l'Enclos until 1951.

The prison has had its fair share of famous occupants, most notably the French poet Paul Verlaine (1844-96) and Karl Marx. Verlaine's fellow poet and lover Arthur Rimbaud was walking down the street on July 10, 1873 to take the train to Paris when he was threatened by Verlaine waving a pistol. Verlaine had already shot him in the wrist earlier in the day. Rimbaud sought protection from a police sergeant, and so Verlaine was brought to the Amigo. The original charge was attempted murder, but Rimbaud managed to have the charge reduced to malicious wounding. Indeed, he pleaded to have the case dropped entirely. Rimbaud did not hang around for the court case, and left the country as soon as he was released from hospital. The doctor who examined Verlaine confirmed that he had "pederastic habits". He spent the night in the company of "a well-dressed drunk, the worst kind", while his mother sadly waited at the Hôtel de Courtrai. The following day he was transferred to the Petits Carmes prison to await trial. He was put to peeling potatoes; lunch consisted of barley with horse-fat. The main inconvenience was the lack of alcohol. Verlaine spent some three months at the Petits Carmes after his conviction before being moved to Mons to serve out his two-year sentence. In *Mes prisons*, published long after the event in 1895, he makes light of the conditions in jail. He immediately started to write frantically and to plan his future literary career. Paper and pen were hard to come by. He even claims to have written poems using a matchstick and coffee as ink.

Karl Marx in Jail

The Karl Marx family stayed at the Grand Hôtel de Saxe at 51 Rue Neuve on their arrival in Belgium in 1845. The Prussian authorities had issued a warrant for his arrest on February 1, so Marx, who was living in Paris at the time, came to Brussels to request political asylum. The Belgians had received word that Marx planned to publish a banned newspaper, *Vorwärts*, from Brussels, but he was admitted after a long interview with the police commissioner, after he promised not to publish anything on the contemporary political situation.

The Marxes stayed for some weeks at a hotel, Le Bois Sauvage, in the Place St. Gudule, before renting rooms at 35 Rue Pacheco from March 13. Marx was chronically short of money. Friedrich Engels sent him 1,000 francs, a substantial sum of money in those days, which enabled Marx to live for a while in the style that he was accustomed to. (An average worker had to support a wife and three children on 14 francs a week at the time.) Engels arrived in April 1845. While Marx rented rooms at 5 Rue de l'Alliance, Engels moved into no.7. Marx always hoped that he would soon earn a large amount of money with his writing. Engels was by now also in financial difficulties. At one time he had to pawn his possessions at the Mont de Piété in the Rue du Lombard. He wrote to his brother-in-law in April 1846:

> I have 150 francs of bits at the pawnbrokers which I have to get out of there before my old man comes here—so I must have access to that sum of money. The whole mess has come about because I haven't earned a penny the whole winter with my writing work—and I had to live with my wife exclusively from what I got from home, and that wasn't much. Now I have the manuscript ready, this won't easily happen again.

Marx held meetings of his Deutscher Arbeiter Verein (German Workers' Union) at Le Cygne in the Grand-Place. Towards the end of his stay, he inherited a large sum of money, some 3,500 francs. He went back to the Hôtel Le Bois Sauvage in February 1848. On February 24, there was a revolution in France, and the Belgian authorities began to expel all foreign subversives. In the night of March 3, a large number of Germans were seen coming and going from Marx's rooms. The police searched the place and found some communist publications. Marx and his wife were arrested and appeared at the Palais de Justice in the Rue de la Paille before being taken to the Amigo prison. Marx's aristocratic wife, Jenny von West-phalen, was taken in for "vagabondage" because she was unable to produce her papers when stopped in the Grand Sablon. The story that she was shut up with common prostitutes is only true in part; in fact, she paid to be given better quarters.

RUE DU LOMBARD

Running across the Rue de l'Étuve is the Rue du Lombard, originally Vold-ersstraat (Fullers Street). The Lombards were usurers who lent money at in-terest rates of 22 to 32 percent. Archduchess Isabella banned them and in 1618 founded the Mont-de-Piété (pawnshop), where the poor could borrow money at six per cent interest.

The Brussels regional assembly, or Conseil de la Région de Bruxelles-Capitale, is housed at 69 Rue du Lombard. The building was designed by L. Bonduelle in 1920, and used to house the provincial government of Brabant, before it was split into two provinces. The federalization of the state has given rise to a Kafkaesque collection of councils and assemblies, with the same representatives often sitting in several bodies (see p.xxvi). The Brussels government reflects the system in the other two regions: there is a parliament, and there are two community assemblies, one each for the French- and Dutch-speakers dealing with what are known as "personaliz-able" matters: those that directly affect the individual citizen, such as ed-ucation, employment, tourism, health, etc. The two community assemblies also meet together as the Assemblée Réunie de la Commission Commu-nautaire Commune. The Brussels regional assembly differs from the Flemish and Walloon regional parliaments, in as much as it can only pass *ordonnances* rather than *décrets*. Certain *ordonnances*—mainly in relation to public works and transportation—can be annulled by the federal govern-ment if they are considered contrary to the interests of Brussels as the capital of Europe.

The first Brussels parliament was elected in 1989. In 2004 ten parties gained representation, the largest being the Parti Socialiste or PS. The FDF or Front Démocratique des Francophones, set up in 1964 to defend the interests of Brussels' French-speakers, has joined forces with the Parti Ré-formateur Libéral (PRL) to form the Mouvement Réformateur (MR), the other major party in Brussels. The extreme right (Flemish nationalist)

Vlaams Belang is also represented. Out of a total 89 members, 72 are French-speakers and 17 Dutch-speakers, but this does not accurately reflect the number of Dutch-speakers in Brussels. The assembly elects five ministers to the Brussels Regional Government, which has a president and two ministers for each language community.

RUE DE LA VIOLETTE: LACE MAKING

On your way to visiting Manneken Pis, you will be struck by the large number of lace shops on every side. The lace industry was at one time a mainstay of the local economy, but these days it has been largely overtaken by machine-made lace, and many techniques are in danger of being forgotten.

The industry began in the 1500s and reached its peak in the following century. At its height 22,000 women and children were employed in the Brussels area alone. The principle is to embroider on a background of fine net using either bobbins or needles. Separate sections of lace are also attached to the background to make larger pieces. Patterns are mostly flowers, but it has also been common to embroider historical figures to make complex scenes. The lace merchants supplied the patterns on paper in order to ensure uniformity and to prevent competition between the lacemakers. The basic material is a very fine linen thread, although lace can be made with any fine thread, cotton, gold, hemp or whatever. The industry became a major export earner in the seventeenth century, to the extent that the English government imposed taxes in the time of Elizabeth I to limit the drain on the balance of payments. In 1662 the importation of Belgian lace was banned completely. English merchants encouraged Belgian lacemakers to work in England, but found they were unable to match the quality of the linen thread. Consequently they had to resort to smuggling the lace, and selling it as "Made in England".

Industrialization inevitably changed the process of lacemaking. The English invented a loom to manufacture *tulle* as a basis for lace around 1800, and lace could be made entirely by machine from 1881. Tourists can choose between the very expensive traditional items, or machine-made ones. The Musée du Costume et de la Dentelle, at 6 Rue de la Violette, is the place to go if you are interested in this typical Brussels craft.

PLACE VIEILLE HALLE AUX BLÉS AND THE FONDATION JACQUES BREL

The small square where the Rue du Chêne and the Rue de l'Escalier come up the hill from Manneken Pis is the traditional starting point for the Ommegang, the annual procession around the city centre. The medieval Korenhalle has been replaced by the Fondation Jacques Brel, dedicated to keeping the Belgian *chanteur's* legacy alive.

Jacques Brel (1929-78) is one of the few Belgians to have gained world fame, with songs such as "Ne me quitte pas" and "Mon plat pays", even if many of his fans think that he was French. He did not originate from a Flemish-speaking family, as many would believe, although both his parents were of Flemish ancestry. His father, Romain Brel, came from near Ypres, from a middle-class French-speaking family. Brel's mother, Lisette, was from Schaerbeek in Brussels and also came from a French-speaking background. Brel himself had a poor command of Dutch, and his attempts at translating his songs into Dutch (for instance, "Marieke") were littered with errors; Dutch was his worst subject at school.

Brel's family moved frequently in his early life. He was born in 1929 at 138 Avenue du Diamant, in Schaerbeek, near the Chaussée de Louvain. Shortly after, his parents moved to 55 Avenue des Cerisiers, and then in 1931 to a cheaper place at 66 Boulevard d'Ypres. By 1935 the family had settled at 25 Boulevard Belgica not far from the Koekelberg cathedral; in 1941 they were at 7 Rue Jacques-Manne in Anderlecht. Brel was a poor student at school and had to repeat two school years before being able to graduate. At the same time, he had an intense fantasy life and a great love of acting, which was encouraged at the school he attended from the age of twelve, the Institut Saint-Louis, on the corner of the Rue du Marais and the Boulevard du Jardin Botanique. After school, the boys would hang around watching the girls walking along the Botanique, never daring to speak to them. One of his early, unpublished songs, "Bruxelles", written in 1953, captures their adolescent longing:

... Il y a le Jardin Botanique
Qui fait la nique
Aux garçons de Saint-Louis
Qui attendent sous la pluie
Les filles dont ils ont rêvé

Devant le phare du Bon Marché
Qui ne cesse, qui ne cesse de tourner...

...There's the Jardin Botanique,
Which mocks the boys of Saint-Louis,
Who wait in the rain
For the girls they dream of,
In front of the lighthouse of the Bon Marché [supermarket],
Which never ceases, never ceases, to turn.

Brel married young and went to work in the family cardboard factory, Vanneste and Brel, at 18-20 Rue Verheyden. (The factory has now been taken over by the Swedish concern SCA.) The prospect of spending the rest of his days as an under-manager in a cardboard factory seems to have been the stimulus for his decision, in 1953, to go to Paris to try his luck as a singer-songwriter. The omens were not promising. The songs that Brel had produced until then were full of run-of-the-mill lyrics about true love and searching for God. He had even come last-but-one in a talent contest in Knokke a few months before.

Brel wanted to write novels and poetry, but did not consider himself a good enough writer. In Paris he decided to stop accompanying himself on the guitar and piano (he was self-taught) and instead act out the stories that his songs were telling. No one had ever seen a singer put such intense physical energy into performances. His sincerity and passion, with the support of skilled accompanists and arrangers, propelled him to super-stardom by the end of the 1950s.

Brel did not think of himself as a particularly talented performer. He put his success down to hard work and the support of his family—very Belgian attitudes. He was the total professional, never singing without a live backing, and often recording a new song at the first take. He also suffered from severe stage fright and often vomited before a performance. To the French, he became the personification of the excessive, uncontrolled, baroque Belgian spirit.

His lyrics, celebrating the lives of ordinary people as though they were characters in an opera, made him into a universal figure. Brel's work combined the romantic with a Belgian realism that distinguished him from the more literary style of his French contemporaries. There is also a pervasive pessimism in his writing: he feels the sorrows of the ordinary man and woman, he knows that dreams rarely come true, that there is not much happiness to be had in this world. And yet there is always the pursuit of love and tenderness, and the distant hope that one day we might understand who or what God is.

Brel was an immensely self-contradictory and restless spirit, whose fluid identity and personality worked on many levels. His tirades against the bourgeois—"the bourgeois are pigs", "death to the bourgeois"—came not from some facile Marxism, but from a deep dislike of anyone who wanted a secure, settled life. He imagined (for no obvious reason) that his parents had robbed him of his childhood, and that only children and adolescents had real integrity. The symbol for this state of innocence was the Far West, which he had read about in his youth. Madeleine in real life ran a florist's on the Boulevard Anspach. The same song refers to them waiting for the Tram 33 (which ran from the Gare du Midi to Boitsfort) to eat French fries at Eugène's. This was evidently written when Brel was still poor. The line in his song "Madeleine", how she is "my very own America" (*mon Amérique à moi*) echoes the same fantasy, as well as the common preoccupation with emigrating to the USA and its legendary wealth. *Far West*, his last film, entails a search for gold by characters from the Wild West, much of it filmed in Brussels. The themes of hatred of all adult organizations, the importance of fraternity amongst men, and the ignominious state of women, are typically Brelian, in this chaotic but highly imaginative film.

Between 1967 and 1973 Brel acted in and directed ten films of very uneven quality. The best of these are *Mon Oncle Benjamin*, about a libertine country doctor, set in the eighteenth century, acted by Brel, and *Franz*, an autobiographical work about an adult living out his childlike fantasies. Directed by Brel, it deals with his typical themes of the necessity of tenderness, the pursuit of impossible love, the inevitability of failure, of despair, foolishness and death.

Having proved himself as a singer, composer, actor, and film director, Brel went on to gain a commercial pilot's license and even considered becoming a flying instructor. In 1974 he set off in a yacht, intending to sail around the world in five years. His journeys were interrupted by the onset of lung cancer, but he still managed to find his own Treasure Island in the Pacific, Hiva-Oa in the French Marquesas, his last years spent in exile with an exotic beauty from Guadeloupe. On his death in 1978, he was buried on Hiva-Oa, a few yards from Paul Gauguin, who had preceded him there by some three-quarters of a century.

Brel made an impact on the English-speaking world only equalled by Édith Piaf among French-language singers. The American musical, *Man of La Mancha*, a stage version of the Don Quixote story, which he translated and performed in French, has the typically Brel line: "To dream the impossible dream... to reach the unreachable star," but he didn't actually write it.

Brel only really identified himself with his birthplace, Brussels. In his own mind he was the eternal *ketje*, the young *Bruxellois*, rather disdainful of other Belgians. His penchant for the outrageous and provocative made him something of a hate figure for the Flemish. The song "Les Flamandes" (1959) seemed to make fun of dull, dependable, Catholic Flemish women, even if Brel claimed that he used the word *Flamandes* for its sound rather than meaning. The next supposed slight to the Flemish, "La, la, la" (1967), included the line, "merde pour les Flamingants" (to hell with the Flemish nationalists). This was as nothing compared to one of his last songs, "Les F...", which made out that the *Flamingants* were Nazis during the war and Catholics in between, an image that came from Brel's experience of growing up under the Occupation. Yet Brel did not have any real hatred of individual Flemish people. He felt strongly about his Flemish roots, and his life and career clearly express those roots. For Brel it is always the organization, and not the individual, that deserves to be attacked. His songs always speak of his deep humanity, not of petty hatreds.

Jacques Brel was certainly not a great poet, and did not count as a *littérateur* in Brussels and Paris. He did, though, develop an excellent feeling for assonance and alliteration, for internal rhyme and rhythm. The simplicity and repetitiveness of his lyrics in some way hold the key to his universal appeal. You simply cannot fail to understand the message of a song like "Ne me quitte pas", even if you do not have a word of French. Still, there is no substitute for watching Brel perform on film as a way to understanding what he was all about. Otherwise his songs can seem over-orchestrated and overblown.

Brel's career was mainly pursued from Paris; hence there are not so many obvious traces in Brussels. There is a metro station named after him, in Anderlecht. It is the closest station to the Rue Verheyden, where his parents had their *cartonnerie*. The Fondation Jacques Brel, located at 11 La Vieille Halle aux Blés and run by his daughter France Brel, energetically perpetuates his legacy. There is a permanent exhibition and an extensive archive.

One can still see some of the houses where he lived: in 1953, at 29 Avenue Brigade-Piron, Molenbeek; then 21 Rue de la Peinture, Dilbeek. In 1962 the Brels were at 31 Boulevard Général-Wahis in Schaerbeek. With greater riches coming his way, Brel could afford to move his family to a spacious duplex in the Avenue Winston Churchill with views over the Bois de la Cambre. Brel's wife, Thérèse, or "Miche", still lives there. The address is not given out.

RUE DES BOGARDS

The Couvent des Bogards was a Franciscan monastery created by invalid weavers in the fourteenth century. *Bogards* or *beghards* were the male equivalent of the *béguines* (see p.5); they had close links with the weavers from their first appearance in the city in 1270. While the *béguines* led a contemplative life, the *beghards* were wandering mendicants who most probably inspired the English word "beggar". Their building was located near the Rue du Poinçon end of the street. The French later turned it into a military prison, and it then became a stable.

The Académie des Beaux-Arts de Bruxelles incorporates the chapel of the Couvent des Bogards. Most of its building dates from 1845; the academy moved here in 1876. René Magritte, Paul Delvaux, Van Gogh and James Ensor all studied here. Ensor (1860-1949) disliked the Académie and left after a year. His most famous picture, *Christ's Entry into Brussels* (1888), a sort of wild parade in favour of Jesus, is far from Brussels, in the J. Paul Getty Museum in Malibu, California. Among the many graduates of the Académie, the most improbable must be Pierre Culliford, the creator of the Schtroumpfs, the little blue dwarves better known in English as Smurfs, who built an empire in the 1960s. Their specialty is to substitute the word "smurf" for other words in their conversation. Culliford, whose *nom-de-plume* was Peyo, was from a long-established Anglo-Belgian family. His teachers said he had no future as an artist...

RUE DES PIERRES

The Rue des Pierres, which runs to the west of the Grand-Place, gets its name from the *steenen* or medieval stone houses that once stood here; at this time only the wealthy could afford to build in stone. On the corner of the Rue des Pierres and the Rue du Marché au Charbon (Coal Market Street) is the so-called *cracheur* (spitter) or "Son of Neptune", who emits a steady stream of water from his mouth. The *cracheur* is one of the few remaining public fountains in the city.

One of Brussels' former entertainment palaces, the Ancienne Belgique, had its front entrance at 23 Rue des Pierres. The first theatre, the "Vieux Düsseldorf", started up in 1906, became the Bruxelles Kermesse in 1913, and took on its present name in 1937. The Ancienne Belgique was more of a cross between a nightclub and a music hall than a theatre. The audience sat at tables with their food and drink, and on occasions, when they had no interest in the performance, they just carried on talking. No one could be accepted as a star in Belgium until they had appeared at the Ancienne Belgique. Jacques Brel made his début there in January 1955 and appeared from time to time until 1965.

The owners of the Ancienne Belgique, the Mathonet family, set up branches in other Belgian cities. Perhaps because of over-expansion, the theatre went bankrupt in 1971. It has been used as a cultural centre for the Dutch-speaking community, with its entrance at 110 Boulevard Anspach, since 1979.

VAN HELMONT: *PHILOSOPHUS PER IGNEM*

Parallel to the Rue du Midi is the Rue Van Helmont, recalling the chemist Jean-Baptiste Van Helmont (1580-1644). The son of a state counsellor of Brabant, Van Helmont had the opportunity to go to Louvain University at an early age to study the arts, medicine, and alchemy. He seems to be have been remarkably precocious:

> At the age of seventeen, I started to give lessons in surgery at the Medical College in Louvain... After a while I abstained from continuing my

lessons when I realized my audacity and lack of reflection: I had assumed that one could learn from books that which can only be acquired from visual examination, manual practice, long familiarity and an acute judgement. I became presumptuous when I was suddenly invited to take on this task and saw my teachers watching and judging my lessons.

Van Helmont mainly devoted himself to practical medicine, remaining a lifelong devotee of the Swiss physician and alchemist Paracelsus. From 1609 to 1616 he lived in Vilvoorde, where his wife had land. He goes on:

> After ten years of travel and studies, I withdrew to Vilvoorde, far away from the crowds in order to have less contact with the outside world and to be able to observe the vegetable, animal, and mineral kingdoms, everything that is worth analysing, by dissecting corpses and analysing them...
>
> Finally I learned that the properties of the body are connected to certain principles; that one cannot understand the body without lifting these veils, and so I sang a hymn to the Lord...

Van Helmont believed in certain unseen forces underlying physical phenomena, which he gave names to. The term for which he became celebrated, "gas", was derived from the Greek *khaos*, by which he meant the abstract principle or soul of a substance. He was perhaps the first to conduct experiments in transforming physical substances into gases, and weighing them before and after, a century before the French chemist Antoine Laurent Lavoisier. Because of the crudity of his equipment he was not able to realize the implications of his own revolutionary procedures. He still held to the notion that physical substances have their own soul. Thus if wood is burnt, the gaseous part is the spirit of the wood. It was the British scientist Robert Boyle who realized that gases can be transformed into solids and *vice versa* through combining different substances. Van Helmont's other great achievement was to construct a primitive thermometer, a glass tube with a sphere at either end filled with red-coloured vitriol, which could be moved by heating one of the spheres.

Van Helmont's youthful recklessness got him into trouble with the Inquisition, who suspected him of being an occultist, and finally he had to confess to adhering to the superstition of Paracelsus. He spent much of his later life under house arrest and was unable to publish anything for twenty years. There is a statue of Van Helmont at the Place Nouveau Marché aux Grains on the Rue Antoine Dansaert.

Chapter Four

CATHÉDRALE ST. GUDULE: SAINTS, SINNERS, AND CARTOON HEROES

"The church whose name sounds like a bell."

John dos Passos

When the Église Collégiale Saints Michel et Gudule became a cathedral in 1962, the papal authorities decided that it should be called the Cathédrale St. Michel; St. Gudule was not on their list of saints. Some felt that the Belgian Cardinal Suenens had not done enough to keep the name Gudule. Some maps now call it Cathédrale Saints Michel et Gudule, others just show "Cathédrale". *Bruxellois* continue to call it Sainte Gudule, as they always have.

As Roger Mols points out in *Bruxelles et les Bruxellois* (1961), Brussels has never been a very religious city, its cathedral arriving very late by any standards. The city first came under the bishopric of Cambrai, and then from 1559 under Mechelen. *Bruxellois* have generally been tepid and conformist in their belief: neither anti- nor pro-clerical. The city's politics after independence were dominated by the secularist parties: the Liberals until the Second World War, and then by Liberals and Socialists.

If St. Michael is the official patron saint of Brussels, St. Gudule has always been the more popular. St. Gudule was the daughter of a count at Moorsel who died in 712; her symbol is a lamp. The story goes that before dawn she would go to pray before a shrine of St. Saviour. The devil, infuriated by her piety, blew her lamp out. She knelt down and prayed, and the lamp was lit again. Miraculous acts of healing were attributed to her. She became so popular that, in 984, Duke Charles of Lorraine, decided to bring her relics to Brussels by force, where they could be safe from pagans.

The church was first named after St. Michael, and its origins could date back as far as the eighth century. In 1047, Count Lambert II gained a permanent place in Brussels folklore when he decided to transfer the relics of St. Gudule from the church of St. Géry to the new church of St.

Michel. The population of the lower town became greatly agitated when it was announced that the relics of their protector were to be moved, mainly because they saw the profits they were making from all the pilgrims coming in search of miracles about to disappear. As the count's party of priests and soldiers moved off with the relics, the women of St. Géry pulled out bundles of reeds from the riverbank and set to lashing the soldiers' faces with improvised whips, the battle raging until the procession moved up the hill towards St. Michel. Until the eighteenth century it was the custom on the anniversary to hang out reeds and pairs of trousers from the windows of the houses in the St. Géry district.

The church stands on a steep hill, the Treurenberg or "Hill of Sorrows", astride a Roman *diverticulum* or byway. The first church or churches were certainly made of wood, and no trace remains. Archaeological investigations during the recent renovation of the cathedral have uncovered remains of a second Romanesque stone church built in 1072. A seal representing a Byzantine-style frontage corresponding to this church was in use in Molenbeek-St. Jean until the seventeenth century. The third church was started under Duke Henry I, and the first part completed in 1226. The Romanesque-Gothic choir was finished in 1259, the triforium around 1300, the south side in 1403, and the north side by 1450. The southern tower was completed in 1451, the north tower in 1480. The south portico appeared between 1475 and 1499.

The basic structure is in the form of a Latin cross with eight side chapels. The popularity of the cult of the Miracle of the Host meant that a larger side chapel had to be constructed on the south side between 1533 and 1539. Another chapel to the Virgin saw the light of day in 1653. Eventually all the side chapels were extended and rebuilt. The cathedral saw its worst moments with the attack of the iconoclasts on June 6, 1579, when statues and paintings were destroyed, and crypts desecrated. The French revolutionaries stole or wrecked much of what was left. The interior of the church now has much in common with other Brussels churches: Gothic on the outside and baroque on the inside.

The English traveller Henry Smithers described the inside of St. Gudule as it was in 1817:

> In the side aisles are sixteen chapels, ornamented with pictures, descriptive of the sixteen sacred Hosts, said to have been stolen and stabbed by the Jews... During the dominion of Napoleon a telegraph was erected on the tower of this Church. The view of the City from this tower is very pleasing. The architecture of this Church is striking, more particularly as the shades of evening advance; but the fine effect of the Gothic is much injured by the miserable white-washed dwellings with which the building is surrounded, in violation of every sentiment or feeling of correct taste.

The practice of whitewashing houses started under the Austrians and was intended to discourage vermin. The French made it compulsory in 1808 and the custom still continues in the countryside.

Victor Hugo was full of enthusiasm for the *chaire de verité*:

> The stained glass of St. Gudule is of a kind hardly known in France, real paintings, real scenes on glass with a wonderful style, with figures like Titian and compositions like Veronese. The pulpit carved in wood by Henry Verbruggen dates from 1699. It's all of creation, all of philosophy, all of poetry, represented by an enormous tree which holds a pulpit in its branches, and a whole world of birds and animals in its leaves. At its base Adam and Eve are chased away by a sad angel and followed by joyful Death, separated by the tail of the serpent. At its summit, the cross, the Truth, the infant Jesus and under the foot of the child the crushed head of the serpent. This whole poem is sculpted and chiselled from oak in the most powerful manner, the most tender and most spiritual. The whole is prodigiously elaborate and prodigiously beautiful. The fanatics of simplicity can deal with it as they wish, it's there. This pulpit is one of those rare moments in art where the Rococo and the beautiful intersect.

Alexandre Dumas *père* had an entirely different opinion: "Undoubtedly in bad taste, but a bad taste full of power and imagination. The author of this *chaire*, Henri Verbruggen, spent twenty years making it for the Jesuits of Louvain. Maria Theresa bought it from them, and gave it to the church of St. Gudule."

To the left of St. Gudule is the Rue du Bois Sauvage or Wilde Woudstraat (Wild Wood Street), which was originally called Wilde Wouterstraet (Wild Walter Street) after a certain Wautier van der Noot who was assassinated here in the fourteenth century. It has also been variously called Rue Derrière St. Gudule, Rue de l'Éventail, and Rue du Soufflet. A remnant of the city walls still stands in the garden of the deaconry between nos.14 and 15. In front of the cathedral runs the Boulevard de Berlaimont. This grand-sounding boulevard started out life as a cul-de-sac known as 't Eeten Gat or Le Trou à Manger (Eating Lane). The builders working on the cathedral came here to eat their meals in the fourteenth century. They also made temporary shelters where they discussed their plans for the following day. The shelters or *loges* built by master builders and sculptors were part of the beginnings of the tradition of freemasonry. A group of English Benedictine exiles had a nunnery in the Eeten Gat from 1599 to 1794.

The Miracle of the Rue des Sols: An Anti-Semitic Legend

In medieval times the area between the Rue des Sols and the Rue des Douze Apôtres (next to the Mont des Arts) was the centre of a small Jewish population who lived from trading and money-changing. The Jews moved here from St. Géry to be under the protection of the nearby Coudenberg Palace.

The story of the Miracle of the Rue des Sols is related in Victor Devogel's *Légendes bruxelloises*: in 1365 Jonathan, a Jew from Enghien, who was angry that his fellow-Jews were converting to Christianity, came looking for someone who would steal some hosts from the church. Eventually, Jean de Louvain, a recent convert living in the Rue Stoevaerts, agreed to his plan in exchange for a huge sum of money (sixty gold sheep), broke into a church, and stole one large and fifteen small hosts. The Jews supposedly stabbed the hosts, insulted them, and so on, at which the hosts started to bleed. The miracle was widely talked about, and eventually came to the attention of the magistrates. The ringleaders were tortured and put to death, and the rest of the Jews forced to leave Brabant. The bleeding hosts were displayed in reliquaries in St. Gudule and Notre Dame de la Chapelle and an annual procession instituted. From 1530 the procession was held regularly on July 20 and since then the Brussels *kermesse* or fair has always started from this date. The Rue Stoevaerts was renamed Rue des Sols after the coins that Jonathan gave to Jean de Louvain. The phenomenon of bleeding hosts had already been reported in other parts of Europe and seems to have been part of a general anti-Semitic hysteria at the time. It is likely that the hosts turned red because of some fungus. As a belated reparation, the Archbishopric of Mechelen-Brussels finally recognized that the charges against the Jews had no foundation, in 1968, 600 years after the event.

RUE ST. LAURENT: RED LIGHT ZONE

To the left of the Boulevard de Berlaimont, down a steep hill, is the Rue des Comédiens, named after the French actors and entertainers who opened a theatre here in the seventeenth century. Turning right, you come into the Rue St. Laurent, once the centre of legalized prostitution in the city until the Second World War.

Jacques van Melkebeke recalls in his childhood reminiscences, *Imageries bruxelloises*:

> On other occasions, we ran along the legendary Rue St. Laurent, from one end to the other, listening with embarrassment and unease to the muted groans and tappings against the windows... There my friend Edgard received a serious practical lesson from his father embracing both morals and economics. "My son," he said, taking him through some dangerous artery, as here and there a concert of pressing cries raised itself, "never come here... these are bad women... and what's more, I believe it's outrageously expensive!"

The recorded origins of prostitution in the city are linked with the public baths *de stoven* or *les étuves* —where men and women bathed together. They were evidently not just places to have a wash. The "Steam Bath Street", or Stoofstraat as it was called, is one of the oldest in the city. This was the location of the public baths in the Middle Ages; there were others nearby. A bell would be rung when the water was hot. The baths were equated with brothels in many people's minds. Jan van den Dale (*c.*1460-1522), a Brussels rhetorician, has left an interesting account of these establishments in his short work *De Stove*, published after his death in 1528. After discarding clothes, clients entered into the second room where young women sprinkled warm lavender water over them and massaged their limbs. Then they went into the steam room, in which water was thrown over a stone stove on the same principle as a sauna. After a wash with soap they went to lie down on a bed to drink wine with the young ladies. Prostitutes hung around outside waiting for customers. The term *stoofwijf* or *stoofmeid* (the women who worked in the steam baths) seems to have had a similar connotation.

The public executioner in the fifteenth century—*le bourreau de Bruxelles*—was charged with controlling prostitution in the city. The ordinances were not particularly stringent. It was forbidden to solicit after the evening bell had sounded, or to place lights in brothels. The prostitutes practised witchcraft against their over-successful competitors, and kept the finger of a hanged man under their beds as a protective talisman.

Philip the Good, Duke of Burgundy, brought in much stricter regulations. Pimps could have their right hands cut off and be exiled for ten years, although no one seems to have actually suffered such a punishment. The need for *les filles publiques* was generally accepted, especially for the military stationed in the city. In 1596 Grand-Duke Albert calculated he needed three whores to service 200 men. In the eighteenth century it can be reckoned that about one in six women were prostitutes or involved in prostitution, about the same figure as in Paris at the time.

The French brought in a new system of registration in 1800, whereby *les putes* had to undergo compulsory examinations in hospitals at regular intervals. In 1844 prostitutes received a *carnet* or identity card allowing them to practise their profession, and had to attend twice-weekly medical inspections. The police were allowed to inspect brothels at any time. At the same time there was a campaign against the white slave trade. It emerged from court cases in Britain in the 1880s that young English girls were being lured to Brussels by promises of jobs in bars and cabarets, the so-called *affaire des petites Anglaises*. Societies for the suppression of the white slave trade were set up to put a stop to the trade. Things have not changed that much, except that the women nowadays are mainly from Eastern

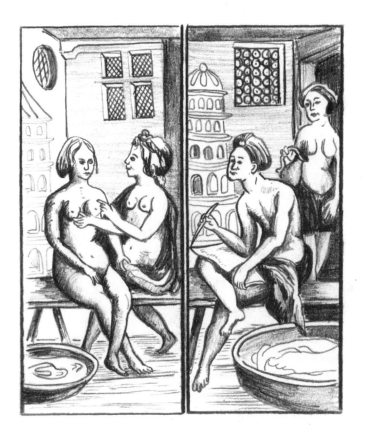

Europe and West Africa. The most notorious whoremonger was King Leopold II. In 1885 it emerged during a trial in London that he had been paying a *madame* £800 a month for a supply of girls aged between ten and fifteen, guaranteed virgins.

The system of regulation in Brussels finally lapsed in 1948, as it was considered to discriminate against women. Prostitution itself has never been illegal in Belgium, although soliciting and pimping are not legal. The prostitutes' point of view is well represented by Neel Doff (1858-1942), in her novel *Keetje* (1921). Doff had come to Brussels with her family from Holland. As her family was perpetually short of money, she was sent out to work the streets from the age of sixteen:

"Keetje, my God, the little ones haven't been able to go to school for two days: how can they... without eating?"

"Eh?"

I got off my old sofa, and took out the whole prostitute's kit from the cupboard, which a girl who had died of tuberculosis had left with us. I put on the high-heeled bottines, the dress with three flounces and a train, put some black mascara under my eyes, a couple of red spots on my cheeks and some greasy rouge on my lips. I put all my hair on top of my head to make me look older, because in the meeting places, the madames chased me away when they saw my sixteen-year-old mug, for fear of the police. I didn't have a hat or shawl.

Keetje's mother follows her around as she looks for a customer. Finally, after five hours of walking, she has earned her family ten francs:

I let my dress drag in the dust, I wiped away the rouge, and groaned as I supported myself on my mother with the other hand on a shop front. I said nothing of my disgust with these unknown men, my desire to insult them every time I had to give myself to them, and the anger which made me even want to bite them when they took possession of my body. A strange kind of modesty between us, never to touch on this question...

Neel Doff was luckier than the rest. Soon after she became an artist's model, and later on in life a celebrated novelist. Her first work *Jours de famine et de détresse* (1919) was under consideration for the Prix Goncourt. Unfortunately it has never been translated into English. The second volume in the Keetje trilogy has been published in an English translation in the US.

At the crossing of the Rue des Sables (Sand Street) and the Rue du Marais (Marsh Street), on the eve of St. Laurent's name day, August 10, the Guild of St. Laurent plants a May tree (traditionally called the "arbre Saint Laurent"). The tree is paraded from the Place St. Cathérine via the Grand-Place to the area whose patron saint is St. Laurent, who could also be the patron saint of barbecues as he was grilled over burning coals. The area was first known as Orsendael in the Middle Ages and then as the Bas-fonds (the lower ground), being at the foot of the Coudenberg. The *quartier* of

St. Laurent and St. Élisabeth has more or less crumbled under the pickaxe, the population has gone elsewhere, but those who have a link with the area come back on August 10 to plant a May tree.

The privilege of planting the tree was granted to the guild by Duke John III some 700 years ago as a reward for defending some Brussels *bourgeois* in a fight with the "Peetermannen" (followers of the guild of St. Peter) of Louvain. The exploit has been immortalized by planting the May tree every year from 1311. Every year the *Louvainistes* sent emissaries to try to prevent the planting of the May tree but the *Bruxellois* never let their guard down and the tree was always planted at the right time and place. But then in 1939 the cortège was waiting at the church of St. Marie when a fight broke out nearby. Everyone went to look. During the short diversion the Peetermannen loaded the tree onto a truck and went off full-speed back to Louvain, so a nearby shrub was used instead. (The *Bruxellois* dispute this story). The following year the Germans had already occupied the city so nothing could be done to gain revenge.

RUE DES SABLES: THE COMIC STRIP MUSEUM

The Centre Belge de la Bande Dessinée (Belgian Strip Cartoon Museum) is housed at 20 Rue des Sables. The building was once a department store run by Charles Waucquez, who moved here in 1902. The design by Victor Horta shows the classic features of Art Nouveau: the bold use of industrial-style architecture with bare steel girders and a large light open space in the centre. After 1965 it proved impossible to find a new tenant. Water started to seep in through the roof, the mosaic flooring disintegrated, squatters broke in and burnt the wooden fittings. Fortunately the place was saved, mainly through the insistence of a former colleague of Horta's. It reopened in 1989 as the comic strip museum.

The Centre de la BD (as Bande Dessinée is invariably abbreviated) has both permanent and temporary exhibitions. The area devoted to Hergé and Tintin is not that great and is likely to shrink further. The Centre de la BD (for the moment) has some rare examples of the very earliest cartoon magazines Hergé contributed to before Tintin had even been thought of. There is a statue of Tintin and Snowy in the entrance hall, on loan from a private collector. Outside the entrance is a statue of Gaston Lagaffe, created by Franquin, one of the most prolific Brussels cartoonists, also the progenitor of Spirou, Modeste et Pompon, and Marsupilami. The question of whether there would be a Tintin museum remained unresolved for many years. The Fondation Hergé bought land in Louvain-La Neuve, south of Brussels, in 2001, and started work on a purpose-built museum in 2007, which will not only house the Hergé collection, but also serve as a research centre for cartoons. The provisional inauguration date is in May 2009. The museum will be in the centre of Louvain-La Neuve, home to the French offshoot of the Catholic University of Leuven, easily accessible by train from Brussels-Midi station.

Along with Hergé, Franquin, and E.P. Jacobs, Joseph Gillain or Jijé, who worked for a time on the *Superman* series, is counted as one of the greats of Belgian BD. More internationally recognizable is Morris (pen name of Maurice de Bevere), who created the cowboy figure of Lucky Luke in 1947. Morris, Franquin and Jijé all went to the US in 1949 and were involved in setting up *Mad* magazine. René Goscinny, who had been in the US since 1945, wrote the scenarios for *Lucky Luke*. He is better known for his work on *Asterix the Gaul*. The nonchalant Lucky Luke is still going strong, although he has had to lose the eternal cigarette dangling from his mouth.

Pierre Culliford's Smurfs have their own section in the Centre de la BD, with models of Smurf houses. A manual *How to speak Smurf* by the Linguasmurf method is on display (you just say Smurf as often as possible). There are also rotating exhibitions of major cartoonists on show. For the serious cartoon fanatic, there is a library, as well as a shop selling all sorts of memorabilia. The centre houses some 30,000 cartoon albums.

The exhibition highlights the fact that BD is no longer a Belgian preserve; the whole genre is somewhat in decline in Belgium, while in the last few decades the French have taken the lead. It is interesting to note that the first serious BD magazine in France, *Pilote*, was started in 1957 with Belgian staff who trained the French illustrators. Here we can appreciate the extraordinary creativity of Belgian cartoonists as well as gain some idea of how they started out. Many of the Olympians of the Ninth Art are Flemish. Marc Sleen (b. 1922), associated with the Ghent newspaper *De Gentenaar*, holds the world record for the number of cartoon albums, some 217, drawn by one cartoonist. He retired in 2002. The Brussels Region has purchased the building where Marc Sleen first gave birth to Nero in 1947, opposite the Centre de la Bande Dessinée in the Rue des Sables. The opening of the Sleenhuis (or Nero Museum as it is colloquially called) will be one of the high points of the Année de la Bande Dessinée (Year of the Comic Strip) planned for 2009 and recognition of the important role that Sleen has played in encouraging bilingualism in Belgium. A scene from a Nero cartoon can be admired on the Place Saint-Géry.

Virtually all the prolific cartoonists set up their own studios to lighten their workload. Another Flemish cartoonist, Jef Nys (b. 1927), has produced no fewer than 240 albums and sold 53 million copies, almost entirely in Belgium. The current top-selling cartoon series in Dutch, *Suske en Wiske* (known as *Bob et Bobette* in French) was started by Willy Vandersteen, an assistant to Hergé on *Tintin* magazine, and sells four million copies in Dutch alone every year. Hergé insisted that he adopt his *claire ligne* style (see below). Comic strips account for eighty per cent of all publishing sales in Belgium and 2009 will see a major effort to gain more recognition for Brussels as the world centre for cartooning. The first school for comic strip art was created in St.-Gilles at the Institut Saint-Luc in 1968.

On the French-speaking side, the Brussels-born Edgar P. Jacobs, a friend and assistant of Hergé's, was one of the most influential figures in the history of the Bande Dessinée. He was best known for his cod-English detective characters, Blake and Mortimer. His treatment of historical topics and the use of elaborately shaded colouring opened up the way for what is recognized as modern cartooning. His work contrasts markedly with Hergé's, who believed in *la claire ligne*, the clear line, which uses no shading and keeps details to a minimum. One can immediately distinguish Hergé's own work from that of his collaborators by the amount of detail and variety of colours in the drawings. Hergé's commitment to *la claire ligne* was strengthened by the influence of the Chinese artist Chang-chong Jen, the "Chang" of *The Blue Lotus* and *Tintin in Tibet*.

HERGÉ AND TINTIN

Hergé (1907-83) was born Georges Rémi in Etterbeek, at 33 Rue Philippe Baucq. His pseudonym derives from his reversed initials, RG, as they are pronounced in French. His early years were marked by a strict Catholic upbringing and fervent love of the Boy Scouts. He was a restless child, obsessively making up stories that he doodled on any available piece of paper. He was evidently destined to be an artist, and his parents sent him to the Collège St.-Luc school of art to receive a proper training. The college was strictly Catholic, and there was no life drawing. Hergé left after one day.

With the help of a scoutmaster Hergé soon got a job with a newspaper, *Le Vingtième Siècle*. After a few years' apprenticeship, he was entrusted, at the age of 21, with the creation of a children's supplement, *Le Petit Vingtième*. Tintin saw the light of day in January 1929, with the first instalment of *Tintin in the Land of the Soviets*.

Le Vingtième Siècle (The Twentieth Century) was no ordinary newspaper, representing the more extreme variety of right-wing Catholic opinion. It was not only hostile towards Jews, communists, and freemasons, but also regarded capitalists, politicians, and everything modern with suspicion. Hergé admitted in later life that the editor, the Abbé Norbert Wallez, was a quasi-fascist (*fascistisant*). Hergé often called himself apolitical, but as a young man he had a strong attachment to the right-wing Rex movement, which was named after Christus Rex—Christ is King—rather than being monarchist.

Tintin in the Land of the Soviets is crude by Hergé's later standards, in every sense of the word. Tintin appears as a red-baiter, anxious to show the Bolsheviks in their true colours. Hergé was strongly influenced in his portrayal by reports sent back by a Belgian diplomat, all of which were later confirmed as being accurate. The next Tintin saga, *Tintin in the Congo* (1931), has a strongly colonialist flavour. Our hero massacres the local wildlife and even blows up a rhinoceros with a stick of dynamite. The depiction of Africans as completely infantile is such that the album is banned in many countries, although it is available in Belgium. It is Hergé's most popular album in the Congo. Hergé was careful to obtain the best available books on the countries he was writing about (he did not travel there in person). Local museums also provided inspiration, such as the well-known Inca "fetish" in the Musée du Cinquantenaire, whose theft signals the starting point for *The Broken Ear* (1937).

Over time, Hergé came to realize that Tintin would have to be completely apolitical, and all references to Belgium removed, if the character was to succeed on the international stage. The turning point in his career came with the fifth album *The Blue Lotus* (1936). Hergé engaged a young Chinese artist, Chang-chong Jen, to help him write a story about China. Chang not only persuaded Hergé to create a tract against the Japanese invasion of his country, but also helped him to improve his drawing technique. *The Blue Lotus* drew protests from the Japanese ambassador, but otherwise was acclaimed as a huge success. Hergé also made up for his dubious political past by satirizing fascism in *King Ottokar's Sceptre*.

Hergé flourished during the war, doing much of his best work, in spite of paper rationing. His success lay not only in his whimsical sense of humour and an innate talent for drawing, but just as much in his extreme perfectionism which drove him to work excessively hard, for he not only produced Tintin but also several other comic strips.

In September 1944, on the evening that the Welsh Guards liberated Brussels from the Germans, he was taken in for questioning by the police at midnight, and spent one night in jail. His crime had been to carry on producing his cartoons for the newspaper *Le Soir*, which had been taken away from the rightful owners, the Rossel family, and so was known as *Le Soir volé* (the stolen *Le Soir*). Hergé got off lightly, although the trauma of being hounded as a collaborator eventually affected his health. The editor of the newspaper in question was condemned to death, later commuted to a term of imprisonment. Thanks to his connections and the reluctance of the authorities to prosecute a children's cartoonist, Hergé was able to work again after three years, unlike many journalists whose careers were ruined, or who were forced into exile.

It was not long before Hergé suffered a nervous breakdown brought on by overwork and the stress of being labelled a collaborator. Sudden disappearances and periods of recuperation continued for the next ten years. Like Tintin, Hergé suffered for his excessive virtuousness and devotion to duty. One psychiatrist he consulted told him to "slay the demon of purity" if he wanted peace of mind. In the end, he had to admit that he did not really have much faith in the Catholic church; his leanings were more towards Taoism and other Eastern forms of spirituality, something clearly reflected in the twentieth Tintin album, *Tintin in Tibet*, a celebration of his friendship with Chang-chong Jen. He was finally reunited with his Chinese mentor in 1981, after an interval of forty-seven years and two years before his death.

The centenary of Hergé's birth—2007—was marked by numerous exhibitions, and the unveiling of a Tintin fresco at Brussels-Midi station. There is also a scene from The Calculus Affair on the side of a building in the Rue de l'Étuve near Manneken Pis (see cover), one of more than thirty such frescoes on the sides of buildings in central Brussels. In this picture Tintin, Snowy and Haddock are tiptoeing down the fire escape of a hotel in Borduria where they have been drinking with some local criminals.

The long-awaited Hergé Museum will open in Louvain-La Neuve in 2009 (see p.58), and 2009 or 2010 should also see the release of the first Tintin film directed by Stephen Spielberg. If the first film is successful, more may follow.

Chapter Five

CITY OF PALACES: ROYAL BRUSSELS

"I went to see the Prince's Court, which is an ancient, confus'd building, not much unlike the Hofft at the Hague…"

John Evelyn, 1641

The Coudenberg ("cold hill"), where the Place Royale is now situated, has traditionally been the location of the ruler's palace since Duke Lambert II (r.1041-62) built his castle here, to get away from the unhealthy River Senne. New bits were added on as they were needed, but the whole complex burned down in 1731, and an entirely new layout of streets took its place. The present-day Palais Royal is an amalgamation of several different buildings, started by the Dutch king, William I. The influence of the Dutch can also be seen in the buildings that house the various national academies of sciences and letters, between the Rue Ducale and the Boulevard du Régent, with the Brussels regional government offices next door. The Belgian parliament and senate are in the Palais de la Nation on Rue de la Loi at right angles to the Rue Royale. The Cour des Comptes (Treasury) is close to where it was in the days of the Dukes of Brabant, in the Hôtel d'Arconati on the Place Royale. On the other side of the Place Royale, the Flemish regional government has taken over the Hôtel Errera, a building that figures largely in the American sociologist Renée C. Fox's memoirs, *In the Belgian Château* (1994).

LIFE AT THE PALACE

Duke John I (1261-94) followed the custom of inviting troubadours to his court from Provence, and wrote a number of *minneliedjes* (troubadour songs) himself, in Flemish, Provençal and Swabian. These mostly concern his favourite pursuits of jousting, feasting, drinking and seducing noble young ladies. Among the writers active during his reign were the French-speaker Adenet le Roi (his epic *Cléomades* is dedicated to the duke), and the great Flemish mystic writer Hadewijch, a noblewoman from Antwerp who lived in Brussels. Adenet did not stay long at John's court, which was predominantly Flemish-speaking at the time, but rather found a new patron in Guy of Dampierre, the Count of Flanders, who favoured French.

John I was a competent, if not brilliant, poet. An example of his work gives an idea of what most interested him:

Eens meien morgens vroege	One May morning early in the morning,
Was ic upgestaen;	I got up;
In een scoen boemgardekin	in a pretty orchard
Soud ic spelen gaen:	I wanted to go and play;
Daer vant ic drie joncfrouwen staen;	There I found three young ladies,
Si waren so wale gedaen...	They looked so beautiful…
Harbalorifa, harbalorifa.	Harbalorifa, harbalorifa.

John I's descendant, Duchess Jeanne, married the much younger Wenceslas of Luxembourg. Jeanne died in 1406, at the age of eighty-four; Wenceslas died at the age of forty-three, in 1383, the same year that the Florentine adventurer, Buonaccorso Pitti, left this fascinating account of life at the Coudenberg:

> The Duke of Brabant was in Brussels with many great lords holding jousts and tournaments, dancing and gambling. In the end I lost the 2,000 gold francs which I had brought with me from Bernardo di Cino, by staking 300 florins at a time on who would throw the highest numbers with two dice. The previous night I had lost 500 francs that I had borrowed from the duke, and so I gave up, as I had only 550 francs at my house.
>
> The duke and the other lords got up and entered the hall where there were many lords and ladies dancing, and as I stood there I was happy to see a young beauty of fourteen years, unmarried, daughter of a great baron, who came to me and said: "Come and dance, Lombard. Don't feel bad because you've lost; God will surely help you." And she gave me her hand. I followed her. The duke called me over and said: "What have you lost tonight?" I answered: "I've lost the remainder of the 2,000 francs which I brought with me to Brussels." He said: "I believe it, and

if I had lost that much I wouldn't be putting on such a good face as you are; go and enjoy the feast, and only good fortune will follow you."

The next morning I put 500 gold francs in a purse, and took them to the duke, saying: "Give me leave; I wish to find better fortune elsewhere." He answered: "If you want, then try again with these 500 francs and see if your luck turns in your favour; and if you lose then give them to me another time, when you are wealthier." I thanked him, saying that I had a great need to go to England, and did not wish to play again. He replied: "Take these 500 francs with you and give them to me another year when you have regained what you have lost." Then he called one of his courtiers and instructed him to make out a letter making me a special servant of his person.

Buonaccorso returned later on and won his money back.

The Burgundians

Duchess Jeanne left no successors. The daughter of Marguerite of Brabant (Jeanne's sister) and Louis de Male, Count of Flanders, also called Marguerite, had married the Duke of Burgundy, Philip the Bold. While Marguerite of Flanders was named as Duchess Jeanne's successor, the people of Brabant preferred Philip the Bold's son, Antoine, the first Burgundian to become Duke of Brabant and master of most of the southern Netherlands in 1406. Antoine of Burgundy was killed at the Battle of Agincourt in 1415; it was said that he had been in such haste to come to the aid of the French that he went into battle with neither armour nor helmet.

The economic situation went downhill. Mass unemployment, inflation and a devaluation of the currency led to rioting in 1416. Antoine's successor, John IV, unable to master the increasingly chaotic political situation, temporarily stood aside for his younger brother, Philippe de Saint-Pol, who in 1421 gave the city a new charter, known as "la Loi", greatly increasing the power of the *métiers* or artisans (see p.3).

Philippe de Saint-Pol succeeded as Duke of Brabant in 1427, but died three years later. From 1430 Brussels entered a more stable period, under the rule of Philip the Good, whose reign lasted until 1467. The territory of the dukes of Burgundy increased rapidly. By various means, Namur, Hainaut, Luxembourg, Zeeland, and Friesland all came under Burgundian domination. The duke favoured Brussels as an administrative centre, and his presence and that of his court naturally brought some renewed prosperity even if weighing heavily on the city finances. While the official capital of Burgundy was Dijon, Philip the Good found Brussels a more convenient place to remain for much of his reign. The presence of one of the Chambres des Comptes, or royal treasuries, meant that there was always a large number of the duke's officials in Brussels. Philip attempted an early sort of Thatcherite free-market revolution, cutting the amount of taxes that had to be raised, opening up the markets to foreigners, and combating restrictive practices by the butchers' guild. Unlike Margaret Thatcher, however, the duke favoured the arts and letters, his collection of books forming the basis of the modern-day national library of Belgium. His personality made him well loved, even if his policies did not suit everyone.

New industries took the place of the luxury cloth trade, and Brussels became a major centre for the manufacture of tapestries. In 1475 the first printing works opened, producing letters of indulgence. The city also became noted for its goldsmiths. In general, however, the economic situation was far from favourable, and by the end of Philip the Good's reign, the city was teetering on the edge of bankruptcy again.

The accession of Philip's son, Charles the Bold ("Le Téméraire") marked an abrupt turn for the worse. Charles disliked the *Bruxellois* and transferred his capital in the Low Countries to Mechelen. Charles' boldness was his undoing. His reckless aggression towards France led to his total defeat and death at Nancy in 1477. The result of his temerity was that the dukes of Burgundy no longer ruled over Burgundy; the Low Countries, "nos pays de par deça" ("our lands on this side") as they called them, were now the centre of their activities.

THE HABSBURGS

Charles the Bold's daughter Mary now had to face Louis XI's campaign to conquer the Low Countries. Brussels was not only under attack from Flanders and from France, but also had to contend with civil unrest between the *lignagers* (patricians) and *métiers* (artisans) within its walls. Famines and plague increased the misery of the citizens. Following Mary of Burgundy's death in 1482, her husband, Maximilian of Austria (a Habsburg), took the reins of power until his son, Philip the Handsome, could succeed to the throne. Philip chose as his wife Jeanne, daughter of Isabelle of Castille and Ferdinand of Aragon; their son Charles was born in 1500 in Ghent.

Brussels regained its position as capital of the Low Countries and some degree of economic stability returned. The future Charles V remained at Mechelen with the regent, Margaret of Austria. From the time of his assumption of power as archduke in 1515 until his resignation in 1555, Brussels was his main residence and the uncontested capital of the

Low Countries. By virtue of being the grandson of Ferdinand of Aragon, Charles inherited Spain in 1516, after his mother Jeanne was declared insane. She suffered from delusions of grandeur, which was odd considering that she was Queen of Spain, and is always known as Jeanne La Folle in French.

In 1519 Charles V was elected Holy Roman Emperor, with not only vast dominions in Europe, but also the Spanish Empire for good measure. Charles always thought of Brabant as his home; he spoke French and some Flemish, but hardly any German or Spanish. The connection with Spain proved to be a catastrophe for the Belgians, as we shall see. But Charles V understood the Belgian mentality well, and remained popular to the end of his tenure. By generously doling out jobs and favours to the indigenous nobility, and playing different political factions off against each other, he was able to keep the country under control without having to use force.

In Brussels, Charles reduced the power of both the artisans and the *lignagers*. From 1532 anyone of noble birth could become an *échevin* (mag-

istrate). The imposition of higher taxes without consultation of the artisans led to rioting in the same year. Further limitations on the privileges
of the city followed; Brussels could not expect to hold on to its medieval
status under an absolutist emperor. Yet under Charles V and his sister,
Mary of Hungary, Brussels became wealthy again. Visitors were amazed by
the riches on display. Albrecht Dürer wrote in 1520:

> I saw the things which have been brought to the King from the new land
> of gold (Mexico), a sun all of gold a whole fathom broad, and a moon all
> of silver of the same size, also two rooms full of the armour of the people
> there, and all manner of wondrous weapons of theirs, harness and darts...

There was genuine sadness when Charles abdicated in 1555, ex-
hausted by forty years of continual travelling and debilitated by illness
(mainly gout and asthma). With his son and successor, Philip II of Spain,
Bruxellois were to have even more reasons for regret.

THE COUDENBERG

Philip the Good's move to Brussels had necessitated the extension of the
Coudenberg, which became one of Europe's most impressive palaces.
Philip had a great hall built that extended into the present-day Place
Royale, the Magna Aula, measuring 140 feet by more than fifty. On top
of the main hall were two storeys of state offices. The hall had a wooden
ceiling, with no internal pillars supporting the roof. Here the ruler could
hold his assemblies as well as celebrations.

The hall was the scene of Charles V's farewell address in 1555, which
seems to have genuinely moved his audience, as many were in tears.
Charles apologized for any injustices that he might have committed during
his reign (without any reference to the Spanish Inquisition, one might
add). There was a gasp of dismay when Charles' son Philip II of Spain was
presented to them, and he had to confess to not knowing any French.

The Italian Antonio de Beatis gives an account of his visit in 1518:

> We also saw the Catholic King's palace [the Coudenberg] where his
> father King Philip [Philip the Fair, Duke of Burgundy] was born. It con-
> tains a large and very lofty hall where they joust without saddles when

the weather is too bad for jousting outside in the great square in front of the palace.

Beside it lies a great park with stags and goats and other animals, and a garden made in the form of a huge maze with many rooms and paths over two paces wide and walls twelve spans high closely plaited and woven from certain shoots which are found in the depths of woods; they bear leaves like those of the hazel but smoother and shinier and the effect is most beautiful.

There is also a fine tennis court surrounded by sloping half-roofs and beneath these and over the walls large numbers of spectators can look at the game... There are some rooms where we noticed a most ingenious secret device: a niche in a corner, carefully decorated and constructed in the same wood I have mentioned, which also serves to conceal a door leading into another room in such a way that if it were not pointed out you would never have guessed that there was a door there at all. There is also a large room containing a bed 34 spans di canna broad and 26 spans long with bolsters at the head and the foot, sheets and a white quilt, and we gathered that the Count had it made because he liked to hold frequent banquets and to see his guests get drunk, and when they could no longer stand on their feet, he had them thrown on to this bed.

We also saw a splendid kitchen there in the middle of which was a vast fireplace, divided by a wall two rods high, in such a way that a fire could be made against either side and thus two fires could readily be used at the same time.

The dukes of Burgundy also extended their park behind the palace, which now reached all the way to the second set of city walls, corresponding to the present-day Boulevard du Régent, with the Treurenberg at one end and the Porte de Namur at the other. The dukes could ride through their park and enter the Cathedral of St. Gudule through a rear door unnoticed.

The ruler also had his own secret garden behind the palace, known as La Feuillée. Charles V built a new structure of banks of greenery resembling a maze, so that his garden received the name La Labyrinthe, and also had a swimming pool constructed. Don Calvete de Estrella, who accompanied Philip II, on his first visit to Brussels in 1549, describes Charles V's park as follows:

A closed garden—called La Feuillée—filled with trees of a single species, interlaced and trimmed with skill and variety, quite unheard of. There are nothing but alleys, porticos, entrances, bowers… where a delicious freshness reigns. You could call it a new labyrinth of Crete, full of ponds, canals and fountains.

John Evelyn visited in 1641 and wrote at length on the park:

From hence we walked into the Parke which for being intirely within the walls of the Citty is particularly remarkable; nor is it less pleasant than of in the most solitary recesse so naturally is it furnish'd with whatever may render it agreeable, melancholy, and country-like. Here is a stately heronry, divers springs of water, artificial cascades, rocks, grotts, one whereof is composed of the extravagant rootes of trees cunningly built and hung together. In this Parke are both fallow and red deare.

From hence we were led into the Manege, and out of that into a most sweete and delicious garden, where was another grott, of more neate and costly materials, full of noble statues, and entertaining us with artificial musiq; but the hedge of water, in forme of lattice-worke, which the fontanier caused to ascend out of the earth by degrees, exceedingly pleased and surpris'd me, for thus with a pervious wall, or rather a palisad hedge, of water, was the whole parterre environ'd.

There is likewise a faire Aviary, and in the court next it are kept divers sort of animals, rare and exotic fowle, as eagles, cranes, storkes, bustards, pheasants of several kinds, and a duck having 4 wings. In another division of the same close, are rabbits of an almost perfect yellow colour.

The Coudenberg played host to countless exiled rulers and aristocrats; for this reason it became known as "L'Auberge des Princes" (The Inn of Princes). A century after Charles V's abdication, Queen Christina of Sweden made a memorable visit here, after renouncing the throne at the age of twenty-eight in order to become a Roman Catholic and travel the world. Her first six weeks in Brussels, from December 23, 1654, were spent at the Coudenberg, after which she moved to the Palais d'Egmont in the Rue aux Laines. Her conversion ceremony took place the day after her arrival in the private rooms of the governor-general of the Spanish

Netherlands, Archduke Leopold-Wilhelm. The rest of her time she spent going to balls and receptions, going round town with her ladies-in-waiting and playing billiards. Everyone was eager to talk to the charismatic exile. She had an excellent command of French, and was so talkative it was hard for anyone else to get a word in. After ten months she left for Innsbruck to repeat the same ceremony of abjuration, accompanied by the Jesuit father who had first received her into the Church.

THE END OF THE COUDENBERG

The Coudenberg Palace no longer exists. During the night of February 3, 1731 a vat of sugar being heated up to make caramel boiled over. The cooks tried to put out the fire themselves, while the nightwatchman had drunk too much and could not be woken up. When the fire brigade finally arrived, the water froze in their buckets, and eventually the entire structure burned down. A large part of the library of the dukes of Burgundy was saved, as well as many art treasures, but many priceless works were lost. The palace was left in a ruined state until 1774, when it was decided to build a new residential area on the site of the old palace. The governor-general's court in the meantime had moved to the Hôtel de Nassau, whose chapel is now a part of the Bibliothèque Royale. The chapel wall with a carving of St. George killing the dragon can be seen from the outside.

The job of organizing the rebuilding of the area of the royal palace fell to Count Starhemberg, minister plenipotentiary of Empress Maria Theresa, rather than to the governor-general, Charles of Lorraine. The design of the buildings was entrusted to a French architect, Barnabé Guimard. Guimard's plans foresaw the creation of a grid of streets around the Parc de Bruxelles, with buildings all in a similar classical style.

PALAIS ROYAL

The official residence of the Belgian monarch has never found much favour with the royal family, because of its proximity to the streets around about. The Dutch King William I created the palace by combining two private houses, the Hôtel Belgiojoso and the Hôtel Bender, into one, with an arcade and a classical pediment in between. The results were considered unsatisfactory, and another architect, Tilman-François Suys was appointed in 1825 to remodel the building so that both sides were uniform. The whole was remodelled and extended between 1904 and 1912, but the effect is still very dark and heavy. When the king is working in the building, the Belgian flag flies above, but he mostly prefers to stay in his Palais de Laeken.

The Hôtel Belle Vue, on the right-hand side, appears to be part of the royal palace but is in fact a separate building that has been joined on to the palace with a gallery. A wine merchant, Philippe de Proft, had it built as a hotel in 1777. It was Wellington's headquarters in 1815 and was fought over by the Dutch and Belgians in 1830, when it was riddled with bullet holes. It then became Brussels' most expensive hotel for a while. Now it houses the Musée de la Dynastie, an exhibition that is worth a visit to gain some idea of the different rulers of Belgium and their regal exploits. King Baudouin, who ruled from 1950 to 1993, has a special memorial. His brother Albert II, is now on the throne, although many expected that he would stand aside for his son, Crown Prince Philippe. Baudouin was an arch-Catholic, married to the Spanish Countess Fabiola. Unfortunately they were unable to have children, so his brother took over the throne. Baudouin's principles were such that he refused to sign a bill legalizing abortion in 1990, and instead abdicated for one day to allow the bill to pass. His devotion to duty and sincerity won him the respect of the country, and there was genuine grief at his early death in 1993 at the age of sixty-three from a heart attack.

PARC DE BRUXELLES
The Parc, opposite the royal palace, was to begin with a continuation of the Forêt de Soignes. When it was enclosed by the second set of city walls, it covered around 100 acres. The present-day Parc de Bruxelles (Warande in Dutch) is only a small remnant of the earlier space and is laid out in the shape of a masonic symbol, with the top of a pair of dividers on the Rue de la Loi end. The word *warande* is Flemish for an enclosure or warren, which the current park certainly does not resemble, for it is very much in the formal French style, with statues and fountains and not much grass to sit on. The original Warande was a less formal affair; 1,218 trees had to be cut down, and 3,284 replanted, to create the present park, which is about half the size of the royal hunting park.

The Parc has its fair share of stories. In 1781 a nightwatchman noticed a man trying to force his way through the hedge into the park. On re-straining him he found that he had hold of none other than the Emperor Joseph II, who, it seems, was in the habit of going for a midnight walk, and was hoping to find some peace and quiet in the park. In 1717, Peter the Great was staying in the Coudenberg, when it was still standing. After imbibing to excess, he fell into a fountain in the park (a plaque was put up to mark the event).

If you walk through the park you will notice the oddly shaped statues, reminiscent of ancient Greek "herms", without arms or legs. A few have their noses missing. For a long time it was said that Lord Byron had been in the habit of breaking the noses with his walking stick when he stayed nearby in 1816. Many years later, the Austrian statesman, Count Metternich, confessed to being the culprit. He was sent to Brussels in 1791 as part of his education, when he was eighteen. He returned to the city in 1848 for a while after an uprising and stayed at what is now the Maison Communale de St. Josse-ten-Noode.

RUE ROYALE

The Place Royale, where this avenue begins, looks out over the lower city. For most of Brussels' history one would not have seen this view, but thanks to the demolition undertaken by the city government in the 1950s nothing stands in the way of the panorama. The church behind you is St. Jacques-sur-Coudenberg, first constructed in a purely classical style. A bell-tower was added later to give it a more church-like appearance. The first place of worship here was an oratory put up by the Duke of Brabant around 1100. It was replaced by a Gothic creation, which burnt down in 1738, and then by the present structure.

The statue in the middle is of Godefroid de Bouillon (1061-1100), sometimes called Godefroid the Bearded, who led the First Crusade that managed to defeat the Saracens against all the odds at Antioch. He was offered the crown of first King of Jerusalem in 1099 but preferred to take the title of Avoué du Saint-Sépulcre (Defender of the Holy Sepulcre). He died of typhoid the following year. Victor Devogel relates in *Légendes bruxelloises* how, on January 19, 1101, a watchman looking out over the city walls from the Porte St. Gudule saw what appeared to be an army of Turks approaching along the Chaussée de Louvain; the men all had beards and blackened faces and wore oriental robes. Then they gave a signal; these were the remnants of the Brussels contingent sent on the First Crusade, who had been given up for lost by their wives and families. As one might expect, the women told the men to take it easy and put their feet up. To commemorate the event, on the evening of January 19 women were put in charge of the household and allowed literally to wear the trousers. The custom, known as Vrouwkens Avond or La Veillée des Dames, was celebrated up until the First World War by some patrician families.

The Place Royale conceals a well-kept secret, namely the underground cellars of the Palais du Coudenberg, the original residence of the dukes of Brabant. When the square was built, the cellars were left as they were to save money. It is sometimes possible to visit the cellars; the tourist office can tell you when. There were proposals in 2001 to turn the space into a car-park, hardly credible considering Brussels' recent history.

RUE ISABELLE: CHARLOTTE BRONTË AND THE PROFESSOR

Another of Brussels' vanished streets, it would hardly be heard of today if it had not been the breeding ground for a great piece of English literature, *Villette*. The street itself used to form a triangle with the Rue Terarken and the Rue des Douze Apôtres, and ran at a slight angle from the present Rue Royale downhill. Adjoining the Rue d'Isabelle (as it was originally called) was the Jardin du Grand Serment des Arbalètriers, the Guild of Crossbowmen, responsible for building Notre Dame des Victoires on the Sablon.

Constantin Heger (1809-95) was the son of a jeweller in the Rue Royale, who had ruined himself trying to save a friend from financial difficulties. The young Constantin went to Paris and found work as the secretary to a barrister. On a visit to Brussels in 1830 he found himself in the middle of the Belgian Revolution; Heger went off to find some gunpowder and fought the Dutch in the Parc de Bruxelles. He married soon after, but his wife and child died in a cholera epidemic during 1832. His second wife, Zoé Parent, whom he married in 1836, was in charge of a *pension* at 32 Rue d'Isabelle. Together they started a *pensionnat* or boarding school for young ladies.

The Hegers charged 300 Dutch florins a year for boarders, 150 for day students. Heger was intellectually gifted and a fine teacher. A few years later, in February 1842, Patrick Brontë, a Yorkshire vicar, brought along his two daughters Emily and Charlotte, and entrusted them to the Hegers' care. Charlotte was soon smitten with Constantin; one of her earlier poems entitled "Master and Pupil" shows her feelings:

I gave, at first, attention close

Then interest warm ensued;
From interest, as improvement rose,
Succeeded gratitude.
Obedience was no effort soon,
And labour was no pain;
If tired, a word, a glance alone
Would give me strength again.

With such motivation, Charlotte quickly became proficient in French. M. Heger kept her *devoirs,* or essays, which have been published as *The Belgian Essays* (1992). He was an extremely strict teacher, and generally completely rewrote Charlotte's work. While Charlotte was entirely receptive to his criticisms, Emily Brontë was not pleased to have her work written all over. After nine months the sisters were called back to Yorkshire, as their aunt had died. Charlotte returned on her own in January 1843, and was retained to teach English at an annual salary of 400 francs. Constantin was aware of her obsession with him and avoided her. Mme Heger equally stayed out of her way. Charlotte continued to send passionate letters to Constantin, who never replied to any of them and usually threw them in the wastepaper bin. His wife, for some reason, rescued them, and the whole collection ended up in the British Museum in 1913, as a gift from the Hegers' son Paul. The Hegers' *pensionnat* became world-famous and attracted tourists from far and wide. Constantin was delighted to tell visitors that he was indeed "the professor", while his wife disliked the depiction of Brussels in *Villette.* The building at 32 Rue Isabelle was demolished in 1909 to make way for the Palais des Beaux Arts.

Charlotte's views on the Belgians were almost as negative as Baudelaire's. Belgium appears as Labassecour, or Farmyard, in *Villette*, a reference to the Belgians' coarse manners. The Rue Isabelle is called the Rue Fossette (Dimple Street) in *Villette.* Charlotte worshipped Heger, while having nothing good to say for anyone else. In 1842 she wrote to Ellen Nussey:

If the national character of the Belgians is to be measured by the character of most of the girls in the school, it is a character singularly cold, selfish, animal and inferior—They are besides very mutinous and difficult for the teachers to manage—and their principles are rotten to the core—we avoid them—which is not difficult to do—as we have the brand of Protestantism and Anglicanism upon us.

In a letter to her brother Branwell, she says: "Nobody ever gets in a passion here—such a thing is not known—the phlegm that thickens their blood is too gluey to boil... The black swan Mr Heger is the sole veritable exception."

One could say that she suffered from culture shock. The fact that she was a Protestant and a provincial in a Catholic country weighed heavily on her. Charlotte often disparaged the Catholic Church, calling its rituals "mummery" and the priests "idiotic and mercenary".

Anyone reading the first version of *Villette*—*The Professor*—could easily have found the Pensionnat Heger. In the first version it is an English teacher, William Crimsworth, who is the object of one of his student's attentions. The following passage comes at the beginning of the story, when he is waiting to have his first interview with the owner of the Pensionnat:

> I saw what a fine street was the Rue Royale and, walking leisurely along its broad pavement, I continued to survey its stately hotels, till the palisades. The gates and trees of the park, appearing in sight, offered to my eye a new attraction. I remember, before entering the park, I stood awhile to contemplate the statue of General Belliard and then I advanced to the top of the great staircase just beyond and I looked down into a narrow back-street which, I afterwards learnt, was called the Rue d'Isabelle. I well recollect that my eye rested on the green door of a rather large house opposite, where, on a brass plate, was inscribed "Pensionnat de demoiselles".

The Professor was rejected by nine different publishers and was only published in 1857, two years after Charlotte's death. Compared to *Villette*, it appears a much more juvenile work, lacking the intensity and controlled despair of the second version. A story without much dramatic incident about two working schoolteachers, with female emancipation as one of its main themes, did not find much favour with publishers of the time. Charlotte had suffered the loss of her sisters and brother in the time between the two versions, which made all the difference to the tone of the two books.

One can only speculate on Constantin Heger's influence on Charlotte Brontë. She said herself that he was "the only master I have ever had." Heger came from a rigorously classical tradition; his main contribution was to make Charlotte think more abstractly about concepts. He admired her gift for logic, but found her too stubborn. No.32 now lies under the entrance hall to the Palais des Beaux Arts. A plaque to Charlotte Brontë was unveiled in 1980 in the Rue Ravenstein, to the left of the Palais des Beaux Arts.

NOTRE-DAME-AUX-NEIGES AND VICTOR HUGO

The Rue de l'Enseignement and the Rue de la Révolution follow in part the course of the former Rue Notre-Dame-aux-Neiges, which went in a boomerang shape from the Rue Royale to the Place des Barricades. The road originally led from the Porte St. Gudule (a notorious prison) on the Treurenberg to Schaerbeek before it was cut off by the second city walls in 1370.

A small chapel called Notre-Dame-aux-Neiges was built in 1621: the Virgin Mary had caused snow to fall in the summer as a sign that a chapel should be built there. The area had many lacemakers who would come and pray that their lace would be perfect and white as snow. The entire area of Notre-Dame-aux-Neiges was razed in 1875 and 1876 for public health reasons.

In 1861, Victor Hugo, on one of his regular trips to Brussels, moved into 64 Rue du Nord, the landlady being one Catherine Rosiers. His mistress and muse, Juliette Drouet, lodged nearby at 91 Rue Notre-Dame-aux-Neiges, in an insalubrious district that was demolished in 1875. Hugo's visits to Brussels were a time for fun and games. Thus his diary entry for April 8: "The Dutchwoman, 3 francs. 11.30 at night, 42 Rue de l'Hôpital, third floor." Then April 9: "Welcome to Jeannette, a new Flemish servant, who doesn't understand a word of French, 1 franc." On April 14: "9.30 am. Bis. Tota. Johann 1fr50." (Twice. Everything. Jeannette). Hugo wrote his diary entries in a mixture of Spanish, Latin and French code, to put Juliette, who was bound to read them, off the scent. "Toto" then turns his attention to his landlady. April 28: "Mlle C. Rosiers, piernas (legs)." May 3: "B.C.R." (Baisé Catherine Rosiers)." On June 18, he is with the Dutchwoman Hélène: "Helena nuda. Rubens. Anniversaire de Waterloo. Bataille gagnée."

During May and June 1861 Hugo stayed near Waterloo with Juliette, working on the chapter of *Les Mis-érables* which has the battle as its background, with the intention of making the writing as authentic as possible. His Belgian publishers, Lacroix & Verboeckhoven had agreed, with some reluctance, to advance him 300,000 francs for his forthcoming blockbuster. The first part was launched with a dinner at the publishers' offices in the Impasse du Parc (now the Rue des Colonies), on September 16, 1862, at which every one of the eighty guests had

their photo taken. The book was a sensation, and made both author and publishers millionaires. Lacroix & Verboeckhoven let success go to their heads; after the Franco-Prussian war of 1870 they even went bankrupt.

Victor Hugo's son, Charles, had his home at 4 Place des Barricades. The Belgian freedom-fighters mounted barricades here from which they could fire on the Dutch during the 1830 revolution. His mother, Adèle Hugo, died there in 1868; his father was a frequent visitor. The location is indicated by the sign *L'Homme qui Rit* (The Laughing Man). Until 1875, the area between the Place des Barricades and the Rue du Congrès comprised many "impasses" or slums, with their ever-present prostitutes. One entry in Hugo's diary notes that "at 2 Rue du Rempart du Nord, behind the Place des Barricades, you can get a cigar, a shot of gin, a cup of coffee and a woman all for 25 centimes."

Adèle Hugo held a weekly dinner at the Place des Barricades, where Baudelaire was often present, in the hope of finding a publisher for his work. The poet disliked Hugo's children ("des poisons") and was put out by the necessity of finding a clean shirt to wear. The French lyric poet, Paul Verlaine, visited the Hugos in August 1867 but was not impressed by the location. He noted in *Croquis de Belgique* (1895):

> The place resembles the least picturesque backwater you could imagine, with its abominable architecture from the end of the Premier Empire...
> A peaceful spot if there ever was, with its stucco, and pleasantly orna-

mented with a fair number of trees, no commerce and all comfortably-off bourgeoisie. I rang the doorbell just like everyone else here.

The meeting was a great success. Hugo flattered his young guest by reading some of his poetry out loud.

The Place des Barricades was also the scene of Hugo's last days in Belgium. He had come in May 1871 to deal with his son Charles' inheritance. Late in the evening of May 27, a group of students (including the son of a government minister) started to shout "Death to the traitor! String him up!" and to throw stones at his windows, in protest against an article he had written in support of the Paris Commune. Hugo, in his *Carnets*, makes out that the mob were out to murder him, yet none of the neighbours seemed to notice anything. Only when the crowd had dispersed did the police arrive. By commenting on French politics, Hugo had broken the conditions of his residence in Belgium. The Belgian Senate issued the expulsion order. He left for Vianden in Luxembourg never to return.

MONT DES ARTS AND THE UNIVERSITÉ LIBRE DE BRUXELLES

The Rue des Sols, which runs alongside the Mont des Arts, the steep slope leading up to the Place Royale, is associated with the so-called Miracle de la Rue des Sols, a legend concerning the theft of the host by the Jews in 1365 (see p.79). The street was also the site of the palace of Cardinal Perrenot de Granvelle, the man largely blamed for the excesses of the Inquisition in the 1570s. With a certain touch of irony, the secular Université Libre de Bruxelles was started in the same building by the freemason Verhaegen in 1834. Brussels had missed out on the opportunity to have its own university in 1423, the city fathers deciding that the presence of a university would corrupt the morals of their daughters, so it went to Louvain instead. The palace of Cardinal Granvelle was demolished to make way for the Galeries Ravenstein. New buildings were constructed for the ULB in Solbosch between 1921 and 1925, in Ixelles.

In medieval times the area between the Rue des Sols and the Rue des Douze Apôtres (of which there is only a tiny remnant now) was the centre of a small Jewish population who lived from trading and money-changing. The Jews moved here from St. Géry to be under the protection of the nearby Coudenberg Palace. Up until the building of the Mont des Arts, there were four streets called Ioden Trap or Jewish Steps running horizontally across the Mont des Arts, even though no Jews had lived there for a long time.

The present-day Mont des Arts, flanked by the Palais des Congrès and the Bibliothèque Royale Albert I, has been here since the 1950s. Older *Bruxellois* will tell you about the Mont des Arts of their youth, when it was known as the Quartier Latin of Brussels. The film historian, Eric de Kuyper, reminisces in *Passie voor Brussel* (1995):

> It was a strange little park, that had something Swiss about it, with its waterfalls and rocks. The best part were the two streets that ran either side. They were a little lower than the park and one of them made me think of a winding old, hollow way along the edge of a forest… It was a dark street with old houses and little shops selling antiques… Because the park looked a bit stiff and official, the street was that much more idiosyncratic and mysterious: it was as though you were coming down into the city by a secret path, after the openness of the Parc de Bruxelles and the Place Royale.

The Swiss-style Mont des Arts was built for the Universal Exhibition of 1910 by the architect Vacherot, while the city decided what to do with the site. When the authorities proposed to replace it with the current version there was a huge outcry. It seemed that no one in the city wanted it to be demolished, but, as is the way here, the destruction went ahead. The railway line between the Gare du Midi and the Gare Centrale runs underneath the Boulevard de l'Empereur at the foot of the hill. The new gardens were laid out from 1954, while the Palais des Congrès and the Bibliothèque Royale were not finished until 1969. The archways and the flat spaces around the park are appreciated by rough sleepers and skateboarders.

Chapter Six
THE SOUTH: MYSTICS AND HERETICS

"Blessed be those who keep their hearts high, and their swords straight during the black days that are to come! "

Charles de Coster, *Thyl Ulenspiegel* (1867)

Many guidebooks point out that Brussels has more green space than any other capital city, except Washington DC, with the figure of thirty or forty square metres per inhabitant often given. If statistically true, this green space is concentrated in the prosperous southern suburbs of the city. When the Romans came there was forest all over southern Belgium, the Silva Carbonaria, a source of charcoal for the metalworking industry. The Forêt de Soignes, which stretches over the southern *communes* of the city, became the property of the Dukes of Brabant in 1197, and was reserved exclusively for hunting. Here and there monastic communities found tranquillity for their devotions. The woods were also a hideout for Protestants during the Reformation when the Spanish Inquisition was active.

JOHN OF RUYSBROECK AND GROENENDAEL

The Forêt de Soignes extends far into the *commune* of Rhode-St.-Genèse, an area popular with wealthy French-speakers, but not one of the nineteen central *communes*. On the northern side, at the end of the Chaussée de la Hulpe, is a museum dedicated to John of Ruysbroeck (1293-1381), known as Ruysbroeck l'Admirable in French, who is credited with laying the foundations of Western mysticism, as well as being a major figure in Flemish literature. As far as anyone knows, he came from the village of Ruysbroeck, about six miles south of Brussels. His uncle was a canon of the Cathedral of St. Gudule and arranged for his education in the cathedral school. Thereafter Ruysbroeck became a chaplain at the cathedral.

The fourteenth century was a time of upheaval in the Catholic Church: the Pope was exiled to Avignon, and heretics were increasing in number. John of Ruysbroeck was disgusted by the greed and hypocrisy of the higher priesthood and the nobility: "all for money" was his judgment. He also abominated any kind of heresy. His struggle with another mystic, Bloemaerdinne or Heilwege Blommaert, is well known, but the nature of her beliefs is obscure, as none of her writings have survived. Even John of Ruysbroeck never actually mentioned her by name. Bloemaerdinne is only known indirectly through what is said about her in John of Ruysbroeck's biography *De origine monasterii Viridisvallis* (The Origin of the Monastery of Groenendael) written in 1420 by Pommerius, one of Ruysbroeck's followers at Groenendael. The passage concerning the female heretic runs:

> When [John of Ruysbroeck] was still a secular priest there lived in Brussels a woman who adhered to a perverse belief and who was vulgarly known as Bloemaerdinne. She was so highly regarded by the common people that one imagined that when she approached the altar to receive Holy Communion she was flanked on either side by two seraphs. She wrote a great deal over the free spirit and the most abominable carnal love, which she called seraphic. Therefore she was considered to have discovered a new teaching. When she gave instruction and wrote she sat in a silver seat, which after her death, it is said, was offered to the Duchess of Brabant out of wonderment. The people believed that cripples could be healed by touching her dead body. Our Ruysbroeck, a man filled with a God-fearing spirit, took pity on such errors, and resisted these corrupting beliefs. And though she counted many followers, he

took up the shield of truth and unmasked her misleading and heretical writings, which she was in the habit of writing down every year as having been given to her by God...

It seems that Bloemaerdinne turned divine love into something more physical. The myth has it that Bloemaerdinne's supporters won the day, so Ruysbroeck withdrew to the monastery of Groenendael in the forest in 1343. Bloemaerdinne had already died in about 1335. There is also the theory that Ruysbroeck's sarcastic comments upset the canons of St. Gudule.

The heresy of the Free Spirit was very prevalent in Brussels during the fourteenth century. Some held the pantheist belief that God is present in everything. One group, the Homines Intelligentiae, believed they were directly inspired by the Holy Spirit and could no longer sin. One of their leaders, Aegidius Cantor, was accused in 1410 of going around naked, carrying a plate of meat on his head to a pauper. Nudist sects existed in the thirteenth century and posed something of a problem for the Church. Such groups were also often accused of not observing Lent, but the records show that the charges against heretics were mostly quite conjectural.

Ruysbroeck set up his community in Groenendael along with some like-minded colleagues. Many came to seek him out to ask for his teaching. He has left about 250 works, all written in "unmixed Brussels Dutch", from which one can gain an accurate idea of his philosophy. During his lifetime there was a movement favouring a more personal relationship with God. Ruysbroeck, unlike the corrupt priests he had left behind in Brussels, felt that the individual had to strive to have an experience of God, by turning inwards and also by turning outwards by reaching out to others: "without deeds of love we cannot be united with God." He found the Forêt de Soignes an inspiring place for his meditations. He observed: "Those who do not praise God here will remain dumb for ever." He often used metaphors derived from plants and animals in his writings. Many of his ideas can be found in his forerunner, the mysterious Hadewijch, a great poetess who may have come from Antwerp to Brussels in the twelfth century. The Flemish term *minne* or love is central in both their writings. Hadewijch was certainly the better poet, but virtually nothing is known about her. Ruysbroeck had a strong constitution, and lived to be eighty-eight. His order was disbanded by the Austrians in 1783 and the monks dispersed. A piece of his pelvis is preserved in the parish church of Ruys-broeck.

ERASMUS AND THE REFORMATION

It would be no exaggeration to say that the Reformation, or rather, the suppression of the Reformation by the Habsburgs, has determined Belgian identity right down to the present day. Even now, when less than one-tenth of the population go to church, everyone has to define themselves as pro- or anti-Catholic by their political affiliation, their trade union, and their sickness fund. Even the boy scouts and girl guides cannot escape the confessional nature of Belgian society (alongside the Catholic and Social-ist sections there are also the Pluralist Scouts and Guides).

At the beginning of the sixteenth century there were few signs of the coming storm. The building and embellishment of churches, funded by the laity and the state, had reached new heights in the second half of the previous century. Alongside the monasteries and convents, there had long been believers who held unconventional ideas about religion, and who wished to live in quasi-monastic communities without being controlled by the official Church. The *béguines* and their male equivalents, the *beghards*, were often suspected of heresy by the Church during the Middle Ages, but generally left alone if they did not cause trouble. The intelligentsia in Brus-sels would also have come into contact with reform-minded individuals such as Bohemian Hussites, the Swiss Waldensians, and English Lollards.

There was certainly discontent in the seminaries with the established Church, and it took just two extraordinary individuals to demolish the foundations of medieval Christian practice. Erasmus of Rotterdam (1469?-1536) had worked for many years to bring about a renewal of the faith, using his profound knowledge of the Greek New Testament to show how far the medieval Church had strayed from true spirituality. Uniting the study of the Scriptures in the original languages with the rediscovered clas-sical tradition would, he hoped, bring about a marriage of reason and spir-ituality. The idea that believers should read the Bible for themselves, rather than rely on commentaries, was far more potent than Erasmus' attacks on the corruption of the Church. From 1510, the whole education system in the Low Countries was re-organized along Erasmian lines.

Erasmus had no wish to split the Church, and naïvely believed that the Church would reform itself. Martin Luther (1483-1546), with his

Ninety Propositions, in 1519, rejected virtually everything the Church stood for, out of hand. The papal bull, *Exsurge domine*, condemning Luther, followed by the burning of Luther's books at the 1521 Diet of Worms, put Erasmus in a dangerous position. For his own safety he left Louvain and came to his friend Pieter Wijchman's house in Anderlecht (31 Rue du Chapitre, near the St. Guidon metro station) for five months from May 1521. The house was originally called De Swaene (The Swan) and had only been built in 1515. In 1920 it was due to be demolished, but fortunately it was saved and is now a museum with furniture, paintings and books from Erasmus' time, as well as a library.

Erasmus had powerful protectors including many of the crowned heads of Europe; for a short time between 1522 and 1523, an Anderlecht priest of Dutch origins became Pope Adrian VI, the last non-Italian pope before John Paul II. While he was in Anderlecht, Erasmus wrote letters complaining about the rumours circulating that he was dead or seriously ill:

> [The rumour went] that when I was taking care of my health by staying
> in the countryside at Anderlecht, I was keeping myself hidden away,
> when in fact I went on horseback practically every day to the city, and
> even returned to Louvain without unbridling my horse. More than once

I was [supposedly] keeping to my bed in Louvain, the victim of a fever resistant to any treatment; or I had fallen off my horse at the gates of Brussels, or perished after some paralysis, when, for many years I had never been in better health.

Every day I went to pay my respects to the bishops, even though, as it happens, I don't feel in the least bit like a courtier when I make these homages. I would take lunch with the cardinal, chat with the nuncios; I would visit the ambassadors, and they, in turn, would visit me in Anderlecht. I have never hidden myself away less in my life.

Erasmus' digestion improved and he suffered less from fever. He joked that he had turned from a city dweller into a country bumpkin, "ex urbano factus rusticus" while "rusticans Anderlaci" (rusticating in Anderlecht).

Erasmus could not escape being lumped together with Luther as an arch-heretic, even though he detested Luther's violent and obscene language. In 1521 he left the Low Countries forever for Basel. While Erasmus' biblical humanism appealed to the educated classes, Luther's writings had a tremendous impact among the rest of the population. The new religious ideas were debated in churches, taverns and virtually anywhere that was not completely cut off from the outside world. The high level of literacy among the Belgian population meant that the new vernacular translations of the Bible were widely read. It now seemed that anybody could interpret the Bible as they wished, something that was not at all acceptable to the Church.

Luther's idea that there should be no intermediary between believers and God had immense repercussions in practice. The priesthood, who had to be supported by the rest of the population, could be dispensed with. Resentment against the multitude of mendicant friars had already led the authorities in some towns to pass ordinances against excessive alms-giving and to establish funds for the genuinely poor. The cult of the saints and the Virgin Mary, which had no basis in the scriptures, was no longer necessary. The magical trappings of liturgy, the doctrine of transubstantiation, the selling of indulgences, would all be swept away.

The appeal of Luther's ideas was such that the Church authorities stopped the priests from preaching against him, since this only helped to bring his doctrines to the notice of a wider audience. The main centre of reformism was Antwerp, in particular among the Augustinians. Two of their number were brought to Brussels and executed on July 1, 1523. The population was horrified to see "two good men" put to death for their ideas. The repression of heresy made the reformists more cautious—the real explosion did not come until 1566. In the intervening years some 228 heretics were put to death in Brabant and perhaps ten times as many prosecuted.

The city authorities in Brussels, and elsewhere, had little enthusiasm for pursuing heretics. The edicts or "placards" against heresy, issued by Charles V, raised serious problems for the Belgian towns. Heresy was quite different from other crimes, in that it was equated with high treason, and had to be punished by death and confiscation of goods, but the latter was an infringement of one of the citizens' basic privileges. While other edicts could be modified in accordance with local legal practice, the edicts against heresy had to be applied literally, thus infringing the judicial independence of the cities. Prosecutions for heresy had formerly been the domain of the ecclesiastical courts but were now to be dealt with by the secular courts, since the authorities reasoned that too much time would be wasted debating points of doctrine in the ecclesiastical courts, while the civil authorities would pass a quick death sentence.

Charles V considered that a ruler bore "the primary responsibility of guarding and ensuring the observation of the Catholic religion." In the fifteenth century it was widely believed that blasphemy would lead to famines and war, so rulers would do all they could to promote religious observance. From about 1530, Anabaptists from Münster started to appear in Brussels, followed by Mennonites, and then Calvinists. Their first sermons took place in the Rue des Bogards (off the Boulevard Lemonnier) in the 1540s. From 1562, meetings, or conventicles, were held in de Heeghde, the part of the Forêt de Soignes that lies within the modern-day Brussels city limits. The domination of the reform movement by Calvinists was significant, since they believed that no one was obliged to obey worldly rulers, while the Lutherans followed a more conciliatory line towards the secular powers.

Charles V had abdicated in 1555, to be succeeded by his son, Philip II, husband of Mary Tudor of England. Philip had little time for the sensibilities of the Belgians. Rather than dispensing patronage to local nobles, as his father had done, almost his entire court was made up of Spaniards. A war with France gave him the excuse to garrison Brussels with Spanish military who quickly made themselves hated by everyone. In 1559 Philip returned to Spain, leaving the illegitimate daughter of Charles V, Marguerite of Parma, as governor of the Low Countries; at the same time, the Cardinal Perrenot de Granvelle was put in charge of a secret council, the Consulta, to advise her. The atmosphere of revolt was stirred up by the *rederijkerskamers* (chambers of rhetoric), which handed out or nailed to doorways scurrilous poems lampooning clerics and officials, and put on plays. As Richard Clough, a Welsh merchant living in Belgium at the time, put it: "There was at that tyme syche playes (of Reteryke) played that hath cost many a 1000 man's lyves..."

Resistance to the despotic Spanish regime centred around William of Orange and the Counts Egmont and Hornes. The Council of State obtained the recall of Cardinal de Granvelle, who was blamed more than Philip for the persecution of the Calvinists. Their pleas for a less intransigent line against the reformists, seconded by Marguerite of Parma, the governor-general, fell on deaf ears. Although the Inquisition was temporarily suspended in 1566, iconoclasm was already breaking out. Philip sent the Duke of Alva to restore order. As he said: "I would rather die a hundred times than rule over heretics."

The Inquisition

Alva instituted the Council of Troubles to try the ringleaders of the anti-Spanish party. The Counts of Egmont and Hornes were decapitated in the Grand-Place in June 1568 (see p.19), Egmont later becoming the subject of a play by Goethe and an overture by Beethoven. Hundreds of citizens were executed, yet the Inquisition was carried out by other Belgians rather than by Spaniards. At this time it was a capital offence to own a forbidden book, harbour a heretic, debate points of Scripture with laymen, or fail to denounce a heretic. Anyone who spent much time reading the Bible came under suspicion. Prisoners found themselves in a hopeless situation. Those who were accused were presumed guilty. Confessions would be extracted by torture on the rack. The fortunate ones were strangled first before being burned; the unfortunate were directly burned at the stake. In true Belgian style, the more pitiless the repression, the greater the resistance. Shopkeepers closed up shop; goods confiscated from heretics found no buyers. The authorities kept careful records of their activities. The following appears in the accounts of the *amman* (one of the city officials):

Payments to the public executioner:
August 18, 1500: payment for questioning Lauken van Moeseke, who
had blasphemed against the Host... August 30, 1500: payment for a red-
hot iron rod to be driven through the aforesaid Lauken's tongue...
payment for Lauken to be beheaded and his body exposed on the wheel
at Sint Quirinus.

By 1573 the Dutch rebels, led by William the Silent, had occupied
large swathes of Belgian territory. Alva's successor, Luis de Requesens,
tried to pursue a more moderate course, proclaiming the pope's general
amnesty for the Protestants. His sudden death in 1576 left Brussels in
the hands of the Council of State. The city was now threatened by mutinous Spanish armies roaming the countryside as well as the garrison
within. From 1577 to 1585 Brussels remained in a state of insurrection
against the Spanish. By 1580 the city was completely dominated by the
Calvinists, and the Catholic religion could no longer be practised
openly. The city declared its independence from Philip II; the churches
and convents were pillaged and their occupants driven out. The revolt
did not last long. Soon the *Bruxellois* had to face a formidable new ad-
versary, Alexander Farnese, son of Marguerite of Parma. Without any
significant military aid, Brussels quickly capitulated. Farnese wisely re-
frained from reprisals, a general amnesty was declared, and the rebels
were given safe passage to Holland. In exchange, the Catholic religion
was re-established and the damage done to the churches was to be repaired "at as small a cost as possible". The population had remained
mainly Catholic in any case, so there was little difficulty in restoring
the status quo. This was also the moment that Belgium and the Netherlands definitively split into two separate countries. Brussels itself had to
accept an ordinance in 1586 restoring the system of city government to
what it was under Charles V.

The consequences of the Counter-Reformation for Belgium were dev-
astating. The intellectuals, entrepreneurs, and many skilled artisans, who
largely favoured Protestantism, left for Holland or England. While the
Dutch profited hugely from this brain drain, Belgian society was literally
decapitated—some have called it the "Spanish lobotomy". Literature and
science, in particular, fell into a mediocrity from which they only started
to recover in the nineteenth century. Belgium was inevitably dragged down

along with Spain in the stultifying atmosphere created by the ruthless repression of free-thinkers.

ANDERLECHT: MARTYRDOM OF A SUPPORTER

To most foreigners, Anderlecht means football. FSC Anderlecht has its
home at the Stade Constant Vanden Stock, not far from Erasmus' house.
It is by far the best-known football club in Belgium, although not always
the most successful. Since 1946 Anderlecht has won 25 Belgian First Division championship. On the European stage the club's best years were in
1976 and 1978 when it won the UEFA Cup. Anderlecht was also involved
in bribing the referee in a match with the English club Nottingham Forest
in 1984, for which those responsible were never punished.

The average supporter is sixteen to eighteen years old and a student,
although support comes from all sectors of society. The tendency is to
imitate the British, and the idea of organized football hooliganism has certainly come from across the Channel, although with less ferocity. The local
groups are known as "sides"—the Anderlecht "O-Side" fight it out with
the Standard Liège "Hell-Side". Even their theme song is in English:

> We come from Brussels,
> We are the O-side.
> We're gonna sing,
> We're gonna win,
> We're gonna f*** you...
> (Quoted in Serge Govaert, *Violence et foot*, 2000)

Anderlecht has a varied population, with Moroccans around the Gare
du Midi at one end, and some very middle-class areas with fine architecture around St. Guidon. This is also the site of the abattoirs in the Rue
Ropsy Chaudron, with the striking statues of two bulls at the entrance. On
Friday, Saturday and Sunday mornings there is a market here, with all
kinds of food, drink, and other goods on sale.

Anderlecht was home to one of the most popular poets in the French
language, Maurice Carême (1899-1978), who was born in Wavre, in
Brabant. He came to Anderlecht to teach at a primary school, a post he
gave up at the age of forty-three to devote himself entirely to poetry.
Carême's work is both technically brilliant and characterized by honesty

and simplicity. Some of his writing is concerned with religious themes, some is specially written for children. He celebrates his own happiness with his family and with everyday life, and his profound attachment to his native Brabant. No one can fail to be moved by such poems as "La Maison Blanche", where he praises the native soil:

> Brabant loved by the gods like no other land on this earth
> But whose modesty forgets the need
> To underline its blessings and shout to the distance...
> When death crosses my hands
> While my spirit enters your hills
> May I always rest on your broad breast
> Like a child that sleeps forgotten in the hay.

La Maison Blanche was his home at no.14 Avenue Nellie Melba, which now houses the Fondation Maurice Carême. As well as poetry, Carême published a novel, *Le Martyre d'un supporter* (Martyrdom of a Supporter, 1928), which deals with the mental disintegration of an Anderlecht supporter.

THE SOUTHERN COMMUNES: UCCLE

Uccle covers a substantial part of the southwestern corner of Brussels, and is the largest *commune* of the nineteen in the agglomeration. Much of it was woodland, part of the continuation of the Forêt de Soignes, known as de Heeghde, until the inexorable expansion of the city from 1850. These days Uccle is Brussels' most diverse *commune*, with every type of social class represented.

The name Uccle is supposed to derive from a Frankish word *hukkla*, meaning "little heights", and appears as Hucle in a charter from 1055. The original church of St. Pierre, built on a low hill, was supposed to have been consecrated by Pope Leo III, when he passed through the area in the company of Charlemagne in 804, but this is more a matter of legend than fact. The first Romanesque church was demolished in 1776, and a new classical-style church in red brick, designed by Jean-François Wincqz, took its place. The presbytery and the local magistrate's court, also constructed in the eighteenth century, together make up an attractive square, the Place Homère Goossens. Near St. Pierre is a Russian Orthodox Church built to commemorate the Tsar and his family.

Uccle consisted historically of several estates. The Stalle estate, lying between the Chaussée d'Alsemberg and the Rue de Stalle has a fourteenth-century church, Notre Dame de Bon Secours. Another estate, in the area now known as St. Job, was known as Carinoo or Carloo, after a castle, which once stood on the site of the Place St. Job. The castle chapel has been incorporated in part into the new Église de St. Job, built in 1911, and contains the tombs of the Van der Noot family, who were actively involved in the 1830 revolution. Every third Monday in September there is the annual fair of St. Job, where farm animals are on display. Uccle also boasts a special breed of hen, the "Barbue d'Uccle".

Descending the Chaussée d'Alsemberg from Altitude Cent, you will see on the right at no.621 the bizarre frontage of the *estaminet* Au Vieux Spijtigen Duivel (At the Sorry Old Devil). At the end of his stay in Brussels, Charles Baudelaire came here a few times to write some of his vitriolic lines about Belgian life. Most of all, the café is associated with the Flemish poet Jan van Nijlen (1884-1965), who composed a large part of his output here. The original name of the café was De Haet en Nijdt (Hate and Envy), and it seems that the Au Vieux Spijtigen Duivel was originally the café on the other side of the road. There is a legend that the devil in

the café sign fell off the coat of arms of a guild of fencers who had St. Michael as their patron saint.

Near the southern end of the Chaussée d'Alsemberg is the railway station of Uccle-Calevoet. Jan van Nijlen made it the subject of a well-known poem—"Klein station in oorlogstijd" ("Small Station in Time of War", 1947)—which begins:

> The useless station of Calevoet
> lies small and sombre on a winter's day
> half red stone, half black soot and rust
> only half a train passes here once a day.
>
> The rails are straight and red and rusted
> an empty bottle lies on the platform,
> a cock tries to crow, but only coughs,
> it's quarter to four, or rather quarter to six…

There is also his verse on the month of March in Calevoet:

> Only a couple of blackbirds were singing properly,
> an apple-tree with three flecks of blood,
> next to it, naturally, budding lilacs:
> how careless is your Spring, Calevoet.

Forêt de Soignes

This last remnant of the primeval forest that covered southern Belgium before the Romans came has inspired a good deal of writing. Many English-speaking writers refer to it as "Soigny", but it is not to be confused with the small town of Soignies in Hainaut province. In the Middle Ages the forest was reserved exclusively for hunting by the dukes of Brabant. The Austrians started to plant large numbers of beech trees in the eighteenth century, giving the forest a rather uniform appearance it did not have before. William I, king of the United Netherlands, then entrusted the Forêt de Soignes to the Société Générale in 1822, the trading company he had set up. After the Revolution in 1830 the Société found itself in a difficult situation, being closely identified with the Dutch king, and therefore lent money to the revolutionaries, so William I promptly took away the land he had given the company in the Netherlands. The Société sold off large parts of the Forêt de Soignes for farmland, so that by 1843, when it was reacquired by the city, almost two-thirds of it had gone.

The poet Robert Southey visited the forest not long after Waterloo, writing in his *Journal of a Tour in the Netherlands in the Autumn of 1815*:

> The forest of Soigny is very striking. It has none of the beauty of a natural forest; but because it is an artificial one, it has a character of its own, not always becoming, impressive where it is upon a large scale. The trees are so straight that they look as if they had grown under the superintendence of a Drill Sergeant. An oak which stands on the verge of the forest, where it has room to spread its arms in natural growth, really appeared like a deformed and monstrous being, from its utter unlikeness to all the other trees. They stand in many parts so close that the interstices look only like straight lines of green light.

Henry Smithers relates the well-known story of the broom-maker (*Observations Made During a Residence in Brussels*, 1819):

> The Emperor Charles V in 1521, when on a shooting party in the forest of Soigny, had parted from his suite: he came to the cottage of a peasant at Boitsfort and asked somewhat to eat. Not knowing him they gave him some roasted hare. "Provided that," said he, "you say nothing to Charles, or he would have me put in prison." At length his companions found the Emperor in the cottage. The cottager astonished, threw himself at his feet to ask his pardon. The Emperor encouraged him and ordered him to come to Court with a load of brooms, making of which was his occupation, and having liberally recompensed him, he granted permission to him and the inhabitants of Boitsfort, to cut in the wood of Soigny, branches to make brooms, a privilege which they still enjoy.

The incident is still known as the Miracle du Coin du Balai.

The silences and mystery of the forest have inspired numerous descriptions. Auguste Rodin (1830-1914), who worked on the statues on the Bourse between 1871 and 1877, often came here:

When I was in Belgium, whatever the weather, from the morning I often went out with my wife... Most often it was to the Forêt de Soignes. I passed whole days there. For a long time, my thoughts resided in this cathedral of vegetation. Each time I saw her again, I found her beautiful, but never of the same beauty. Through seeing her, I took on her character.

It was there that I began to look at the world with my own eyes, to love nature deeply, to discern and taste her nuances; I understood that one only has to see, to feel and then one renders something of beauty.

WATERMAEL-BOITSFORT

More than half of the middle-class suburb of Watermael-Boitsfort is in the Forêt de Soignes. The name Boitsfort, or Bosvoorde in Dutch, is perhaps derived from Boutsvoorde, meaning the ford in the uneven land. Watermael maybe derives from the Frankish word for water and a depression in the land (*mahlo*). This was open countryside until the First World War. After the war, two garden cities were built, Le Floréal and Le Logis, by workers' cooperatives.

Boitsfort has changed drastically with the greater volume of traffic that passes along the main roads. From 1939 to 1953, Hergé (creator of Tintin) had his studio at 17 Avenue Delleur, which is a busy highway these days, and 6 Avenue Delleur was the model for Hercules Tarragon's house in *The Seven Crystal Balls*. Hergé and Edgar P. Jacobs hung around outside drawing it until they realized it had been taken over by the German SS. Prof. Calculus was, incidentally, directly modelled on the Swiss balloonist Auguste Piccard, who lived in Brussels for some time. Calculus is Tryphon Tournesol in French; the name Tryphon was borrowed from a local cabinetmaker. The insurance broker, Jolyon Wagg in the English version, Séraphin Lampion in the French, is based on an insurance salesman who came to visit Hergé one day.

Running into the Avenue Delleur is the Avenue Émile van Becelaere, home to Franquin, creator of the cartoon character Gaston Lagaffe, the eternal bungler, and several other well-known characters. Gaston is immensely popular in the French speaking area, but hardly known outside. The cemetery of Watermael-Boitsfort has some illustrious residents: the Nobel Peace-prize winner Auguste Beernaert; Charlotte Brontë's "Professor" Constantin Heger; and the artist Rik Wouters among others. The station of Watermael-Boitsfort has become world-famous as the model for Paul Delvaux's hallucinatory scenes of nudes and trains in the night. He was eventually made honorary station-master. He painted many other parts of the *commune*, in particular the Pont d'Élan. The same bridge appears in Hergé's *The Black Island*.

LA HULPE

This *commune*, which is not within the central Brussels region, has traditionally been a place to enjoy nature. Magritte and Delvaux liked to come here to draw inspiration from the forests, while the writer Camille Lemonnier had a cottage where he could get away from the city. The name seems to derive from a stream called La Helpe, now known as the Argentine or L'Argent from its clear waters. Paul Delvaux's father came here to fish for trout.

Baron Ernest Solvay, who made his fortune from inventing a commercial process for the production of soda, had an estate here standing on a part of the Forêt de Soignes that had been sold off in 1833. The German playwright Carl Sternheim (1878-1942) built a villa next door, La Claire Colline, named in honour of Tolstoy's Yasnaya Polyana (which actually means Clear Field). While the German army occupied Belgium during the First World War, there was also a group of German socialists and pacifists in Brussels who were on the side of the Belgians. The best-known figures in this group were the Sternheims, and the expressionist writers, Gottfried Benn and Carl Einstein.

The Sternheims moved to Brussels in December 1912. They lived at the Villa Piccola near the station of La Hulpe in 1914 in order to oversee the building of a villa on the piece of land they had bought. Sternheim suffered a nervous breakdown and was released from military service. The Sternheims then had to leave at the end of the war because of the anti-German atmosphere. Sternheim moved back to Brussels in 1930, after marrying Pamela Wedekind, but with Hitler's accession his work was banned and he had no more income. Between 1935 and 1938 he lived at three addresses in the Avenue Longchamp with his housekeeper Henriette Carbonara. His final address was 52 Rue Emmanuel van Driessche in Ixelles. He eventually died in November 1942 of pneumonia brought on by lack of heating.

AUDERGHEM AND HUGO VAN DER GOES

Auderghem, an area between Watermael and Woluwe, first came to prominence when the widow of Duke Henry III, Aleidis, for a short time regentess, established a Dominican convent here in 1270. Val Duchesse prospered under the patronage of the dukes but was burnt down by a mob in 1563. The convent was then suppressed by the French and sold off, but some parts are still visible. The well-known priory of La Rouge Cloître originated from a hermitage, De Bruxkens Cluse (Hermitage of the Little Bridge). A wooden monastery, the Roode Cluse (Red Hermitage) was built in 1368, then renamed Rouge Cloître (Red Monastery), from the ground-up red tiles that covered the walls to protect them from rain.

Rouge Cloître is associated with the painter Hugo van der Goes, who retired here at the end of his career. He was born in Ghent around 1425 and died in 1482. Trained under Jan Van Eyck, he reached his peak as a painter by 1460 and was employed by Charles the Bold, duke of Burgundy, for the festivities during his marriage to Margaret of York at Bruges in 1468. Van der Goes fell in love with a Ghent woman, whom he depicts as the Biblical Abigail in his paintings. He gained her hand in marriage, but she died soon after. The shock made him give up his career as a painter in Ghent, and he retired to the Rouge Cloître. He went on a journey to Cologne, but on the way back showed signs of going mad. He constantly said that he was eternally damned, and would have killed himself if he had not been restrained; he could not be cured and died soon after. His epitaph was simple: "Here lies the painter Hugo van der Goes. Regretted by the arts, for he knew no equal." The tombstone was destroyed when the church was rebuilt in the following century. The monastery was severely damaged during the religious troubles of the sixteenth century; the part that can still be seen is the main building from the sixteenth century.

WOLUWE

The area of Woluwe (sometimes written Woluwé) was historically three villages: Woluwe St. Étienne, Woluwe St. Lambert, and Woluwe St. Pierre. The first has been swallowed up into Woluwe St. Lambert, although the name Woluwe St. Étienne still persists. Woluwe first appears as Wolewe, which could mean "well" and "water". The first church of St. Lambert dates back, according to legend, to the ninth century, while the current church is a mixture of different parts, some from as early as the twelfth century. A neo-Romanesque church was built up against the original in 1938. About half of Woluwe St. Lambert belonged to the Benedictine nuns of the Abbaye de Forest between the twelfth and sixteenth centuries, including the area still known as Roodebeek; the *commune* was still covered with forests until around 1600. The urbanization undertaken at the end of the nineteenth century on the orders of Leopold II meant that what had always been a country area was to have new avenues driven through it. Woluwe St. Lambert has retained its character with many green open spaces, and is generally rated as one of the most prosperous *communes* in Belgium. It was also found to be the cleanest according to a survey carried out by the Belgian consumers' association in 2001. The Woluwe area has a high concentration of European Commission functionaries.

The most popular place of pilgrimage in Woluwe St. Lambert in earlier times was the shrine of Marie la Misérable, or Lenneke Mare in Dutch. The legend of Miserable Mary inspired a play of the same name by Michel de Ghelderode. Somewhere around 1300 there lived in Woluwe St. Pierre a young girl, Marie, known for her beauty and purity. Rather than marrying she chose to retire to a hermitage, where she constantly prayed to the Virgin. A young nobleman from the area came repeatedly to ask her hand in marriage, but she refused. So the young man thought up a plan to get his revenge; when Marie went to a rich relative's house he arranged for a precious cup to be slipped into her bag. She was denounced and sentenced to death for theft, then buried alive with a stake through her chest. As she expired, thirteen beautiful virgins appeared in the sky to honour her martyrdom. The young man immediately went mad, and no holy site in Brabant was able to help him. He only regained his senses when he came to ask for forgiveness in the chapel erected on the spot of the martyrdom. There are those who deny that Marie was ever a historical person, but there is no doubt that the chapel of Notre Dame des Sept Douleurs, Our Lady of Seven Sorrows, who is symbolized as a heart with seven arrows, was built some time after 1300 in Brabant Gothic style. The chapel is popularly known as the Chapelle de Marie la Misérable. The church was restored in the 1970s, but it retains its seventeenth-century fittings, with a triptych showing the life of Marie.

WOLUWE ST. PIERRE AND EDDY MERCKX

Woluwe St. Pierre is a middle-class *commune*, which includes the Parc de Woluwe and several other green spaces. At the southwestern end is an area where all the streets are named after birds. This was the cradle that nurtured the greatest cycling talent the world has ever seen, one Édouard (Eddy) Merckx, the "poet of the pedals". Eddy was born in the village of Meensel-Kiezegem in Flemish Brabant in 1945, but twelve months later his parents moved to Brussels to take over a grocer's on the Place des Bouvreuils, while living in the nearby Avenue du Chant d'Oiseau. The young Eddy decided to become a professional cyclist at sixteen and showed extraordinary tenacity and courage in reaching the summits of a notoriously tough sport. His record of five victories in the Tour de France, and 400 victories overall, is never likely to be surpassed. His will to win led his teammates to give him the nickname "Le Cannibale" (The Cannibal). Merckx was also unusual in that he succeeded in a sport that was entirely dominated by riders from the Dutch-speaking areas of Belgium. He moved to Kraainem when he became wealthy enough; there is now a metro station named after him in Anderlecht.

CHOCOLATE TRAMS AND AMÉLIE NOTHOMB

On the other side of the Parc de Woluwe is the superb Musée du Transport Urbain Bruxellois, a celebration of public transport in the city, with lovingly restored trams and buses. It is generally open only in spring and summer, and at weekends there are groups of enthusiasts who trade in postcards and other public transport memorabilia. Trams were not a Belgian invention. A French engineer living in the US, Alphonse Loubat, first had the idea of burying the rails in the street surface and using chamfered wheels on horse-drawn carriages in 1852. The first horse-drawn tram service ran between the Porte de Namur and the Bois de la Cambre from 1869. The "hippomobiles" converted to electricity from 1894; the drivers were, and still are, known as *wattmen*. Several tram companies started up, with investment from Great Britain and the US. The trams gradually looked less like horse-drawn carriages and more recognizably tram-like. Along with the tram companies was the well-loved *vicinal*—a network of light railways run by the Société de Chemins de Fer Vicinaux. The last *vicinal* ran in 1978.

The well-known *trams chocolat* (named after their colour) were run by the Société Générale de Chemins de Fer Économiques before the First World War. John dos Passos mentions them in his memoir on his childhood. Many trams were replaced by bus services after the war, and the current network is a pale shadow of its former self. But anyone who visits the Musée du Transport Urbain cannot help but be taken over by the romance of a typically Belgian, and very practical, mode of public transport.

Amélie Nothomb (b.1967) exploded onto the French literary scene in 1992 with a mature bestseller, *Hygiène de l'assassin*, a study in cruelty and perversity based around a Nobel Prize-winning writer on his deathbed. Since then she has become the most popular writer in the French-speaking world. Nothomb was born in Japan to a Belgian diplomat and considers herself partly Japanese. Her account of returning to work in Japan, *Stupeur et tremblements* (1999), was made into a film, *Fear and Trembling*. She first came to Brussels to take a degree in Romance Philology at the Université Libre de Bruxelles. She states that she has "given birth" to many novels on the tram 94 and bus no.71 (she keeps an apartment in Ixelles where she stays when she is not in Paris). "I believe that my frantic use of the STIB (the Brussels public transportation company) has played a big role in my work. You see people on public transport who are so ugly that you want to get up and congratulate them and say: Bravo. Your interpretation of ugliness is most interesting." Her only novel set in Brussels, *Antéchrista*, partly plays out at the ULB, but she has also contributed to a study of Belgian French fries vans. Her eccentric habits are a matter of much interest. She is rumoured to live on rotten fruit and cheese and was once forced to eat a rotten pear live on television.

Chapter Seven

ART FOR SALE: BRUEGHEL,
SURREALISM AND HIGH CULTURE

"You don't need to feel you have been sold, until you have been bought."
Marcel Broodthaers

With the fall of Antwerp in 1585, Holland and Belgium definitively split into two countries. The status quo before the Protestant revolt was restored in Brussels, the damage done to the churches to be repaired as quickly as possible. In 1598, Philip II handed over the Spanish Netherlands to his daughter, Isabella, who was to rule with her husband, the Habsburg Archduke Albert. Their heirs would be rulers of Belgium. The couple were greeted as saviours, for at least Albert was not a Spaniard. They were energetic and keen to restore Brussels to its former glory as the capital of the Low Countries. Isabella also favoured pomp and frequent celebrations, which made her especially popular. The processions and feasts that had been suspended during the years of the troubles could start again. The wealth on display at the time can be seen in the series of six pictures commissioned by the archduchess from Denis Van Alsloot, now to be seen in the Victoria and Albert Museum in London. Under Albert and Isabella, Belgian Baroque came to its full flowering. There was a huge demand for new statues and pulpits for the churches ravaged by the iconoclasts, as well as for new buildings for all the religious orders coming into the city. This was also the era of Pieter-Paul Rubens and his pupil, Antoon Van Dyck.

Unfortunately, Archduke Albert died in 1621, leaving no heirs. Isabella continued to rule alone until her own death in 1633, when the Spanish Netherlands reverted to Philip III of Spain. A succession of more or less ineffectual governor-generals continued the war against the Dutch and French. Finally, in 1648, the Spanish had to recognize the complete independence of the Netherlands by the Treaty of Münster. Under the conditions of the treaty the Dutch gained complete control over the Scheldt estuary, cutting Antwerp off from the sea and thus dealing a mortal blow to the Belgian economy. The Eighty-Year War with the Dutch devastated much of Belgium, although Brussels itself was never directly threatened.

LOUIS XIV: BRUSSELS BOMBARDED
Just when it seemed that peace would return at last, a new threat appeared in the shape of the French King Louis XIV (r.1643-1715). By virtue of his marriage to the Infanta of Spain, he now claimed the Spanish Netherlands for himself. Louis XIV attempted to attack Brussels in 1668, 1677, and 1684, but was prevented from actually entering the city. His frustration was such that in 1695 he ordered the bombardment of the city with red-hot cannon balls, in the vain hope of lifting the siege of Namur by the English. Some 4,000 houses, churches and convents were destroyed in one single night; in the Grand-Place only the town hall was left standing. Napoleon called the destruction of Brussels "pointless and stupid". The city was largely rebuilt within five years, and the narrow medieval streets could now be widened. Not many buildings now remain from before the bombardment.

The designs of the French on Belgium had not finished. Charles II of Spain, on his death in 1700, left his territories to the grandson of Louis XIV, Philip of Anjou. The union of France and Spain under one crown threatened to upset the balance of power in Europe, and a Grand Alliance was organized by William III of England to prevent it. The Maréchal de Villeroy, who had bombarded Brussels in 1695, was defeated at the Battle of Ramillies in 1706. Shortly after, the Duke of Marlborough entered Brussels and installed his brother as governor. The Habsburg Charles III of Austria became ruler of the Low Countries, while Spain went to Philip V. By another treaty in 1715, the Dutch were allowed to install garrisons on Belgian territory to safeguard against further invasions from France, the so-called "Traité de la Barrière".

THE BRUEGHEL FACTORY
Pieter Brueghel The Elder (1526?-1569) came to Brussels six years before he died, following his marriage to the twenty-year-old daughter of his teacher, the Antwerp painter, Pieter Coecke Van Aelst. His father-in-law had only consented to the marriage on condition that the couple moved to Brussels, because of Brueghel's reputation as a playboy and heavy

drinker (hence his nickname: "The Droll"). Brueghel's wife, Mayken, bore him three children, Pieter Brueghel the Younger (1564-1637), Jan Brueghel (1568-1625), known as "Velours" or "Velvet", and a daughter, Maria. Mayken only lived until 1578, so the children were brought up by their grandmother in Antwerp.

Brueghel the Elder was born the son of a peasant, probably in Flemish Brabant. Following his apprenticeship he travelled in France and Italy before settling in Antwerp. He excelled at landscapes and allegorical paintings, which show the influence of the older Dutch master Hieronymus Bosch, in particular in his *Mad Meg* (1562). His representations of village life in Brabant, sometimes with Biblical themes, are full of wit and spontaneity. The church in *The Parable of the Blind* (1568) is on the outskirts of Brussels at Sint-Anna-Pede, which has an open-air Bruegelmuseum. A fountain with a small representation of three of the blind men in the painting has recently appeared outside the Church of St. Nicolas on the Rue au Beurre near the Grand'Place in the centre of Brussels. Brueghel painted the village people just as they are, with the symbolic elements that were popular in his time. Brueghel the Younger largely concentrated on making copies of his father's most popular works. He also had a sideline painting scenes of hellish torment and sorcery, hence his nickname "d'Enfer". Jan "Velvet" was more versatile, specializing in landscapes, flowers and animals. He and Rubens were the main court painters for Albert and Isabella.

Whereas only forty of Brueghel the Elder's works have survived, Brueghel the Younger, or rather his workshop, produced around 4,000 copies of works by his father and others. This was not considered particularly reprehensible, since customers wanted something recognizable rather than original. The copies were made with *cartons* or pre-drawn patterns transferred on to a prepared oak board by making pinholes in the paper, or drawing on the back with charcoal and pressing onto the board. Out of Brueghel the Elder's popular paintings, 127 copies are known of *Winter Landscape with Birdtrap*, and so on.

One can compare *The Fall of Icarus* (an authentic painting by Brueghel the Elder) in the Musée des Beaux Arts, with a copy made by his son, in the Musée Alice et David van Buuren, in Uccle. Brueghel the Younger has added a representation of Icarus that was not in the original. The painting inspired W. H. Auden's poem "Musée des Beaux Arts," written in December 1938 when he was staying nearby:

About suffering they were never wrong,
The Old Masters: how well they understood
Its human position; how it takes place
While someone else is eating or opening a window or just walking dully
along;
...
In Breughel's Icarus, for instance; how everything turns away
Quite leisurely from the disaster; the ploughman may
Have heard the splash, the forsaken cry,
But for him it was not an important failure; the sun shone,
As it had to, on the white legs disappearing into the green
Water; and the expensive delicate ship that must have seen
Something amazing, a boy falling out of the sky,
Had somewhere to get to, and sailed calmly on.

Notre Dame de la Chapelle, the church where Brueghel the Elder and his wife are buried, stands at the end of the Rue Haute where they most probably lived. The origins of the church date back to the twelfth century; it has always been the parish church for the working-class Marolles district. The aisles and nave were added in the fifteenth century. The unusual black shingled clock tower was designed by Antoine Pastorana to cover the damage caused by the 1695 bombardment of the city. There is also a well-known statue of Nuestra Señora de la Soledad, Our Lady of Solitude, which the playwright Michel de Ghelderode has written about in *Mes Statues* (1978):

She represented the land of Theresa of Avila in the eyes of our masters,
in the demolished oratory of the Dominicans from whence she came...
They left her one day all alone, the lady in dark *failles*, with her rosary,
and the cadaver of her son suspended above her. No one prays to her,
except for some solitary people, because she keeps her distance... Just
think that Our Lady of Solitude, virgin of extinct auto-da-fés, keeps in
her *failles* the odour of holocausts.

MUSÉE DES BEAUX ARTS
Belgium's premier art museum, located near the Place Royale, owes its existence to Napoleon Bonaparte. After finally overcoming the Austrians in

1794, the French confiscated the artistic treasures of the monasteries and sent some 270 items back to Paris to form part of the collection of the Louvre, which had been founded just a year before. The director of the Academy of Painting, Sculpture and Architecture of Brussels, Bosschaert, was allowed to select 100 paintings deemed superfluous to the Louvre's needs, and set up the first Musée des Beaux Arts in the palace of Charles of Lorraine, located in the square behind the contemporary museum. More works discarded by the Louvre came Bosschaert's way until, by 1811, there were 305 works in the museum. Then, in 1815, the French were obliged to restore all the looted artworks to their respective countries, according to the terms of the Treaty of Vienna.

The Musée is almost entirely devoted to Belgian art, organized by time periods and styles. The Musée d'Art Moderne is accessible from the Musée d'Art Ancien through a series of descending steps. In order to keep the two collections in one location a large hole was dug into the Place des Musées, which is effectively obscured from the street by a stone balustrade. This allows daylight to penetrate down to the lowest floors, and the idea works well. As one would expect, the Musée d'Art Moderne has a large number of Magritte paintings, thanks to generous bequests from Georgette Magritte, and Irène Scutenaire-Hamoir, a friend of the Magrittes, although many of the most famous ones are now in the United States.

Dada and Surrealism

Surrealism in Belgium, and around the world, is identified with the figure of René Magritte (1898-1967), one of the great creators of images in the twentieth century. He was, however, only one of a network of artists and writers based in Brussels who launched Surrealism in 1924. Magritte originated from Lessines in the area of Charleroi, in the suburb of Châtelet, to be precise. When he came to study at the Brussels Académie des Beaux Arts in 1916, he made contact with radical artists. The First World War made many question the values of Western civilization, while the Russian Revolution pointed to a new future.

Before Surrealism there was Dada, a nihilistic movement originating in wartime Zürich that tried to dismantle traditional aesthetics in order to rediscover an authentic reality. Brussels had its own Dadaist, Clément Pansaers (1885-1923), who started writing a Dadaist work, *Pan-pan au cul du nu nègre* in 1916 before the term Dada was even known (it was not actually published until 1920). It has all the Dadaist elements of parody, far-fetched aphorisms, wordplay and calligrams. Pansaers made contact in 1919 with Tristan Tzara (1896-1963), a founding Dadaist, and agreed that he was a Dadaist too.

Dada was too nihilistic to last. Surrealism also aimed to explore and celebrate the processes of subconscious thought but by better worked-out strategies. As André Breton put it in his *Manifesto of Surrealism* from 1924:

> Surrealism: Pure psychic automatism by which one aims to express either verbally, or in writing, or by any other means, the real functioning of thought. The dictation of thoughts, in the absence of any control exercised by reason, outside of any aesthetic or moral pre-occupations.

There was an ethical programme as well. Starting from the premise that human beings are basically good, Surrealism posited that they should be liberated by allowing them to consciously experience their underlying thoughts. Breton and the other early Surrealists had a serious interest in séances and automatic writing. They hoped to unveil revelatory messages by putting themselves into trance-like states. Rational distinctions between truth and untruth, or madness and reason had to be broken down in order to get at the experience itself. In Brussels the ideas developed by the Dadaists were debated intensely by a group of proto-Surrealists. On November 22, 1924, not long after the first Surrealist manifesto appeared in Paris, the Brussels group started the review *Correspondance*. Most issues contained a parody of one or another French Surrealist. In Issue 19, significantly entitled "Keeping our Distance", Breton was himself parodied. Positive statements about the group's thinking, meanwhile, were thin on the ground. They claimed to "adhere to life": "To find life, there should be a revolution through language, by giving life to language by forcing it to excess." Experimenting with language was the main purpose for the group's chief theorist, Paul Nougé (1895-1967). In his turn he influenced Magritte, some of whose work deals with the misleading nature of words applied to objects. The well-known title "Ceci n'est pas une pipe" may have come from Nougé.

No one could doubt that Surrealism and André Breton, the movement's high priest, were one and the same. Magritte and his wife Georgette moved to Paris for three years from 1926, but they did not get on with

Breton, who made fun of Magritte's Walloon accent and was incensed by Georgette's refusal to stop wearing a cross around her neck in his presence. In the end, the economic crisis of 1929 forced the couple to return to Belgium. They settled in Jette, near Magritte's brother Paul and Georgette's sister.

The Magrittes could only afford to rent the ground floor of the house at 135 Rue Esseghem, which now houses the Musée René Magritte. In order to support themselves, René ran a graphics business from a shed in the garden, which he called Studio Dongo, while Georgette worked in an art materials shop. René did his serious painting in the dining room. Every Saturday the Surrealists of Brussels met in his salon. The room has been restored to something like its original state; the walls are painted sky-blue, René's favourite colour. Georgette's piano stands in the corner. The front window appears in the painting *La Condition humaine* (1933), where the view appears on shards of broken glass. Another similar work, *Le Soir qui tombe* (Evening Falls, 1964), was painted when he was living in Schaerbeek, but still with the same window-frame. The fireplace with a steam engine coming out of it appears in *La Durée poignardée* (Time Transfixed, 1954). Capturing the present moment was one of the main pre-occupations of the Surrealists; Breton called it "prospecting for the gold of time." The street lamp outside the window can be seen in *Le Mal du pays* (Nostalgia, 1941). Many of the titles of Magritte's paintings were arrived at through discussion with the Surrealists as a group and Nougé in particular. Magritte was interested in images, while Nougé concerned himself with language and poetry.

Belgian Surrealism diverged from the Paris group in fundamental ways. The Belgians considered that using dreams, automatic writing or trances would not uncover the nature of reality; they would rather stay with the traditional forms of art, and subvert them from within. Magritte was entirely able to produce conventional paintings, while introducing some disturbing element into them that would shake viewers out of their conventional perceptions. The Belgians also preferred to avoid becoming literary stars as individuals, choosing to work as a collective and spread their ideas in more subtle ways. There was also the revolutionary assumption that Surrealism was about living rather than just making art, that art should be a terrorist action that breaks down political and aesthetic barriers.

It is interesting to speculate why surrealism became popular in Belgium so early on. The tendency of *Bruxellois* to parody serious subjects is well known, and between 1870 and 1914 there was a Brussels-based *art swanze* or "joke art" movement whose members put on exhibitions of absurdist art. The desire to subvert authority most probably derives from the foreign occupations of the city. Yet Belgian Surrealism was more conservative than the French variety, and made connections between Surrealism and a quest for spiritual truth.

Magritte became commercially successful and more readily understood in the changed culture of the 1960s. Over time, his concerns changed. He left Surrealism behind and even parodied himself. During the Second World War, he even painted in the style of Renoir, his so-called Période Plein Soleil, as a way of cheering people up under the occupation. With greater wealth coming their way, the Magrittes were able to move to a bigger house 97 Rue des Mimosas in Schaerbeek. Yet he still kept the habit of painting in his living room, dressed in his suit and bow tie. He is buried in the Cimetière de Schaerbeek in lot 16.

Marcel Broodthaers

The Musée des Beaux Arts possesses a great number of works by Marcel Broodthaers (1924-76), arguably the natural successor to Magritte. Broodthaers was a French speaker from the Brussels *commune* of St.-Gilles, lived in poverty for much of his life, and died at an early age as a consequence. He started out as a poet but made no impact and turned to plastic arts in 1964. His lack of materials meant that he had to resort to using everyday items. The Musée has works such as "a piece of coal wrapped in cotton wool", "eggshells stuck to a piece of board", or "casserole full of mussel shells". Judging from his artistic output, Broodthaers must have eaten mussels and omelettes every day of his life. He was greatly interested by the connection between the French word for mussel (*moule*) and *mal*, which means "evil".

Broodthaers was greatly preoccupied with the connection between money and art with titles such as "I weep for Andy Warhol". He also admitted that he was not an artist, hence "I don't try to make something beautiful". On one copy of a Magritte painting he wrote: "Available at your dealer". He also sometimes put on his works "Tirage illimité" ("Unlimited edition"). Where he resorts to Magritte's tactic of writing words on objects that do not match, one could mistake these for Magritte's own work. In 1968 Broodthaers set up a fictitious Musée d'Art Moderne, the "Département des Aigles" or "Department of Eagles"; the eagle—symbolizing Napoleon and the Prussian state—stands for ideology and conventional art. The "Department of Eagles" was a base from which to circulate tracts and publish open letters. In 1972 he created a museum of seventeenth-century art, which was nothing more than crates of postcards. One day he solemnly loaded his crates onto a truck and moved his museum to Antwerp...

COBRA AND THE RUE DE LA PAILLE

Straw for horses was stored here (hence the name) as it was adjacent to the main horse market of the medieval city, now the Grand Sablon. The Jesuits had their monastery at the Galerie de Ruysbroeck end of the street until their papal suppression in 1773. The classical-style Palais de Justice built by the French ran the length of the street in the nineteenth century. It was here that Paul Verlaine was tried in July 1873 for wounding Arthur Rimbaud. Karl Marx was another defendant here. The building was soon to be torn down, to be replaced by the gigantic new Palais de Justice on the Galgenberg, as one can surmise from Verlaine's description:

> I can certify that you only got in there with great difficulty, through endless corridors, over all sorts of tiresome walkways and bridges... A dismal, narrow, scabby courtroom, or rather a hall; the walls, once daubed with whitewash, were flaking, cracked and seemed likely soon to collapse. A statue of Christ suffering from eczema, who seemed to have let his hair grow too long, hung off the wall.

The short-lived but influential COBRA arts collective (COpenhagen BRussels Amsterdam) met in a dingy house at 10 Rue de la Paille in its early days; the movement's manifesto was signed in Paris in November 1948. Christian Dotremont (1922-79), the prime mover, lived here with his wife during the three years that COBRA existed, sometimes without gas or electricity, sleeping on the floor because they could not afford a bed. The founders were six writers and artists: the Belgians Dotremont and Joseph Noiret, the Dutchmen Karl Appel, Constant and Corneille, and the Dane Asger Jorn. Dotremont had started the Revolutionary Surrealist

Group in 1947, at the same time that Breton, the leader of the Paris Surrealists decisively turned against the French Communist Party.

The COBRAs had more of an anti-manifesto than anything else. Dotremont, playing on English, called it: "a *practical joke, practical* in the *pictural, sculptural, poetical...* against the *theoretical* and *dogmatical.*" Dotremont still believed that Surrealism should serve the revolution. Living communally was an important part of the creative process, and for a time the group was remarkably productive. Pierre Alechinsky and others started the International Cobra Research Centre, or Cobra House, in the Ateliers du Marais, in the Ateliers du Marais, at no.80 Rue du Marais. Their art was a violent reaction against the theorizers of Surrealism, reflected in their name, which leaned heavily on primitive and children's art, with strong shapes and colours that burst out of their frames. COBRA art also drew heavily on primitive Scandinavian models. There was also the COBRA journal that ran to nine issues. The movement folded when Dotremont and Jorn both contracted tuberculosis in 1951.

Dotremont published a long poem entitled "10 Rue de la Paille" for the twentieth anniversary of COBRA (1948-68).

Jorn peels potatoes
before painting the eyes
Atlan opens the wine
Noiret the discussion
Alechinsky paints the cupboard
Calonne sets the monocle...

Dotremont led a nomadic life, even if his roots were to some extent in Brussels. He was born in the Grande Place in Tervuren, and returned to Tervuren later in life. He strongly believed in the French Surrealists' original preoccupation with automatic writing, the writer discovering the poem in the process of writing it. Out of his Surrealist poetry he developed a particular style of calligraphy which he called *logogrammes*; they look like a cross between Arabic and Japanese calligraphy.

SABLON
The Place du Grand Sablon was the original horse market of Brussels, lying just outside the first city walls. The medieval name was Zavelpoel or

Peerdemarct. These days the square is lined with expensive antique shops and high-class cafés. The fountain in the centre of the square was donated by the Jacobite exile Thomas Bruce. The Latin inscription may be translated as: "Thomas Bruce, Earl of Aylesbury, enjoyed Brussels hospitality for forty years. In his testament he left funds for the building of this fountain for the beauty and salubrity of this place. 1740." Thomas Bruce signed a contract for the building of the fountain before he died with Jacques Berge, a Brussels sculptor; there was to be an eight-foot high Minerva holding medallions with reliefs of Maria Theresa and her consort, Francis of Lorraine. The statue was finished in 1743, but permission to erect it was not given for six years. The whole was finally put up in November 1751. There are three genii: one is Fame, blowing a trumpet, which some joker has stolen; another holds an overflowing urn representing the River Scheldt; the third represents War.

NOTRE DAME DES VICTOIRES

One of the city's most attractive churches is located on what was once a cemetery belonging to the Hôpital St. Jean-au-Marais, a religious order that cared for the sick. The area was first known as the Saedelwegh, or "saddle way". It was given free of charge to the Grand Serment des Arbalétriers, the Guild of Crossbowmen, in 1318. The name of the church is often associated with Duke John I's victory at Worringen in 1288, but it seems that the two may not be connected. The crossbowmen became more prosperous and could soon afford to extend the church. The choir was completed before 1435, and the nave and transept around 1450. The church is particularly associated with the cult of Onze Lieve Vrouw op 't Stocksken (Our Lady on a Little Stick). The story goes that in the early twelfth century Beatrijs Soetkens in Antwerp had a vision of the Virgin Mary, who was grateful for the building of a chapel on the Sablon by the crossbowmen. She told her to take her image, known as Onze Lieve Vrouw op 't Stocksken, from the cathedral in Antwerp and place it in the Sablon. She took it and placed it on a boat, which drifted without any effort up the Senne to Brussels where the Duke of Brabant and his son awaited her with their retinue. The statue was taken to the Sablon and was given into the care of the crossbowmen.

The original church was begun in 1304 and finished in 1346. The ritual of the Ommegang perhaps began at this time, as the first reference

is from 1359, and was apparently organized in thanks for the ending of the Plague. All the residents of Brussels were obliged to contribute to the cost of this yearly procession, which began from the Korenhalle (Place St. Jean) and went along the Rue du Chêne and the Rue de l'Étuve into the Grand-Place. After a lavish lunch at Le Cygne, the procession then returned along the Rue de la Madeleine to the Sablon. The first procession was made up of the archers and other guilds, magistrates, the male religious orders, bishops, priests, and finally the image of the Virgin carried by the cross-bowmen. She was now called Onze Lieve Vrouw van het Bootje (Our Lady of the Little Boat). More and more groups joined the Ommegang and in 1549 the most magnificent Ommegang of all was held in the presence of Charles V. An eyewitness described 52 guilds, each with their symbol carved in wood and a picture of their patron saint. There were floats representing comic or religious scenes, and then floats of musicians, the traditional giants, a caravan of mythical animals, followed by thirteen magnificent floats showing scenes of the Virgin's life. It is this Ommegang that is recreated every year around the first Thursday in June.

The Ommegang went into decline with the religious troubles and stopped completely in 1580 before the Archduke and Archduchess Albert and Isabella revived the custom in 1615. They also commissioned two paintings by Denis Van Alsloot (now in the Victoria and Albert Museum in London) to show the full glory of the procession. The custom was neglected under the Austrians, but was put on again for the wedding of Napoleon and Marie-Louise in 1810. The procession seemed to be bound for extinction, but a new society, the Cercle de la Société de l'Ommegang was started in 1928 to keep it going; these days it is an important tourist attraction.

The Grand Serment de St. Georges, the Guild of Archers or Crossbowmen, was one of the city's most prestigious organizations in the Middle Ages. Membership was open to freemen of the city who were of good standing. In recognition of their importance they received a practice ground next to the city walls in the Inghelant Straete, below the Coudenberg palace, which became the Schuttershof. Every year next to the church on the Sablon, an archery competition took place to find out who was going to be the "Roi du Serment". The object was to shoot down a wooden bird, the *papegay*, attached to a perch on a tower near the church. Anyone who could shoot the bird down three years in a row became the Emperor of the Grand Serment.

In 1615, the already very popular Archduchess Isabella was invited to have a go and brought down the *papegay* with her first shot, for which she received 25,000 florins. Isabella gave much more in return, and allowed the Grand Serment to build their headquarters next to the new Rue d'Isabelle. The custom of asking the ruler to shoot down the *papegay* has continued to the present day. Archery is officially Belgium's national sport.

PALAIS DES BEAUX ARTS

The Palais des Beaux Arts (now referred to by the more neutral "Bozar") on the Rue Ravenstein was designed for temporary exhibitions and musical performances. The architect, Victor Horta (see p.192), was given the difficult task of having to build the Palais so that it would be no higher than the level of the Rue Royale above. The building is in Art Deco style and was opened in 1928. For the outside world it is best known as the home of the finals of the Queen Elisabeth Competition. Most years, at the start of May, what is generally considered the world's most prestigious music competition after the Tchaikovsky Prize, begins at the Conservatoire at 30 Rue de la Régence. The competition, which bears the name of King

Albert I's widow, Queen Elisabeth (1876-1965), was actually first conceived by the Belgian violinist Eugène Ysaÿe in a letter written in 1904, in which he mentions a prize for music graduates who would be put into isolation for eight or ten days during which they would work up an interpretation for a new concerto without any assistance from their teachers. Ysaÿe presented the queen with the first draft of the competition in 1924, which was to be named the Concours Eugène Ysaÿe, expressing the hope that it would be a means for young musicians to launch their professional careers, rather than to put their teachers in the limelight.

The project stood still for a while, during which time Ysaÿe, King Albert I, and Queen Astrid, wife of the new King Leopold III, all met untimely deaths. The first competition for violinists was held in 1937, starting at the Conservatoire, with the finals held at the Théâtre de la Monnaie. It could hardly have started better, as the winner was the Russian violin virtuoso David Oistrakh. (The contest was dominated by Russians, five of the six top places going to them.) Another Russian, Emile Gilels, won the piano competition in 1938. The 1939 competition was to have been for conducting, but the war stopped it from taking place. There were further difficulties when it was discovered at the end of the war that the director and organizer of the competition, the composer Charles Houdret, had embezzled 12 million francs. Houdret ended up in prison in 1944, but the competition still follows Houdret's format: a first eliminatory round, a semi-final between twenty-four musicians, a final after selecting twelve of them, and then the winners.

A new music chapel, the Chapelle d'Argenteuil or Queen Elisabeth Music Chapel was built in Waterloo in 1939 for training young Belgian musicians. The Chapelle is now used by the twelve finalists in the Concours as a place where they can be kept in isolation from the city. The contest was renamed after Queen Elisabeth after the war. In recent years there have been three main disciplines: violin, piano and voice. Thus in 2008 there is a voice competition, in 2009 it is the turn of the violin, 2010 piano, 2011 voice

The Queen Elisabeth competition is generally rated one of the most difficult in the world. The soloists not only perform a piece they have chosen themselves, but are also required to prepare a piece they have never seen before during a week-long period of isolation from the outside world (presumably to prevent coaching). The judges are selected from the most renowned and respected figures in the discipline under consideration. Everything is done to avoid any hint of partiality. The finals have been held in the Palais des Beaux Arts since 1951; the semi-finals for voice with orchestra competition are also held here.

The Henri Le Bœuf Hall, where the final is held, has a specially designed hollow wooden floor under the podium, which gives the hall its superb acoustics. The semi-finals are mainly held in the Grande Salle of the Brussels Music Conservatory. This is actually quite small, but ideally suited to chamber music. All the sessions are open to the public and are sold out months in advance. As far as orchestras go, communal or language politics have inevitably affected the choice, as all cultural activities come under the Community Assemblies (see p.xxvi). Finding the ideal orchestra in such a small country is no easy task. Since 1999 the Orchestre National de Belgique has accompanied the pianoforte and violin competitions, while the Orchestre Symphonique de la Monnaie (the house orchestra for the Théâtre de la Monnaie) accompanies the voice finalists.

Perhaps the most unfortunate aspect of the Queen Elisabeth Competition is the fact that no Belgian has ever won it; the best a native has achieved is third place. Winning the Concours more or less guarantees a successful career. Some who have not won have also done very well; Mitsuko Uchida, who only managed to come tenth in 1968, is better known than many former winners.

The Concours is an intense experience for everyone who takes part. Temperatures inside the concert hall can reach 38 degrees on a hot day, making the musicians', and especially the violinists' task much more difficult. Some competitors have broken down under the strain. The winners are under contract to give a gala concert at the end, and there are agents waiting to book them for performances around the world. The members of the jury are also sometimes asked to give recitals; on one occasion in 1959 Oistrakh, Menuhin and Grumiaux performed together. Members of the jury will also give master classes to the contestants.

The competition took on a political colouring from 1951, as Soviets and Americans confronted each other in a microcosm of the Cold War. In 1952 the Soviets did not take part because of the Korean War. The Americans did well during the 1950s, while the Soviets won in 1956 with Vladimir Ashkenazy. From 1963 the Soviets dominated completely, but between 1978 and 1987 the Russians boycotted the competition, in spite of the best efforts of the organizers to persuade them to send finalists.

BRUSSELS CINEMA

Underneath the Palais des Beaux Arts is Belgium's national film museum; officially the address is 9 Rue Baron Horta. The fact that Belgium has a film industry has escaped the notice of much of the outside world. The highest-profile representative in Hollywood is no doubt Jean-Claude Van Damme, "the Muscles from Brussels" or "Fred Astaire of Karate", who was born in the western suburb of Berchem-St.-Agathe, with the name of Jean-Claude Van Varenberg. One might add that Audrey Hepburn (1929-93) was born in Ixelles, at 48 Rue Keyenveld, the daughter of a British banker and a Dutch baroness. Her real name was Edda van Heemstra Hepburn-Ruston. She lived in Linkebeek, to the south of Brussels, from 1932 to 1939, before moving to Holland.

The Belgian film industry is inevitably at a disadvantage because of the language question. Belgians themselves have always preferred foreign films; if they do not want to watch Hollywood films, they can watch French or Dutch films. The typical Belgian film is a low-budget affair, and the industry has been supported financially by the state since 1965. Even with state backing, foreign investors have a lot of say in the making of the films.

After 1896, when the Lumière brothers first showed films in the Galerie du Roi, a cinema craze started in Brussels, but like everywhere else in Europe, far fewer people go to the cinema today than used to. From the early generation of film-makers one would have to cite Henri Storck (1907-99), the pioneer of the Belgian documentary school, with films such as *Misère au Borinage*, about mine workers, as the most significant. Out of the current generation, one director stands out above the rest, the experimental film-maker Chantal Akerman (born 1950), who has worked in New York and now lives in Paris. One American critic made the extraordinary claim that she "is arguably the most important European director of her generation." Her films have been variously described as "structuralist" or "minimalist" (not a great deal happens in them). Some of her works have been set in Brussels, notably *Jeanne Dielman, 23 Quai du Commerce, 1080 Bruxelles* (1975).

As far as commercial successes go, *Man Bites Dog*, by three directors, Rémy Belvaux, Benoît Poelvoorde and André Bonzel, won three prizes at Cannes in 1992. The story is about a serial killer who agrees to let a camera team follow him while he does his work; the film crew become his friends and accomplices. The other success of the 1990s was *Toto le Héros* (1991), by Jaco Van Dormael, a film about a man who believes that he was switched at birth with someone else more fortunate than himself. In this and *The Eighth Day* (1996), Van Dormael has used a Down's Syndrome actor, Pascal Duquenne.

One cannot talk about film in Belgium without mentioning the Brussels-based Jan Bucquoy, a satirist or tiresome self-publicist, depending on one's point of view. In the 1980s he made a stir by publishing obscene cartoons of the Belgian king, the cardinal, Tintin and Snowy, and with his Musée du Slip, or Underpants Museum. He is also a trained film-maker and scored a success with his low-budget feature, *La Vie sexuelle des Belges* (The Sexual Life of the Belgians, 1994), which has been widely shown abroad. This was followed by three more in the same series, including *Camping Cosmos*, a satire on Belgians at the seaside, while the third was about the closure of the Renault factory in Vilvoorde. In 2002 Bucquoy brought out *La Vie politique des Belges* (The Political Life of the Belgians).

The Brussels European Film Festival has been held annually at the Flagey Building on the Place Flagey (Ixelles) since 2003. Two Belgian film-makers have won the "Audience Award": Joachim Lafosse for *Ça Rend Heureux* and Vincent Lanoo for *Ordinary Man*. The Flagey Building was one of the first purpose-built broadcasting buildings in Europe. Designed in Art Deco style by Joseph Diongre, it housed the National Institute for Radio Broadcasting (NIR) from 1938 until 1975. The building was restored between 1997 and 2002, and is now one of the main arts centres in Brussels, with daily cinema, theatre and music programmes.

Chapter Eight

THE ROAD TO WATERLOO

"Here his last flight the haughty eagle flew,
Then tore, with bloody beak, the fatal plain."

Lord Byron, *Childe Harold*

Following the War of the Spanish Succession, fought in order to prevent Spain and France coming under one ruler, the political map changed again. The Austrians, who had allied themselves with the British, gained the Spanish Netherlands as their reward. Austrian rule started under difficult conditions. Prince Eugene of Savoy was made governor-general, but never actually exercised his function. His successor, the Archduchess Maria-Elisabeth, restored some of the glory of the Brussels court, but in 1731 the Coudenberg Palace burned to the ground and was not rebuilt.

The accession of Maria Theresa to the throne of Austria in 1740 was the signal for a renewed attack by the French on Belgium. Brussels was occupied from 1746 to 1748, reinforcing the growing influence of French culture on the city. In some ways this was a turning point in the decline of Flemish and the increasing dominance of French. Once peace had been restored, Brussels experienced an economic boom, largely thanks to the sympathetic government of Charles of Lorraine. The large-scale production of cotton on mechanized looms, porcelain, paper and lace attracted more workers, and the population rose from 57,000 to 74,000 in the space of thirty years. Charles was popular as a *bon vivant*; the statue of him in the Place du Musée, opposite the Musée de l'Art Moderne, shows a well-fed and well-satisfied figure.

Brussels played host to a large number of French émigrés, forced to leave their country by the intolerance of Louis XV's regime. At the same time, intellectual life inevitably came to be more and more dominated by the French Enlightenment. After the French occupation of 1746-8, theatre and opera became immensely popular. In 1772 Maria Theresa established the Académie Impériale et Royale des Sciences et Belles Lettres de Bruxelles. The following year, the Jesuits were suppressed by papal decree, and a new Collège Thérésien instituted to educated the children of the well-to-do along Enlightenment lines.

Maria Theresa and Charles of Lorraine both died in 1780. Their successor, Joseph II, had far less sympathy for the Belgians. On his first visit to Brussels in 1781, he found the administration of the country in dire need of reform. He began to impose a serious of radical measures to reduce the influence of the Catholic Church and sweep away the last vestiges of the medieval privileges of the corporations. The convents of contemplatives who were not engaged in any useful work were to be suppressed. Carnivals and processions were banned, something guaranteed to annoy the *Bruxellois*. The entire judicial system was reorganized. The whole range of reforms was imposed from Vienna.

Joseph II's actions naturally aroused intense anger among the entire population. The opposition was itself split between a more conservative party—the Statists under Henri Van der Noot—who wished to retain the privileges of the clergy and nobility, and the Vonckists under Jean-François Vonck, who preferred to concentrate power in the hands of the bankers and industrialists.

The inevitable revolt started and, contrary to all expectations, the Belgians routed the Austrian army at Turnhout in October 1789 and declared independence as the United States of Belgium. Joseph II died soon after; one of his last utterances, to the Belgian Prince de Ligne, was "Your country has killed me." Brussels was in fact in a state of complete chaos. Once Joseph II's successor Leopold II had made sure that no other country would intervene on behalf of the Belgians, he soon managed to convince them that further armed resistance would be useless. Leopold then died shortly afterwards in March 1792, to be succeeded by Francis II. Almost immediately, the French declared war with the intention of absorbing the Low Countries into France.

FRENCH OCCUPATION

The victory of the revolutionary General Dumouriez and his entry into Brussels in November 1792 were greeted with rapture by the Belgians. Dumouriez promised to restore Belgium's liberty, but the ruling Convention in Paris had entirely different ideas. The entire system of government was to be modeled on French lines, the Church suppressed, and the privileges of the nobility abolished. The *Bruxellois* protested loudly, but to no avail. Soon after, the French were heavily defeated at the Battle of Neerwinden, in March 1793, and this time it was the turn of the Austrians to be greeted as liberators. By now the Belgians demanded independence. Francis II refused to accede to their wishes, and made the traditional Joyeuse Entrée—the ceremony by which all rulers swear to uphold the privileges of the city and are greeted as dukes of Brabant—in April 1794. Within two months the Austrians were again defeated at the Battle of Fleurus, and Belgium was now definitively absorbed into the French Republic.

The French saw Belgium as a useful source of revenue for their wars. The Catholic Church was again suppressed, the convents used as warehouses, and the secular cult of Republicanism imposed on the populace. The streets were renamed, and the churches given suitably Jacobin titles: thus the church of St. Jacques-sur-Coudenberg became "The Temple of Reason". Most of all, *Bruxellois* resented forced conscription, and by 1798 bands of guerrillas were harassing the French on all sides. The resistance was rapidly put down. The regime now re-instituted some of the banned processions and reopened some churches to worshippers. While the French were still deeply unpopular, the economic situation started to improve.

NAPOLEON AND THE PALAIS DE LAEKEN

The official residence of the Belgian monarch was built in 1782-4 for the Austrian governor-general, Albrecht von Sachsen-Teschen and his wife Marie-Christine, by the architects Montoyer and Payen according to Albrecht's own designs. The original name of the palace was Schoonenberg. Georg Forster, the German naturalist, visited Laeken in 1790 in the company of the young Alexander von Humboldt, not long after the palace was built. Forster regarded the palace with approval, in particular the peristyle of twelve Corinthian columns, the whole a tribute to Albrecht's good taste.

The mirrors of Paris Gobelin are of gigantic proportions. The gardens are a great success, with a stream joined to the Mechelen canal and cascade... There is a 120-foot tower with 231 steps, from which one can see Antwerp on a clear day.

Forster noted that Albrecht and Marie-Christine had to carry out the instructions of their master Joseph II, often against their own inclinations. It pained him to see the servants packing up the furniture and carpets to be sent abroad. The arch-duke and arch-duchess were in the process of moving out after the Austrian defeat in 1789. The archduchess' favoured pastime was growing plants and herbs, all of which would be lost to her.

Following the arrival of the French in 1794, the palace was abandoned. It was officially the property of the Austrian royal family and as such was confiscated by the new authorities. The whole estate was put up for sale by auction in several lots. One Jean-Baptiste Terrade bought the main buildings for 220,810 francs in September 1803, with the intention of demolishing them and selling off the materials. As luck would have it, Napoleon had seen the palace during his first visit to Brussels in July 1803. When he heard it had been sold, he ordered an agent to try to buy it back along with whatever part of the estate was still on the market. Napoleon engaged two architects, Charles Percier and Pierre Fontaine, to restore the palace, but by this time the orangerie and Chinese Tower had both been demolished.

Bonaparte made his first visit to the Palais de Laeken on 1 September 1804, in the company of Empress Josephine. On his next visit he was accompanied by his second wife, the Empress Marie-Louise. He arrived at the Anderlecht gate to a small cheering crowd. The welcome was more for his wife than for him, because she was of Austrian descent, and the French were now extremely unpopular. The fact that he had been excommunicated in 1809 for annexing the Papal States had most probably affected the Belgian view of him. In 1812 Napoleon exchanged the Palace of Laeken for the Elysée Palace in Paris as part of a deal with the former Empress Josephine. When it became apparent that the emperor would soon lose his empire, he issued orders for the most valuable items from the Laeken Palace to be packed up and taken to Malmaison in Paris. Following Napoleon's exile there was endless legal wrangling between the Belgians and Louis XVIII, his successor, as to who was the actual owner of the contents of the palace. The French argued that everything belonged to the emperor, and that Josephine only had the use of the palace during her lifetime. Even items that were of no practical value, such as curtains, were not returned.

WATERLOO: A NEAR RUN THING

The Battle of Waterloo, fought on June 18, 1815, has gone down as one of the decisive moments in history. In another sense, it was merely an afterthought. The future of Europe was already being decided in Vienna while it went on. For Belgium, the main consequence was to ensure that the union with the Netherlands, decided on in 1814, would continue.

The fact that the battle was fought at Waterloo, ten miles from Brussels, was not entirely a coincidence. The Duke of Wellington had already considered the ridge at Mont St. Jean as the likely spot where he would station his army almost a year earlier, before there was any idea that Napoleon might try to escape from Elba. The Duke's reasoning was that he would have the upper hand here; he would use the terrain so that Napoleon would have to fight uphill.

The British officers billeted in Brussels tried to carry on with life as normal. Basil Jackson, in *Notes and Reminiscences of a Staff Officer* (1903) reports that British soldiers, stationed in Brussels in 1814, had a go at some fox-hunting in the forests round about.

> Reviews of the troops often occurred, taking place in the park whenever any great personage came. Then we had races, fox-hunting and cricket, all of which were patronised by the Prince. The hunting, however, was a great failure; in the first place the Belgian foxes had no idea that they were to run before the hounds, not being trained, I presume, to do so from their birth like our own; moreover, the farmers could not see the propriety of our riding over their land: indeed, the Prince had to pay a considerable sum as indemnification for alleged injury to the crops. This drove us to hunt in the forest of Soignies, but, as the stupid foxes would not run, hunting had to be given up.

When the news came that Napoleon was on the march, Wellington had good reason to feel worried. His army was a ragtag bunch of inexperienced British troops, backed up by Belgians, Dutch, and Poles; to the east, the Prussian army under the seventy-two year-old Marshal von Blücher was a vital element in his plans. The allied troops were quartered in Brussels with the intention of marching on Paris. In the meantime, the French King Louis XVIII was sheltering in Ghent, enduring the so-called Hundred Days exile.

Napoleon had little trouble reassembling the Grande Armée for a last throw of the dice, in the face of a pusillanimous response from Louis XVIII. Although he talked of peace, no one in Europe had much doubt as to his real intentions. Some of his former generals had switched sides, or kept out of the way. The others recognized Napoleon's immense popularity with the common soldier and were prepared to give him their support. His strategy was straightforward: march north with an army of 125,000 men and try to drive a wedge between Wellington and Blücher's troops before they had a chance to come together, and thus capture Brussels. The allies had an apparently substantial numerical advantage. Blücher alone had 120,000 Prussians or Germans, but half of them were untrained, and some might mutiny against the Prussian command. Wellington's army of 88,000 was a mixture of nationalities, of whom only 23,000 were British. Napoleon's troops were almost all French and veterans of his earlier campaigns. If the battle was to be decided on the quality of the troops, then the French looked likely to win.

The emperor's plan worked well to start with. He gained an element of surprise by marching north to the Belgian border in a mere two days. His forces under Marshal Ney had the better of the first engagement with the allies at Quatre Bras, south of Brussels, but had preferred to fall back on Gosselies rather than press on towards the capital. The Belgians and Dutch were generally blamed for running away from the battle in large numbers. Further southeast, Blücher's army was badly mauled at Ligny on June 16. Napoleon believed that the Prussians would retreat to the east, and sent 33,000 men after them, while he expected to drive back the British and march on Brussels.

A Last Dance

The degree of nonchalance with which the British treated Napoleon's invasion is impressive. Wellington, the Prince of Orange and other top brass were attending a ball given by the Duke and Duchess of Richmond in the Rue de la Blanchisserie when news came at two in the morning on June 18 that Napoleon was approaching the Forêt de Soignes. Hundreds of wounded were already streaming into the city from the defeat at Quatre Bras. The revellers left the ball and headed towards their units in the direction of Braine l'Alleud to the south.

The ball has entered British folklore thanks to descriptions in Byron's

Childe Harold and Thackeray's *Vanity Fair*. There was no doubt some apprehension when the news came that Napoleon had arrived at the southern outskirts of the capital. Eyewitnesses described it as a scene of chaos rather than a calm farewell. Most of the troops were already at Mont St. Jean: it was their commanders who were partying. In *Vanity Fair* it is the doomed George Osborne who leaves the ball to meet his end on the battlefield:

> Away went George, his nerves quivering with excitement at the news so long looked for, so sudden when it came. What were love and intrigue now? He thought about a thousand things but these in his rapid walk to his quarters—his past life and future chances—the fate which might be before him—the wife, the child perhaps, from whom unseen he might be about to part...
>
> At that moment a bugle from the Place of Arms began sounding clearly, and was taken up throughout the town; and amidst the drums of the infantry, and the shrill pipes of the Scotch, the whole city awoke.

In *Childe Harold* the ball covers stanzas 21 to 25 in Canto Three:

> There was a sound of revelry by night,
> and Belgium's capital had gathered then
> Her Beauty and her Chivalry, and bright
> The lamps shone o'er fair women and brave men;
> A thousand hearts beat happily; and when
> Music arose with its voluptuous swell,
> Soft eyes looked love to eyes which spake again,
> And all went merry as a marriage bell;
> ....
> And there was mounting in hot haste: the steed,
> The mustering squadron, and the clattering car,
> Went pouring forward with impetuous speed,
> And swiftly forming in the ranks of war;
> And the deep thunder peal on peal afar;
> And near, the beat of the alarming drum
> Roused up the soldier ere the morning star;
> While thronged the citizens with terror dumb,
> Or whispering, with white lips—"The foe! They come! They come!"

The Duchess of Richmond was concerned about whether her ball could go ahead, but the Duke of Wellington assured her: "Duchess, you may give your ball with the greatest safety, without fear of interruption." He had already planned a ball himself for June 21.

For Napoleon and Wellington this was to be the one and only occasion that they would meet in battle. Wellington had been the Corsican's nemesis in Spain, and proved to be so again. The conditions were appalling, it had rained all day on June 17, turning the fields into a sea of mud. Rather than attack straight away, Napoleon waited a little for the ground to dry out.

In the evening Wellington had most of his army stationed on the ridge of Mont St. Jean, near Waterloo. The French massed on the heights of La Belle Alliance, less than a mile to the south. Napoleon seriously underestimated Wellington. He often said that Wellington was a bad general and only capable of defeating Indians. The Emperor also showed a lack of tactical skill: by making a frontal attack on the allied troops he did what Wellington hoped for. At the same time that the arriving Prussians fell on the French right flank, the Imperial Guard marched straight towards British troops lying behind a ridge. The sudden appearance of the British unnerved the French, and for the first time the Imperial Guard broke and retreated. Napoleon's armies were unable to prevent the Coalition from restoring Louis XVIII to the French throne. Napoleon made an unsuccessful attempt to escape to America and was imprisoned on St. Helena.

After the battle the recriminations started between the allies, as to who had saved the day, and who had run away. The Belgians, by all accounts, performed very badly and many deserted. Some were probably pro-French or anti-Dutch, anti-British, anti-Prussian and anti-foreigner. The Dutch under General Chassé, who had fought, unwillingly, in the Peninsular War on the side of the French, did much better, indeed they claimed that without their steadfastness the battle would have been lost. Wellington agreed that it was a "damn near thing" or "damn nice thing"; no one is quite sure exactly what he said.

BATTLEFIELD TOURISTS

The battle had hardly ended when hordes of trophy hunters descended on the field to find souvenirs to sell later on. Waterloo immediately became the place to see on one's travels if one was British. The soldiers had not come alone; many of them had wives and girlfriends tagging along behind, ready to go and rescue their menfolk if need be. There are several graphic accounts of the battle by combatants, the most interesting by Edward Cotton, a sergeant-major in the 7th Hussars who stayed on after the battle and lived at Mont St. Jean. His writings, such as *A Voice from Waterloo* (1845), inspired Victor Hugo's Waterloo section in *Les Misérables*. Hugo himself stayed at the Hôtel des Colonnes during 1861 to do research.

Fanny Burney, who was married to a French general on the allied side, remained in the city while the battle went on and noted:

> Accounts from the field of battle arrived hourly; sometimes directly from the Duke of Wellington to Lady Charlotte Greville, and to some other ladies who had near relations in the combat, and which, by their means, were circulated in Brussels; and at other times from such as conveyed those amongst the wounded Belgians, whose misfortunes were inflicted near enough to the skirts of the spots of action, to allow of their being dragged away by their hovering countrymen to the city…
>
> All the people of Brussels lived in the streets. Doors seemed of no use, for they were never shut. The individuals, when they re-entered

their houses, only resided at the windows: so that the whole population seemed in public view.

As the battle started, the residents of the city were alarmed to see hundreds of foreign troops trying to enter. At first they appeared to be French, but on closer inspection turned out to be deserters and stragglers from the engagement at Quatre Bras. The *Bruxellois* barred all the gates from the south, while many of them fled the city in the direction of Antwerp, panicked by the constant rumours that Napoleon had already won. W.M. Thackeray devotes several pages to the panic in Brussels in *Vanity Fair,* mostly based on his own imagination, as he had not yet been to Belgium.

On the battlefield there were 40,000 dead or dying troops, and 10,000 dead horses. The locals stripped the bodies and buried them in pits. There was a stream of women and civilians towards the battlefield looking for their missing loved ones. Mrs. Eaton, in *Waterloo Days* (1815), describes the scene:

> Thus the road between Waterloo and Brussels was one long uninterrupted charnel-house: the smell, the whole way through the Forest, was extremely offensive, and in some places scarcely bearable. Deep stagnant pools of red putrid water, mingled with mortal remains, betrayed the spot where the bodies of men and horses had mingled together in death...

James Simpson, a Scottish lawyer, gives the following account (*Visit to Flanders*, 1816):

> The first thing which struck him at a distance, was the quantity of caps and hats strewn on the ground; it appeared as if the field had been covered with crows. When he came to the spot, the sight was truly shocking. At first there was a great preponderance of British slain, which looked very ill; but more in advance, the revenge made itself dreadfully marked, for ten French lay dead for one British. The field was so much covered with blood, that it appeared as if it had been completely flooded with it; dead horses seemed innumerable, and the peasantry employed in burying the dead, generally stript the bodies first. Of course these

people got a vast booty, when they ventured out of the neighbouring wood, after the battle; many of them made some hundred pounds. A great quantity of cap plates, cuirasses, and other articles, were collected by them, and sold as relicks.

Hundreds of deserters from the battles of the previous three days were making their way back to Brussels. The British officers urged them to return to their regiments, while the local people barred the gates of the city to them, so they lay down on the pavements of the suburbs. Wellington gave an order that any soldier who was separated from his unit without a pass was to be flogged. There were worse problems: Prussian stragglers had turned to robbing visitors to the battlefield.

There were debates about what the battle should be called: Battle of Mont St. Jean or Battle of Hougomont were mooted, while the French would have liked Battle of La Haye Sainte. Wellington ensured that the battle was named after Waterloo where he had his headquarters, so that the British role received the greater attention.

As soon as the dust had settled, British tourists started to arrive in numbers. Some of the soldiers remained behind and set up as guides or opened hotels. Sir Walter Scott was one of many who hoped to write a bestseller with his reportage *Paul's Letters to his Kinsfolk* (1816):

A more innocent source of profit has opened to many of the poor people about Waterloo, by the sale of such trinkets and arms as they collect daily from the field of battle; things of no intrinsic value, but upon which curiosity sets a daily increasing estimate. Almost every hamlet opens up a mart of them as soon as English visitors appear. Men, women, and children rushed out upon us, holding up swords, pistols, carabines, and holsters, all of which were sold when I was there at a prix juste, at least to those who knew how to drive a bargain. I saw a tolerably good carabine bought for five francs; to be sure there were many words to the bargain... Crosses of the Legion of Honour were in great request, and already stood high in the market. I bought one of the ordinary sort for forty francs. The eagles which the French soldiers wore in front of their caps, especially the more solid ornament of that description which belonged to the Imperial Guards, were sought after, but might be had for a few sous.

Scott also penned the following lines:

> For high, and deathless is the name,
> Oh Hougomont, thy ruins claim!
> The sound of Cressy none shall own,
> And Agincourt shall be unknown,
> And Blenheim be a nameless spot
> Long ere thy glories are forgot.

Byron was not so impressed with Scott's versifying. He wrote in the visitor's book where he was staying:

> "For one brief hour of deathless fame" [Scott].
> "Oh Walter Scott, for shame, for shame" [Byron].

The scene at Waterloo these days makes it hard to imagine the layout of the battle. The British erected an artificial hill, the Butte du Lion, and the French have their own monument. There is a visitor centre, and some oddly amateurish exhibitions, but to have any idea of what happened it is essential to do some reading before coming here. To all intents and purposes, this is just another piece of farmland without any clear landmarks. When he visited Waterloo a few years after the battle Wellington is reputed to have said: "They have ruined my battlefield."

The Duke of Wellington's descendants still benefit from the Iron Duke's success. The Duke has the title Prince of Waterloo, and should be addressed as Your Highness. He has the rights to 2,600 acres of forest near the battlefield for as long as the dukedom does not become extinct, and owns sixty acres outright. All told the Duke earns about US$200,000 a year from his properties here. Some locals have challenged this arrangement in the courts as an anachronism.

BYRON IN BRUSSELS
Lord Byron spent four days in Brussels in 1816 at 51 Rue Ducale. The visit to the battlefield inspired him to write twenty-six stanzas, of nine lines each, of *The Childe Harold* on returning to the city the same evening. His companion Dr. Polidori, relates their excursion:

I ordered our postillion to drive to Mont St Jean without stopping at Waterloo. We got out at the Monuments. Lord Byron gazed about for five minutes without uttering a syllable; at last, turning to me, he said: "I am not disappointed. I have seen the plains of Marathon. And these are as fine. Can you tell me," he continued, "where Picton fell? Because I have heard that my friend Howard was killed at his side, and nearly at the same moment."

Byron and Dr. Polidori ("Polly Dolly"), his personal physician, had landed in Ostend on April 26. Byron's marriage had ended, and there were rumours that he had been sleeping with half-sister; a long spell abroad was indicated. The poet did not behave any differently when he landed on Belgian soil. Polidori notes that as soon as they had checked into their hotel room, Byron "fell upon the chambermaid like a Thunderbolt." In a letter to his friend Hobhouse dated the following day, he reminds him "Don't forget the Cundums." The two set out for Ghent in a huge coach equipped with a bed that the poet had evidently had shipped over from Dover. Outside Ghent a wheel broke; the same happened at Mechelen. Byron ordered another coach in Brussels. It was said that he left town without paying for it, although Polidori claimed that he paid over the odds for it and could not get his money back when it turned out to be not much better than the coach they had brought from England.

Byron arrived hoping to stay in the hotel where Napoleon had stayed on his first visit to the capital, the Hôtel de l'Angleterre on the Rue de la Madeleine, but found it full of English tourists. He went to lodge with a Major Pryse Gordon, who had taken part in the battle, at 51 Rue Ducale on the Coudenberg. There is a plaque to mark his stay. Polidori and Byron also paid a visit to the Palace of Laeken:

We set off for the Chateau du Lac [sic], where we found the hind front much finer than the other for want of the startling dome and low windows. It has all its master-apartments on the ground-floor; they are extremely well laid out both with regard to comfort and magnificence— they were furnished by Napoleon. We saw the bed where Josephine, Marie Louise, and the Queen of Holland, have been treading fast on one another's heels. The hall for concerts divides the Emperor's from the Empress' rooms—it has a rich appearance and is Corinthian. The flooring of the Emperor's is all wood of different colours—checked—having to my eye a more pleasing appearance than the carpeted ones of the Empress. I sat down on two chairs on which had sat he who had ruled the world at one time. Some of his eagles were yet remaining on the chairs. The servant seemed a little astonished at our bowing before them.

The two travellers set off the next day for Cologne. Byron, of course, never returned to England, losing his life at Missolonghi fighting for Greek independence.

JAMES JOYCE

James Joyce (1882-1941) went on an excursion to Waterloo with Nora and his daughter Lucia in September 1926 to gather information for his description of the battle in the first chapter of *Finnegan's Wake*. Lucia apparently had an obsession with Napoleon. At the time they lodged in the Hôtel Astoria on the Rue Royale. By coincidence, the American novelist, Thomas Wolfe, was with the party. He was too shy to approach the great man.

> Joyce was very simple, very nice. He walked next to the old guide who showed us around, listening with apparent interest to his harangue delivered in broken English, and asking him questions. We came home to Brussels through a magnificent forest, miles in extent... Joyce got a bit stagey on the way home, draping his overcoat poetically around his shoulders. But I liked Joyce's looks—not extraordinary at first sight, but growing. His face was highly coloured, slightly concave—his mouth thin, not delicate, but extraordinarily humorous. He had a large powerful straight nose—redder than his face, somewhat pitted with scars and boils.

The Joyce family had started their trip to Belgium with a stay in Ostend. Joyce took a serious interest in learning Dutch and followed 64 lessons in the language. Some Dutch words later turned up in *Finnegan's Wake* in the mouth of the character Sockerson.

Chapter Nine

THÉÂTRE DE LA MONNAIE:
BIRTHPLACE OF THE NATION

"Gentle Bacchus poured some burgundy;
The monster replied: 'I'd rather have faro!' '"

Baudelaire

Theatre has always played a significant role in the life of Brussels. On any one night one can go to twenty-five or thirty performances in the city alone, an astonishing figure for a city with fewer than a million inhabitants. Drama also has strong political connotations. Strangely, the independent Belgian state was, in a sense, born out of a theatre, namely La Monnaie, because of an opera that triggered a popular uprising in 1830 against Dutch rule.

The current Théâtre de la Monnaie dates only from 1856, but the first permanent theatre on the site opened in 1700. There had been open-air theatres since the Middle Ages, using improvised stages. In 1650 a permanent theatre—La Comédie—was constructed on the Montagne St. Élisabeth. The Opera had its own theatre at the Quai aux Foins in 1681. The director of the latter, an ambitious Italian financier by the name of Gio-Paolo Bombarda, who was also the treasurer of the governor-general Maximilian of Bavaria, put forward the idea of building a new theatre on the site of the old mint of the dukes of Brabant, the Hôtel de la Monnaie. Construction started in 1695, with the design by the Italians, Bezzi father and son. The Monnaie mainly specialized in French dramas. A permanent theatre company was formed in 1766, and since the time of Napoleon it has received subsidies from the city. The open square around the Monnaie was the work of the Dutch, who also reconstructed the theatre in 1819.

The Monnaie went up in flames in 1855 but was reconstructed within the space of a year by Joseph Poelaert, famous for his Palais de Justice. This is a far more restrained and attractive building, retaining the original pediment in a classical style. The main change Poelaert made was to get rid of the arcade around the theatre, a promenade popular with the aristocracy. The Hôtel des Postes opposite the Monnaie was built in 1892 and demolished in 1965; the Centre Monnaie shopping arcade has appeared in its place.

The Place de la Monnaie was the site of the Brussels mint for most of its history, the first mint from 1420 situated across the Place with its front on the Rue des Écuyers. The mint moved in 1890 to St.-Gilles. Behind the Monnaie, in the Rue Léopold, is a plaque on the wall at no.5: "The French painter Louis David died in this house on December 29, 1825." David (1748-1825) was considered a genius in his day, but is not so highly regarded now. He has several paintings in the Musée des Beaux Arts, the best-known being *The Death of Marat* (1793).

The area around the Monnaie is set to become another stronghold of Dutch-speaking culture. The new Vlaams-Nederlands Huis, which promotes Flemish and Dutch culture in Brussels, was built on the corner of the Fossé aux Loups and the Rue Léopold with money from the Flemish regional government. The main Dutch public library is already next door to the Monnaie. The building running along the Rue de l'Écuyer to the Rue Léopold is also in Flemish hands.

THE 1830 REVOLUTION
The Monnaie is more famous than anything else for the events of August 1830, which marked the start of Belgian independence. Discontent with the regime of the Dutch King William I had been building up since 1828. The Austrian Netherlands had been assigned to the Dutch after the fall of Napoleon in 1814, but the marriage was not a happy one. William I tried to impose the use of the Dutch language on French-speaking functionaries and generally appointed Dutchmen to important positions in the Belgian government. His campaign against dissent in the press finally led to his downfall. Certain newspapers regularly ran articles critical of the Dutch government, and their journalists were sometimes fined or imprisoned. When the Belgian deputies in the lower house rejected William I's budget for 1830, the king unwisely sacked a number of them. A group of journalists started a subscription fund for the deputies, which resulted in lengthy prison sentences for some.

Against this background, the performance of an opera about the Neapolitan uprising against the Spanish in 1647 had the potential to cause trouble. A fireworks display planned for August 24 was banned by the police, causing general annoyance because the fireworks had cost seven million florins. Graffiti appeared: "Monday: fireworks, Tuesday: illuminations, Wednesday: revolution." Police were posted inside the Monnaie the following night for the performance of *La Muette de Portici* by the French composer Daniel Auber. A crowd hung around outside expecting, or maybe hoping for trouble, while inside, the tenor La Feuillade sang an aria "Amour sacré de la patrie" ("Sacred love of one's country"). In the fifth act as he came to the words "to arms!" the audience ran out of the theatre, and along with the waiting crowd, set off to smash up the house of the director of a pro-Dutch newspaper in the Rue de la Montagne. Others broke into a music shop and grabbed drums and trumpets. To start with, there was little more than a wave of random violence. Someone ran up a French flag from the Town Hall, but this was quickly replaced by the black, gold and red of Brabant. A Committee of Public Safety was set up to keep order, while the middle classes, who were seeing their properties damaged, advised negotiation with the Dutch. The Monnaie held a benefit concert for the dead and wounded on September 12, 1830. This was also the first occasion that the Belgian national anthem, *La Brabançonne* ("Brabant girl") was performed, naturally, by La Feuillade, the same tenor who had sung "Amour sacré de la patrie."

The Dutch king was not prepared to consider autonomy for Belgium, and preferred to resort to force. Outside the city at Vilvoorde, the Prince of Orange, with 5,000 men, could quite easily have nipped the problem in the bud, but he was reluctant to shed blood and left it to his younger brother, Prince Frederick, to deal with the rebels. The Dutch attacked from several sides and got the better of the poorly armed revolutionaries, except at the Porte de Flandre, where their cavalry were driven back by a hail of paving stones, chamber pots, and whatever else came to hand. The rebels had, however, raised an army of volunteers in other Belgian cities who came to the rescue.

The Belgians held out in the centre of the city at the Palais Royal, while the Dutch occupied the Parc de Bruxelles. A provisional government was formed on September 26, and the following day the Belgians were to attack the Dutch in the park. In the early hours of the morning the rebels crept into the park, but as they moved silently along they realized there was not a single Dutchman to be seen. They had all melted away during the night, leaving their heavy equipment behind them. The unexpected turn of events came about through the wisdom or restraint of the Prince of Orange. Although he knew that he had superior military force and could have bombarded Brussels into submission, he saw the futility of unleashing so much death and destruction on a people who would never accept his father's regime.

Belgium proclaimed its independence on October 4, 1830. A constituent assembly was elected the following month. The Conference of London recognized the state in December.

LA MALIBRAN

"La Malibran" is one of the most popular figures in Brussels folklore: a hospital and a street are named after her. She was born Maria-Felicia Garcia in Paris in 1808, the daughter of a well-known Spanish tenor. Her father (who had wanted a son) started to train her when he discovered she was a natural singer, and she was already a star by the age of seventeen. When her family were in New York she unwisely married a fifty-year-old French banker, Eugène Malibran, when she was only eighteen. Although she left him behind in New York soon after, she continued to send him large amounts of money for another ten years.

She made her Brussels début at the Théâtre de la Monnaie in August 1829, when the Dutch were still in power. Here she met the violinist Charles de Bériot, and the two fell in love but could not marry because her husband would not consent to a divorce. Their liaison was a matter of gossip in Paris (where she was living) so she moved to Brussels where she found people more tolerant.

Malibran performed in England from 1825, and was paid unheard-of sums of money. She gave much of it away to deserving causes as well as to her undeserving husband. Her virtuousness was a legend in Brussels where she went to visit the sick in hospital. Her marriage was finally dissolved in 1835 (she had already given birth to her first child in 1833). Then disaster struck: on a tour of England she went horse-riding, one of her favourite pastimes. The horse bolted and she was dragged along by one stirrup and badly hurt, but she insisted on carrying on with her tour. In the end she died in Manchester in September 1836, from what would these days be called exhaustion. After she had been buried in Manchester, her mother insisted that her body be brought back to Brussels, and she is now buried in Laeken Cemetery. The house that La Malibran and Bériot shared is now part of the Maison Communale of Ixelles.

THE MONNAIE IN MODERN TIMES

The Théâtre Royal de la Monnaie is the home of the Belgian National Opera. It also has its own resident symphony orchestra and choir, and is legally obliged to maintain a ballet company. Between 1959 and 1987 it was home to the Ballet du Vingtième Siècle, under Maurice Béjart, who also started a training school for contemporary dance, Mudra, in 1970. Béjart was replaced for a short time by the American choreographer Mark Morris; most of the Belgian dancers were sacked, and there were demonstrations by young choreographers at the gates.

Morris' successor, Anne Teresa de Keersmaeker (b. 1960), has remained in place since 1992. De Keersmaeker combines dance with text, theatre and music in an innovative style that has made her one of the world's leading choreographers. The other leading Belgian choreographer, Wim Vandekeybus (b. 1963), started as a protégé of the Antwerp theatre director and artist, Jan Fabre, and also works as a film director. In 1987 his first performed piece "What The Body Does Not Remember" became an international success and won him the prestigious New York Bessie Award in 1988. His company Ultima Vez performs all over the world. The extraordinary success of Flemish dance and choreography can be attributed to an enlightened subsidy policy on the part of the Flemish Regional Government. Subsidies have attracted foreign choreographers, most notably the American Meg Stuart, who set up her Damaged Goods company in Brussels in 1994.

The Monnaie is one of the smaller national opera theatres, holding only 1,250 spectators, but it is one of the best-supported, with some 14,000 season ticket-holders, and has maintained its reputation for innovation and world-class productions. The theatre operates on the principle that works are presented for a season. It is also the practice to commission pieces from Belgian composers and librettists every year.

CAFÉ CULTURE

Cafés, in the sense of places where one could take the family, hardly existed before 1830. Working people went to *estaminets* to drink themselves into oblivion with an inferior-quality gin called *schnick*. It has been estimated that there was one *estaminet* for every twenty families in 1830. There was also a tradition of *cabarets*, more attractive places where customers could eat, maybe outside in a courtyard. Many of these establishments had a profitable sideline as pickup joints with private rooms. By 1880 there was one drinking den for every thirteen families, and alcoholism was out of control. Higher taxes were imposed on alcohol from 1896, and in 1919 the sale of spirits was completely banned in cafés. The gin industry disappeared overnight, while the consumption of beer and wine took over. The law against the sale of spirits was only repealed in 1984.

Brussels nightlife changed with the opening of the first covered shopping mall in the Galeries St.-Hubert in 1847, and the rapid growth of *café-concerts* and *café-chantants*. Café-owners vied with each other to give their premises a French, English or Swiss interior, while English and German beers became hugely popular in the later nineteenth century. The building of the great boulevards over the River Senne was the starting point for a whole new range of cafés, where families could take their children. The first was the Sésino (now demolished) on the Boulevard Anspach, opposite the Brouckère metro entrance, which opened in 1872, owned by a Swiss. The Sésino was built in elaborate Moorish style with a covered terrace.

One can still gain some idea of the grandeur of these new café-restaurants from the terrace of the Hôtel Métropole, on the Place de Brouckère, the most expensive hotel in Brussels in its day. The surroundings have, of course, completely changed; there was a large fountain in the square, which had to be moved to the Quai au Bois à Brûler in the St. Cathérine area to make way for traffic. A room in the Métropole cost a princely ten francs, and lunch five francs in 1890. The Métropole still belongs to the wealthy brewing family, Wielemans, who originally had it built.

To experience a genuine fin-de-siècle atmosphere, go to the Falstaff, 19 Rue Henri Maus, or to the Cirio, 18 Rue de la Bourse. The latter was started by an Italian, Francesco Cirio, as a wine bar. It has a special *lambic italien*—a mixture of Chianti and Spumante unique to this café. Les Trois Suisses was another popular café—now sadly demolished and replaced by the Philips building—on the Place de Brouckère. The American writer John dos Passos reminisced in his earliest published writings in the *Harvard Journal* (1911):

> There was one café with a thrilling name, Les Trois Suisses, where I would sit solemnly sipping my milk and eating my madelaine, while gnomes and old men with beer mugs leered at me from the walls, from behind placid ladies and gentlemen taking their déjeuner. Then, if you were lucky, the gilt lion at the far end would roar. That glorious event occurred whenever a new barrel of beer was broached, and was accompanied by a flashing of electric-lighted eyes, fearful to behold.

There are still some old *estaminets* down the few remaining *impasses* or alleyways in the centre of town. On the Rue de Tabora, near the church of St. Nicolas, a large neon sign points to La Bécasse—The Snipe—a venerable *estaminet* that once had its own brewery. The alley in which it stood was called Doodengang (Alley of the Dead) in the eighteenth century because coffins from St. Nicolas were taken through here to the cemetery of the Récollets on the corner of the Boulevard Anspach and the Rue de la Bourse. The residents protested at the macabre name and had it changed. The beer is served reverentially by barmen in white aprons in a somewhat airless atmosphere like that of the church itself.

LITERARY CAFÉS

The 1880s marked a time when Brussels could seriously rival Paris as a centre of literary innovation. At the heart of this movement was the group known as La Jeune Belgique, after the journal of the same name, edited by Max Waller. For the short time that it lasted, *La Jeune Belgique* introduced most of Belgian French literature's great names to a wide audience: among others Maurice Maeterlinck, Émile Verhaeren, Albert Giraud, Iwan Gilkin, Charles Van Lerberghe, and many more. The journal became bogged down in endless arguments about literary style with its competitors *La Wallonie* and *L'Art Moderne*, and had lost its standing by the end of the 1880s. At its height, its associates would meet every evening in the Sésino, the first café to appear on the newly built boulevards over the Senne. The

Dutch-speaking literary group "Den Distel" ("The Thistle") held its meetings a few yards away, at the Maestricht Brasserie, which also no longer exists. Among its members were locally-born authors Pol de Mont, August Vermeylen and Isidore Teirlinck.

Coming off the Place de Brouckère is the ancient Rue Fossé aux Loups, originally a ditch running alongside the first city walls. Around 1900, the Café Au Compas (no longer in existence) was a meeting place for non-conformists and revolutionaries such as Georges Eekhoud and Camille Lemonnier. The first Belgian Dadaist, Clément Pansaers, frequented the place. Another Dadaist, Gérard van Bruaene (1891-1964), started his first café off the Rue du Marché aux Herbes, at no.8, when his art gallery failed in the Great Depression. His café, L'Imaige de Nostre Dame, became a popular hangout for artists in the 1930s, and van Bruaene took great pleasure in discovering up-and-coming painters.

The Imaige de Nostre Dame still exists down the Impasse des Cadeaux. These days it has none of the Dadaist connotations of yesteryear and is much the same as the other cafés in the area. Van Bruaene went on to run a number of artistic cafés; the only one to preserve his particular style is La Fleur en Papier Doré at 55 Rue des Alexiens, opened in 1945. The café has preserved a large number of his aphorisms written up on the walls, some witty and others mystifying. A sample of some of his better-known sayings:

> There is no merit whatsoever in being anything.
> We are not sufficiently nothing at all.
> Every man has the right to twenty-four hours of freedom a day.
> The thing that is most foreign to me is myself.

Many other artists and writers have left mementoes of their passing. The literary society, Grenier Jane Tony, is based here and puts on readings in various locations, but the favoured place these days for sophisticated (French) literary evenings is Théâtre Poème at 30 rue d'Écosse in St.-Gilles.

Literary cafés come and go, as rapidly as the groups who meet in them, but one café, or rather restaurant, has remained over the years, L'Estrille du Vieux Bruxelles in the Rue de Rollebeek, one of the few seventeenth-century buildings still standing in the city centre. The Théâtre du Marais put on plays in a small room on the first floor (thirteen feet square), for a time in the 1920s. From 1938 to 1952 it was a meeting place for leading poets such as Norge, Maurice Carême, Paul Éluard and other visitors. The writer Samuel Stehman ran a literary cabaret, Le Trou Vert, here in the 1950s. Johnny Hallyday, the French rock star, whose father worked with Stehman, came along from time to time when he was a teenager; his original name was Jean-Philippe Smet.

The Café Aux Bons Enfants, also on the Rue de Rollebeek, was the meeting place for the influential Dutch-speaking literary group, Van Nu en Straks ("From Now On"), also the name of a literary review from 1893 to 1902. Of the leaders of this grouping, the only one to become widely known was August Vermeylen (1872-1945), the author of *De Wandelende Jood* (1906), translated as *The Wandering Jew* in English. In various translations this had a tremendous impact in Europe, as a brilliant psychological study of a man who appears in different places and times, even if by present-day standards it could be labelled anti-Semitic. Out of the Van Nu en Straks group, Cyriel Buysse and Stijn Streuvels are still widely read.

GALERIES ST.-HUBERT: SHOPPING INNOVATION
The Galeries, designed by J.-P. Cluysenaar and built between 1842 and 1847, was the first covered shopping mall of its kind in Europe. The ribbed design of the roof gave it the nickname "Le paraplu de Bruxelles" (the umbrella of Brussels). It opened at the height of a potato famine, a fact not lost on Karl Marx, who was living in Brussels at the time. The demolition of the existing shops and houses caused outrage, and it took some nine years to expropriate all the owners. One barber by the name of Pameel even went so far as to cut his own throat in his shop. Only one existing business was incorporated into the new shopping mall, a covered flower market, which was boycotted thereafter. The Galeries run from the Rue du Marché aux Herbes to the corner of the Rue de l'Écuyer, the lower half being the Galerie de la Reine, the upper the Galerie du Roi, with the Galerie des Princes branching off to the Rue des Dominicains. The motto "Omnia omnibus" (Everything for Everybody) visible above the Rue de l'Écuyer entrance was taken from La Maison des Orfèvres (Goldsmiths' House) that existed on the site.

The Galeries became the meeting point for French exiles after Napoleon III's coup of 1851. At 10 Galerie de la Reine, Victor Hugo lectured on several occasions to a packed crowd. The Taverne du Passage in the Galerie du Roi also has strong literary associations. To its *habitués* it was known simply as Le Passage. The Dutch poet Jan Greshoff described it:

It's good here in my warm stable.
Good evening, sir. Michel knows in advance
What I want, faithful to your habits.
I wear out one pair of trousers after another on this bench.
Some might say that I was born
And I'll die in this small enclosed corner.

Jacques Brel often came when he was in town; he appreciated the *croquettes aux crevettes* (shrimp croquettes).

Within the Galeries is the Théâtre Royal des Galeries, one of the centres of Brussels cultural life, where Jacques Offenbach wrote a large part of *Orpheus in the Underworld*. The vogue for operetta at the Théâtre des Galeries started with Offenbach in 1860, when he opened with *La Chatte métamorphosée en femme*. While Offenbach presented his operettas, his father was the cantor at the Grand Synagogue in the Rue de la Régence. The operetta craze lasted until 1908, after which the theatre went over to conventional spoken plays.

The classic comedy of Brussels life, *Le Mariage de Mademoiselle Beulemans*, was co-written by the theatre's director, Jean-François Fonson, and a professional playwright, Fernand Wicheler, and was premiered here in March 1910. A satire on Brussels bourgeois manners, it has an extremely simple plot: a young Parisian goes to work for a Brussels beer-bottler and falls in love with his daughter, who is already betrothed to a local. The contrast between the Beulemans who speak Brussels French with its strong Flemish influences, and the sophisticated Parisian speech of the young Frenchman, proved an immense hit with Brussels audiences, for whom this good-natured self-mockery was something quite new. Within three months it was being shown in Paris with great success.

Traditional Brussels comedies, such as *Le Mariage* and *Bossemans en Coppenolle* (1936) by Paul Van Stalle, revolve around petit-bourgeois businessmen; the latter is about two partners in a firm of wall-paper manufacturers, where the son of one partner wants to marry the daughter of the other. The main bone of contention is that the partners support different football teams. *Bossemans en Coppenolle* is different in that it uses a lot of

Brussels Flemish words, and so is not as accessible to those who are not in the know.

Brussels' most famous French-language bookstore, Tropismes, is located at 11 Galerie des Princes. The bookstore has only been here since 1980; previously the premises housed a jazz club, the Blue Note, and before that a *café-concert*, Le Concert des Princes. Juliette Drouet, Victor Hugo's mistress, who had faithfully followed the author into exile from Paris, had an apartment in this building, while Hugo was installed in the Grand-Place with his family. Every morning "Juju" would send hot chocolate to "Toto". Drouet was no stranger to Brussels, as she had started out as an actress at the Théâtre du Parc in 1832.

La Mort Subite: Brussels and Beer

Ask any *Bruxellois* which is the most emblematic café in the city and there can be only one answer: La Mort Subite, on the Rue de la Montagne aux Herbes Potagères (Potherb Mount). The interior was designed in 1910 by Paul Hamesse (who also designed De Ultieme Hallucinatie in the Rue Royale), but this is a café for the serious beer-lover, with beer posters all over the walls. The name of this quintessential café—"Instant Death"— arose from a dice game that was played here: *pitjesbak*. Those who were eliminated from the game suffered *la mort subite*. It has become a recognized brand-name around the world. The café is supplied by the Mort Subite brewery in Kobbegem, Flemish Brabant, which was renamed after the café.

La Mort Subite started out by catering for the workers at the Belgian National Bank nearby. It is also within easy reach of the Théâtre de la Monnaie. Maurice Béjart, who ran the Ballet du Vingtième Siècle for almost twenty years, talks of coming here in his journal: *La Mort Subite: Journal Intime* (1991):

> I arrived in Brussels about a hundred years ago, or the day before yesterday perhaps… From the start, there was one place that tempted me, just behind the Théâtre de la Monnaie, an old café full of old mouldings and faded mirrors whose name explodes in pseudo-erotic-gothic red neon: La Mort Subite. I went in. You drink gueuze here. A distant cousin of beer, which, with its sour perfume of barely fizzy fake cider, agitates your head a little without weighing on your stomach.

Brussels beer has become world-famous in recent years, thanks to the efforts of the regional export councils, and the cognoscenti believe that Belgium produces the world's greatest beers, virtually all bottled. A recent survey of the fifty best beers in the world included thirteen Belgian beers. The strength of the beers can be gauged by the name. Dubbel has been fermented twice, and may be 8-9% alcohol. Tripel, which has been fermented three times and can have an alcohol content of 12%, will leave you legless. The different brand names give one some idea of how lethal their contents can be: Forbidden Fruit, Judas, Delirium Tremens, and so on. For those who prefer something less incapacitating, the best beer is probably Hoegaarden *bière blanche* or *witbier*, a light wheat beer flavoured with coriander, which was until recently made east of Brussels in the town of the same name, but is now brewed in Louvain. It is meant to be cloudy; connoisseurs drink it with a slice of lemon. Perfect for a summer's day.

A specific form of Brussels brewing produces *lambic* beers. Their uniqueness lies in the fermentation, for they are left in the open to be fermented by two kinds of yeast that float over the River Senne and to the west: *Brettanomyces bruxelliensis* and the *Brettanomyces lambicus*. These beers can only be brewed within a ten-mile radius to the west of Brussels because of the unique yeasts and weather conditions. Blended with *lambic*, a rather flat beer with a sour taste, *kriek* is made by macerating sour cherries, or *griottes*, *framboise* with raspberries, and *faro* with the addition of sugar and caramel. The local concoction called *half-en-half* is half faro and half *lambic*. The Café Falstaff serves a joke *half-en-half* (half white wine and half spumante).

Beer was first brewed at home by women in a single cauldron from oats and wheat. To improve the taste and its keeping qualities, herbs were added, and from the thirteenth century hops were substituted to improve flavour and preservation. Because much of the water supply was contaminated, it was usual to drink several litres of beer a day, and workers' contracts specified how much beer they could expect to receive. By the fifteenth century, quality controls were instituted, and limits placed on the opening hours of public drinking houses. The Brewers' Guildhall on the Grand-Place was first built in 1522. By 1700 there were 120 breweries in the central Brussels *commune* alone. The industry went into decline after 1700 with the increasing popularity of tea, coffee and cocoa, and by the time the French arrived in 1792 the brewers' guild no longer existed. The reconstituted guild now occupies the Maison des Brasseurs on the Grand-Place, which houses the Musée de la Brasserie.

Beer-brewing as an industrial activity took off again in the following century, aided by a greater scientific understanding of the brewing process, and the development of pure yeasts. The inconvenience of transporting the raw materials into the city centre eventually led to all the brewers moving out of central Brussels. The classic Brussels beers are brewed on the same principles as in medieval times, although almost all of them are now pasteurized.

In the Middle Ages, lack of knowledge about beer fermentation made brewers believe that there was some magical process at work. The basic ingredients for *lambic* in early medieval times were eleven *sisters* of oats and six *sisters* of rye, a *sister* being sixty decilitres. From the seventeenth century barley was used as well (these days barley is the main ingredient). Wheat is used for *bière blanche* or "white beer", not a Brussels speciality. The malted grain was heated in a cauldron and left to ferment. The resulting "wort" was then boiled with various herbs and transferred into barrels. The ideal barrels used today are sherry barrels of Spanish oak, holding 650 or 750 litres. Since the brewers had no equipment to measure the alcohol content, the beer was labeled according to the amount that could be derived from a certain quantity of grain and water, the tool used to measure the contents being a stick called a *pegel*.

The old Brussels breweries were all located along the Senne, for until the eighteenth century the waters were still relatively pure. Each brewer had a licence to draw water using a simple bucket on a lever, a *putsel*. The brewers observed early on that *lambic* could only be successfully brewed during cold and dry weather; the brewing season was and still is between October and March. At other times there were too many bacteria in the air that could spoil the process. Nor, strangely, were women allowed to be present during the brewing process. If the weather was misty, candles would be lit since it was thought that light was necessary for a successful result.

Along with the basic *lambic*, and its derivatives of *faro* and *kriek*, there have been numerous other experiments, such as banana or raspberry beer, which are not to everyone's taste. The classic beer is *gueuze*, which appeared in 1893 when some brewers had the idea of letting old and new *lambic* ferment in a champagne bottle, producing a sour and fizzy beer with a wine-like flavour. Some believe that the word *gueuze* comes from *geus* meaning beggar or Protestant in Dutch, but it is more likely that it was named after a brewer by the name of Geus.

To observe beer-making today, the best place to visit is the Brasserie Cantillon, at 56 Rue Gheude, near the Gare du Midi. The brewery only started operating in 1938, but everything is done in the traditional manner. The beer museum in the Grand-Place is rather less interesting. The contrast between the beer brewed by Cantillon and other brewers is striking. While the others pasteurize their beer, the Cantillon brewers keep to the old methods, which gives the beer a strong musty aroma. One may be reminded of Victor Hugo's remark about the beer of Louvain: "It smells of dead mice; delightful!"

Charles Baudelaire, who, as we shall see, had little good to say about Belgium, composed a short poem on the subject of *faro* and its disagreeable aftertaste:

Do you drink faro, Mr. Hetzel?
A look of horror crossed his bearded face,
No, never! Faro! I say this without spleen,
It's beer that you drink twice.

Verlaine and Hugo greatly appreciated *faro*, but it is not much drunk these days.

Cherry-flavoured beer, *kriek,* is a traditional summer drink and was usually accompanied by a slice of bread and white cheese. To counteract the sourness of the beer, you would have a lump of sugar and *stoemper* or sugar-crusher; nowadays most brands are already sweetened.

BAUDELAIRE AND THE RUE DE LA MONTAGNE

The Rue de la Montagne was the last stage of the main road to Cologne. It suffered from severe traffic jams from the fifteenth century, and an ordinance was passed in 1549 banning parking (*plus ça change...*). The original Rue de la Montagne went right up to the cathedral of St. Gudule; a part of it is now lost to the Boulevard de l'Impératrice. One side of the street, with an entire row of superb eighteenth-century buildings, was demolished in 1956 to make way for a parking lot. Thirty years later the authorities saw fit to replace it with a row of fake-medieval hotels. Behind the hotels is one of the more surreal sights of the city: larger-than-life size statues of Don Quixote and Sancho Panza look down on a less impressive Arnold Schoenberg. At the start of the Rue de la Montagne, on the Place d'Espagne, Charles Buls, the conservation-minded burgomaster from the later nineteenth century, sits with his back turned on the whole disgraceful spectacle.

The Rue de la Montagne's most famous literary resident was Charles Baudelaire (1821-67), who stayed at the Hôtel du Grand Miroir between 1864 and 1866. By all accounts it was the oldest hotel in Brussels, some kind of inn having existed on the spot from as early as 1250. P.T. Barnum's circus stayed in 1845; Toulouse-Lautrec was a guest in 1885.

Baudelaire had originally intended to arrive in Brussels in October 1863 and had even arranged speaking engagements for the following month, but for reasons unknown his arrival was delayed until April 1864. The motives for his flight from Paris were entirely financial: to escape his creditors and to make some easy money in Brussels. His publisher, Auguste Poulet-Malassis, shared his state of penury, and arrived in Brussels before him.

The Hôtel du Grand Miroir was run by a Parisian willing to tolerate Baudelaire's financial uncertainties. The poet complained about the price of meals (two francs for lunch) and avoided eating there. In 1864, his masterpiece, *Les Fleurs du mal,* was known only to a few, and although his first lecture at the Maison du Roi had been a critical success, the second and third were poorly attended and no more offers were forthcoming. He now pinned all his hopes on Victor Hugo's Belgian publishers, Lacroix and Verboeckhoven, who were making a fortune out of Hugo's success. Unfortunately, Baudelaire had made the mistake of attacking Hugo in print while still in France, so that neither Hugo nor his publishers would lift a finger to help him.

Baudelaire developed a paranoid hatred of everything Belgian, and set to writing a guide to Belgium. His *Pauvre Belgique*, and *La Belgique déshabillée*, extraordinarily vicious attacks on Belgians, or more precisely *Bruxellois*, clearly reveal a state of extreme mental distress. Insomnia, fevers and bad digestion made it difficult for him to work. His only exercise was to walk up and down the Galeries St.-Hubert precisely eight times; for company he kept a pet bat which he fed on milk-sops. Debts permitting, he would eat out at cafés, or otherwise with friends.

He continued to write and have works published, and could have returned to Paris long before circumstances forced him to. On a visit to Namur in February 1866 to see his close friend, the artist Félicien Rops, he had a fit on the steps of the church of St. Loup; on his return to Brussels he was taken to the Institut Chirurgico-Médical St. Jean-St. Élisabeth at 7 Rue des Cendres (now occupied by the Hôpital St. Jean), before going back to the Hôtel du Grand Miroir. The syphilis which was now attacking his brain had rendered him aphasic. Eventually in July 1866, his mother took him back to Paris, seen off by his faithful friends Poulet-Malassis and Rops, where he died soon after.

The following are just some samples of Baudelaire's bizarre views about the Belgians:

Amoenitates Belgicae
She stank like a rotten flower.
I told her (but courteously):
"You ought to take regular baths
To dispel your perfume of ram."
What did this foolish young thing say to me?
"You don't disgust me at all!
—At least here they wash the pavement
And the parquet with black soap!"

The Belgians, my word, push
Imitation to excess,
And if they get syphilis,
It's just to be like the French.

The breasts of even the smallest women,
Weigh half a ton,
And their limbs are like sticks
That remind you of a skeleton.

Further along from Baudelaire's hotel, at 52 Rue d'Arenberg, is the site of what was once a tavern, Au Prince Belge. There is a plaque: "In September-October 1859 Multatuli (Edouard Douwes Dekker) wrote his masterpiece *Max Havelaar* in the café Au Prince Belge which stood on this spot until 1876, when it was 80 Rue de la Montagne."

Multatuli (meaning "I have suffered much" in Latin) was an official in Dutch Indonesia, who had resigned his job and determined to write an exposé of the abuses of the colonial administration in Java. By doing so he left his family on the verge of starvation; fortunately *Max Havelaar* (1860) was a bestseller, and the first significant modern novel in Dutch. He wrote pathetic letters to his wife complaining about not having enough money to pay for coal to heat his room. He had to do his writing in the café downstairs, as it was too cold to think in his garret. The spot is something of a place of pilgrimage for the Dutch. For French-speakers it has not signified much; several guidebooks manage to get the address wrong. Next door, then no.82, was a post office. The service was once rather better than it is now: around 1850 it was open every day from 5 AM to 8 PM, except on Sundays when it was only open from 7 AM to 8 PM.

Chapter Ten

VILVOORDE AND MOLENBEEK: THE

INDUSTRIAL REVOLUTION

"L'Union fait la force"—"Unity is Strength"
Belgian national motto

Support for independence was by no means universal. William I enjoyed a great deal of popularity among the Flemish-speakers and even in some French-speaking areas. The Dutch had been driven out of Brussels in September 1830, and their king would not consider autonomy for Belgium, so there was no turning back. At the Conference of London in 1831, Belgium was recognized as an independent and neutral state. The German prince Leopold of Saxe-Coburg, widowed husband of Charlotte, daughter of William IV—who would have become Queen of England had she survived—was invited to become the first king of Belgium. The choice was a fortunate one. Leopold was highly intelligent and energetic, with great ambitions for his new kingdom.

Belgium's future prospects did not look promising. The threat from France and Holland hád to be neutralized. Leopold found it expedient to marry the daughter of the French King Louis-Philippe. The Dutch king William I attempted a coup d'état, which was only narrowly averted. In 1839 Belgium had to accept the loss of part of Flanders and Limburg, and the independence of Luxembourg, under pressure from the British. The two main political factions, the Catholics and the Liberals, formed governments of national unity until 1839, by which time any threat of invasion seemed to have passed. The constitution of Belgium at the time was perhaps the most liberal in Europe, and large numbers of political refugees from France and elsewhere moved to Brussels where they could find work in academia or as writers.

Following independence there was an atmosphere of patriotism and renewed confidence in the air. The city authorities wanted jurisdiction over the surrounding suburbs on the basis that the canal system and ports could not be run efficiently by several *communes*. Schaerbeek, Ixelles, St.-Josse, and Etterbeek duly became part of Brussels in 1853. In 1864 the Avenue Louise and the Bois de la Cambre were absorbed into the capital. At this time, only the Brussels *commune* and St.-Josse were truly urbanized.

The project to replace the city walls with wide new boulevards, ordered by Napoleon in 1810, finally got under way in 1819. The first gasworks opened in the same year. Continental Europe's first railway line, from Brussels to Mechelen, began operations in 1835. Belgium needed a railway system to be able to export its goods; Antwerp, its main port, was still blockaded by the Dutch.

The reign of Leopold II from 1865 to 1909 was an era of grandiose, some might say megalomaniac, projects that completely transformed the face of the city. A large-scale population shift occurred from central Brussels to the outer *communes* with the clearance of large areas of unhealthy slums. Public transport made it possible for the workers to live on the outskirts of the city. The money for these projects came from the success of Belgian industry, fuelled by foreign investment, especially from Britain. There was also the Congo, a colony eighty times the size of Belgium. From 1885 it was Leopold II's private property; the king handed it over to the state in 1908, the year before he died, following an international campaign against his misrule in Africa. The years 1850-1874 and 1895-1914 were the years of greatest expansion for the Belgian economy. By 1900 Belgium ranked on a par with the US and was only behind Great Britain in terms of its *per capita* wealth. Belgium's prosperity was guaranteed by the Congo, thanks to which it came through two world wars with its economy intact.

THE CANAL DE WILLEBROECK AND THE PORT OF BRUSSELS
Few visitors to Brussels are aware that there is a busy port here, which shifted eight million tons of cargo in 2008. Brussels' original *raison d'être* was its position on the road from west to east, from northern France to Cologne, and on the north-south axis of the River Senne. The first port was established at the point where the Senne became unnavigable and cargo had to be loaded on or off to go any further; in the city itself goods had to be unloaded and transported overland. The Habsburg ruler Charles V took the decision in 1531 to dig a canal to run alongside the Senne, which was prone to silting up and changing course. The Canal de Wille-

broeck opened in 1561. Its creation was a major technological achievement, not least because one of its channels had to pass under the River Senne. Brussels could now ship its goods to Antwerp without having to pay tolls at Mechelen.

Along with the Canal de Willebroeck, an area of quays was developed around the *béguinage*, known as the Bassins. These have all been filled in now, with the exception of the Quai au Bois à Brûler and the Quai aux Briques. At the start of the nineteenth century, the mine owners in the southern province of Hainaut demanded that the canal should be extended to Charleroi. This required the building of 55 locks and a kilometre-long tunnel, but the work only took five years, and the Canal de Charleroi opened in 1832. Within a few years it also became clear that the old port within the city was too small, so a larger port was developed alongside the canals on the western side of Brussels.

Brussels did not develop industrially in the same way as Liège and Charleroi. The Dutch King William I preferred to make it a centre of commerce, banking, publishing and the manufacture of luxury goods. The new Belgian ruler also saw the dangers of creating a large industrial proletariat in the capital, so money was invested elsewhere. In the eighteenth century industry centred around textiles and the cotton printing industry. Cotton imported from India was turned into fabrics, known as *indiennes*, for the European market, while a chemical industry developed in parallel to supply acids, dyes and saltpeter. The city also specialized in the production of faïence pottery, tanning, coach-making, paper-making, and printing.

Along with industry, huge warehouses sprouted up around the new docks, the most impressive being the colossal customs depot of Tour et Taxis, built between 1902 and 1907 on land that had belonged to the Thurn and Taxis family, who once controlled the postal services in the Habsburg Empire. The Tour et Taxis on the Avenue du Port is a remarkable construction, built using a 183,000 square-foot self-supporting metal frame with a saw-blade glass roof that disperses light evenly throughout the building. It has now been restored and is a centre for industrial archaeology as well as being rented out to artists, theatres and anyone who needs a lot of space. The industrialists also required a railway line on both sides of the canal, so the Gare Maritime (Maritime Railway Station) was built between 1904 and 1907 on the west bank of the canal. Downstream from the railway station is the giant Buda Bridge, constructed in 1931. This can be raised to allow ships through and lowered to allow trains to cross.

Industrialization provided jobs for the people, but it was also the cause of immense social problems when there were large-scale layoffs in the factories in the 1880s and during the Great Depression. In 1886 there was rioting in the Charleroi and Liège areas and hundreds died. In the capital there were demonstrations for universal suffrage. The police were ready to put down disorder by force, but few protesters were killed in the capital. Measures were taken to deal with the worst problems. In particular, the practice of paying workers in kind or in the form of alcohol was stopped. The foundations of a system of social security and pensions were laid. The numbers of those who were entitled to vote went up from around two percent of the population to twenty percent, but universal male suffrage for the lower house of parliament was only instituted in 1918.

BRUSSELS CHANGES LANGUAGE

It became apparent that Flemish (i.e. Dutch as spoken in Belgium) was under threat in Brussels in the second half of the eighteenth century, even though the city had always been Flemish-speaking. While most of the population still spoke Flemish in everyday life, French gained more and more ground as the prestige language, most of all after the French occupation of 1746-8 during the War of the Austrian Succession. The next French occupation from 1794 to 1814 naturally diminished the status of Dutch still further. The arrival of the Dutch regime in 1815 might have appeared to be a godsend to the *Flamingants*, as pro-Dutch militants are called, but rather had the opposite effect. The clumsy attempts of the Dutch king to impose his language on the French-speakers contributed in large measure to the revolt against Dutch rule. In Brussels, a large contingent of exiled French intellectuals gave significant support to the anti-Dutch movement, so that William I had to back down from his plans to impose Dutch on everyone.

With the establishment of an independent Belgian state, everything seemed to favour the progress of French. Virtually the entire electorate, 46,000 males, was French-speaking, since only rate-payers could vote. The fact that the Belgian state had been created by a small group of French-speakers, and the lack of a standardized Dutch language in Belgium resulted in French becoming the language of administration. The threat of an invasion from the north, or possibly from France, acted as a strong brake on any linguistic separatist tendencies. Nonetheless, in reaction to William I's attempts to impose Dutch on Belgium, article 23 of the 1830 Belgian Constitution stated that the choice of language was "optional" (*facultatif*), which in practice meant that there was no barrier to the spread of French. All official decrees were to be published separately in Flemish, but only the French version had legal validity. The army was to be entirely French-speaking. Flemish could only be used in the lower courts, and there was no obligation on functionaries to be competent in Flemish.

In the early days of the Belgian state the pauperization and apathy of the Flemish population played a major role in leaving the field open to French. In another sense, the lack of education of the Flemish-speakers was a factor in saving their language from extinction, as one could hardly teach French to illiterates. Economic prosperity was concentrated in the French-speaking area, and the industries and coal-mines were all owned by French-speakers. Flemish was in a state of disarray, without even a standard spelling. The *Flamingants* first had to turn Flemish into a viable language for literature and public life. Writers such as Hendrik Conscience (1812-83), who was actually half-French, set about creating romanticized versions of Flanders' great medieval past couched in simple Dutch which the workers could understand, his most well-known work being *De Leeuw van Vlaanderen* (The Lion of Flanders, 1838). It was said that Conscience taught the Flemish how to read. He was appointed tutor in Dutch to Leopold I's children.

The census figures for Brussels show quite graphically how the balance of power shifted towards French. In 1842 and 1846 the census included the question: "Do you speak French, Flemish or German?" About a third of the population gave French as their language, and almost all the rest Flemish. What is most noteworthy in these censuses is that there is no clear correlation between social class and language spoken. The poorest area, the Marolles, had one of the highest concentrations of French-speakers, dating back to the Middle Ages.

The nature of immigration into Brussels also played a large role in the growth of French. The typical immigrant in the mid-nineteenth century was a skilled and upwardly-mobile worker coming from another town in Belgium or from abroad. Using French was an obvious way of improving one's social and professional situation. Substantial numbers of

French as well as British, Dutch and German immigrants were drawn to Brussels by the prospect of good jobs and pay. The economic crisis in Flanders between 1845 and 1850 was another factor drawing Flemish immigrants to Brussels, but there were also many new arrivals from French-speaking Wallonia.

There was no question about language in the 1856 census, but subsequent censuses gave French, Flemish, German, English, and bilingual as choices. About half the population stated that they were bilingual in 1866, even though it is obvious that most of these were really Flemish-speakers who wanted to speak French to improve their social status, and who could only speak an approximate form of French. Most striking is the large number of domestic servants (about eleven percent of the active population), who would inevitably have adopted French to obtain work. There was a vast influx of female domestic servants, which meant that women outnumbered men in much of the city. At one time there were 154 women to 100 men in the *commune* of Ixelles.

By 1880 it was evident that French-speakers (or perhaps one should say speakers of some form of French) were the majority in the capital. Statistics on "bilingualism" in the censuses could be used to promote French: bilingualism was assumed to be a staging-post on the way from being a Dutch-speaker to becoming a French-speaker. In the popular mind, speaking a hybrid of Dutch and French was considered more desirable than speaking one's own dialect of Dutch. The popular 1910 play *Le Mariage de Mademoiselle Beulemans* (see p.142) illustrates this situation: a brewery-owning family of Flemish origins, speaking *Bruxellois* French, engages a young Parisian on work experience, who falls in love with the daughter. The French they speak uses Flemish word order, although not many actual Flemish words as they would have done in real life, making a hilarious contrast with the intricate, literary sentences of the young Parisian sophisticate. The self-mockery running through the play made it a huge hit in both Brussels and Paris.

A major factor in the process of Frenchification was the organization of the education system. Parents given the choice of sending their children to Dutch- or French-medium schools naturally saw no point in having their children educated in a language that would be of little value to them in the employment market, thus causing a further decline in the use of Dutch. The organization of universal free primary education from

1880 in itself was a powerful factor in promoting French. Charles Buls, mayor of Brussels from 1881 to 1899, made a brave attempt to reverse the trend to purely French-medium education in Brussels, by giving school principals rather than parents the right to determine the language children were to be taught in. His attempt to bring in a more or less bilingual system foundered by 1888 on the opposition not only of parents, but also of the teaching profession, who came from the French-speaking élite. Dutch as a medium of instruction was caught in a vicious circle: children who were taught in Dutch in their earlier years had great difficulty in then switching over to a predominantly French-medium system, so Dutch could never become the language of the educated élite.

THE FLEMISH FIGHT BACK

Attempts to redress the flagrant repression of the Flemish language were slow to take off. A number of Flemish intellectuals organized a *pétition-nement* in 1840 asking for Flemish to be used in some areas of the administration and law-courts, but the authorities quickly realized that these requests had no real popular backing and took no action. A governmental commission proposed, in 1857, to introduce Flemish primary and lower secondary education, and the use of the two languages in the administration, but no action was taken. The main movement against the use of French came, not surprisingly, from Antwerp, where hardly anyone spoke the language. A case in which two Flemish-speakers were guillotined after a trial of which they had not understood a single word, caused widespread outrage. A marked shift came about after the defeat of France by the Prussians in 1870. French prestige suffered a mortal blow and shortly after, in 1873, the first reform of the constitution took place, allowing the use of Dutch in Dutch-speaking areas. In 1878, Dutch also became an official language, but the French-speakers retained the right to use their language in the law-courts and the administration in Flemish areas.

The *Flamingant* movement in Brussels struggled to make its demands heard. Much of its support came from bilingual lower middle-class Flemish immigrants and some intellectuals who saw the injustice of trying to eradicate Dutch in Brussels. Successes were few: the building of the Royal Flemish Theatre (Koninklijke Vlaamse Schouwburg) in 1887, and attempts by Mayor Buls to bring in some degree of Dutch-medium education between 1881 and 1888. The victory of French in Brussels simply could not be prevented.

An entirely new set of circumstances arose during the First World War, when the German occupiers tried to play off the Flemish and Walloons by making Dutch the sole language of administration in the Flemish territories, in the vain hope that they would be unified with Germany, the so-called *Flamenpolitik*. The result was administrative chaos, and a severe setback to the movements for Flemish and Walloon autonomy. Another decisive factor was language use in the Belgian army. The officers tended to speak French, while many of the enlisted men only spoke Dutch. It has been claimed that the ordinary soldiers could not understand their orders, sometimes with disastrous results. The war marked a turning point: the Flemish expected equal treatment with the French-speakers, given their sacrifices in the cause of Belgian freedom. The attempts of Flemish activists to gain equality for their language backfired because of Flemish collaboration within occupied Belgium. For a while French regained its prestige, but after universal male suffrage was introduced in 1918 it was not long before the Flemish were able to push through legislation in favour of the use of Dutch.

On the basis of the census returns for Brussels, the years up to 1930 show fewer people being registered as "bilingual" as the population goes over to speaking more standard French or Dutch. From the 1930s the process of Frenchification became far more deep-rooted, with the offspring of Flemish immigrants giving up their parents' language completely. Brussels officially became a bilingual city in 1932. Until the 1960s the ordinary workers were still quite capable of speaking Dutch, while those who worked in the administration or high-class shops could not or did not wish to speak Dutch. at that time. The picture now is quite different in that many working-class people in Brussels are unable to speak Dutch at all. The more educated classes, on the other hand, and the administration make greater efforts to speak both languages. In practice, most genuinely bilingual Belgians live in or around Brussels, but they now speak standard Dutch and French, rather than the dialects of the past.

One should also not underestimate the impact of the building of the Jonction Nord-Midi between 1910 and 1951. The railway line created a barrier between the poorer and wealthier areas of the city as well as driving many out of the city centre. These days the entire area to the east and south of the railway line, along with the Quartier Léopold, which includes the government and EU offices, can be termed affluent, while the area to the west and north is more mixed.

Dutch gained complete parity with French throughout the country in 1935, with the acceptance of the principle of unilingualism, that is that only one language could be used in one area, but the language issue was not solved by this decision, as we shall see at the end of this book.

The other great divisive issue at the end of the nineteenth century was the question of education. The first law on universal primary education was passed in 1842. The *communes* were expected to provide schooling for the children of parents who wanted it, but sending children to school was not compulsory. The education minister, Charles Rogier, took a further step with the establishment of state-run middle schools and *atheneums* or high schools, in 1850, leading to protests by the Catholics and even from the pope. The interference of the Catholic Church in the education system took on extraordinary proportions. At one point the pope excommunicated the entire University of Ghent for refusing to dismiss a professor who was not a Catholic. The Church wanted all teachers to be Catholics since the children, they reasoned, were Catholics. The political opponents of the Catholic party were the Liberals, many of whom were Freemasons. A law passed by the Liberals in 1879, obliging every *commune* to establish a state-run school and forbidding the teaching of religion in school hours, led the Catholics to organize their own system of schools, the so-called *écoles libres* (free schools). In 1884 the law was changed so that the *communes* could adopt a Catholic school or keep their secular school. Too many hasty and radical measures led to instability in the schools and violent protests in the streets, since schoolteachers could not cross over from one system to the other. The problem is still felt down to the present day; schoolteachers generally stay within one system or the other.

THE CANALS AND L'ALLÉE VERTE

Before the expansion of the port, the canals were home to small yachts for those who could afford to pay the mooring charges. Rowing on the canal was a popular pastime. Further up the canal were the *guinguettes* or riverside taverns at Marly.

The Allée Verte follows the course of a track called the Rue Verte, leading from Molenbeek to Laeken from at least 1400. The area was popular with revellers in the eighteenth century, since beer could be sold here without incurring excise taxes. A hundred years ago it was a place to be seen taking a stroll, when it came down as far as the Place Sainctelette, now a busy traffic junction. The Molenbeek-born author, Herman Teirlinck (1879-1967), uses the Allée Verte as the backdrop for a romantic meeting in the fourth short story of the (Dutch) cycle *De zon* (The Sun, 1906). Teirlinck, under the influence of the Belgian Impressionists, was particularly preoccupied with the description of light and colours:

> Philemon marches along the Willebroeck Canal, where the sun spatters and washes over, broken into thousands of fragments. He walks past the city gates, follows the shadeless quays, and reaches the entrance to the beautiful Allée Verte which, alongside an eight-fold row of elms, leads to the Royal Park in Laeken. Here Philemon stood still... Soon he would walk under the elm trees, where the sun drips down between the masses of branches, and bursts open on the yellowish golden ground in brilliant flickers.

Robert Louis Stevenson (1850-94) took a leisurely cruise along the Willebroeck Canal (*An Inland Voyage*, 1907):

> It was a fine, green, flat landscape; or rather a mere green water-lane, going on from village to village. Things had a settled look, as in places long lived in. Crop-headed children spat upon us from the bridges as we went below, with a true conservative feeling. But even more conservative were the fishermen, intent upon their floats, who let us go by without one glance. They perched upon sterlings and buttresses and along the slope of the embankment, gently occupied. They did not move any more than if they had been fishing in an old Dutch print. The leaves fluttered, the water lapped, but they continued in one stay like so many churches established by law...
>
> At the last lock just beyond Villevorde, there was a lock mistress who spoke French comprehensibly, and told us we were still a couple of leagues from Brussels. At the same place, the rain began again. It fell in straight parallel lines; and the surface of the canal was thrown up into an infinity of little crystal fountains. There were no beds to be had in the

neighbourhood. Nothing for it but to lay the sails aside and address our-
selves to steady paddling in the rain.

Beautiful country houses, with clocks and long lines of shuttered
windows, and fine old trees standing in groves and avenues, gave a rich
and sombre aspect in the rain and the deepening dusk to the shores of
the canal. I seem to have seen something of the same effect in engrav-
ings: opulent landscapes, deserted and overhung with the passage of
storm. And throughout we had the escort of a hooded cart, which
trotted shabbily along the tow-path, and kept at an almost uniform distance in our wake.

The first railway station in the city opened in 1835 at the southern
end of the Allée Verte—above the present Yser metro station—and was in
operation until 1954. The first train to Mechelen set off at a sedate twelve
miles an hour (although it could quite safely do twenty-five miles an hour)
with George Stephenson as guest of honour. The open carriages were much
like horse-drawn carriages, with names such as *fiacre* and *berline*. The de-
partures of the trains were signaled by an ear-splitting noise from a bugler.
Théophile Gautier (1811-72), the French Romantic poet and traveler, ex-
pressed the misgivings of many in his *Un tour en Belgique et Hollande,*
recording a journey to the Low Countries he made in 1836.

> Railways are now all the fashion; they have become a fad, a mania, a
> craze! To speak ill of the railways is to deliberately expose oneself to the
> pleasant insults of the friends of progress and utility. It is making certain
> of being called a retrogressist, a fossil, a partisan of the ancien régime and
> of barbarism, and of being looked upon as a man devoted to tyrants and
> obscurantism.

VILVOORDE AND WILLIAM TYNDALE

The town is first mentioned as Filfurdo in 779. Situated on the confluence
of the Senne and the Woluwe, the Canal de Willebroeck passes through it
to the west of the original village. The name means "many fords"; when the
castle was built the name was reinterpreted as Villa Fortis.

The attack by Flanders on Brussels in 1357 led Dukes Wenceslas and
Jeanne of Brabant to authorize the building of a castle at Vilvoorde. A
prison was built to house important political prisoners, the most illustri-

ous by far being William Tyndale (1494-1536). Tyndale started translating the Bible into English from 1522, an act of heresy as far as the Catholic Church was concerned. When Sir Thomas More became Chancellor of England it was no longer safe to stay in England. He left for the continent and was shipwrecked on the Dutch coast in 1524. Henry VIII, More, and Cardinal Wolsey were determined to find him and have him brought back to England and burnt at the stake. Agents were sent to track him down, but Tyndale was wily. He printed his books with false colophons and did not stay anywhere for long.

By 1535 it seemed that Tyndale was safe from the English authorities, who were now more sympathetic towards him, but More's agents were still looking for him. Tyndale lived openly at the English House in Antwerp; there was an understanding that the Habsburg authorities would not enter the house to arrest English exiles. More's agent Harry Phillips found him in May 1535 and lured him outside with the offer of dinner in a restaurant. Phillips then pointed him out to officers he had brought with him from Brussels. Tyndale was taken to Vilvoorde and questioned for several months. He complained of the cold and the lack of light. Most of all, he wanted a Hebrew Bible and dictionary. He was finally found guilty of heresy in August 1536 and burnt at the stake in October. Since he was not a relapsed heretic he had the privilege of being strangled first before being put to the fire. The greatest irony was that Sir Thomas More, the man who was so determined to see him burnt at the stake, had been executed in June 1535.

Molenbeek and Industrial Archaeology

Called Meulebeek in the local dialect, the character of this area adjoining the western side of the central Brussels *commune* was strongly influenced by the creation of the Canal de Willebroeck and subsequently the Canal de Charleroi. According to the folklorist Louis Quiévreux, the canal even had its own ghost, the *lodder met zijn keuting* (spook with a chain), who would chase its victims until they fell into the canal, and run off cackling to itself. The *lodder* (literally "shaker" in Dutch) was generally a ghostly dog in Brabant in earlier times.

Those who worked in the port became known as *vaartkapoen* or "canal scamps", and carried on a fierce rivalry with the other Brussels ruffians or *ketjes*. They also gained some renown for resisting the Austrian occupiers in the eighteenth century. As a tribute the municipality commissioned the sculptor Tom Frantzen to create an authentic *vaartkapoen* rising out of a manhole cover and tripping up a policeman (at the Place Sainctelette in Molenbeek). Tom Frantzen also sculpted a *zinneke* (mongrel dog) urinating on a bollard in the Rue des Chartreux between the Rue Antoine Dansaert and the Place du Jardin aux Fleurs.

The opening of the Canal de Charleroi in 1832 and the building of the railway brought more new industries to Molenbeek, and it gained the nickname of "Little Manchester". To understand the effects of the industrial revolution in Brussels, it is worth visiting La Fonderie, an industrial museum set up in a disused bronze casting workshop, La Compagnie des Bronzes, at 27 Rue de Ransfort. The innards of the steam-driven machinery set up as sculptures in the courtyard give some idea of the scale of production here. La Fonderie was responsible for casting many of Brussels' best-known statues, among others Manneken Pis, the statues on the Petit Sablon, Leopold II on his horse on the Place du Trône, and Everard 't Serclaes by the Grand-Place.

Various approaches are being tried to deal with the problem of disused factories in Molenbeek, with new housing going up on derelict terrain. Where feasible, warehouses are being converted into "lofts" for housing, popular with Dutch-speaking yuppies. The *commune* is taking on a more gentrified air. It also has a well-established middle-class Moroccan community.

THE BASSINS AND PLACE ST. CATHÉRINE

The area of streets called the Quais was the port of Brussels, when it linked up with the Canal de Willebroeck. The goods were unloaded at the *quais,* such as the Quai aux Pierres de Taille (Freestone Quay), Quai au Foin (Hay Quay), Quai au Bois à Brûler (Firewood Quay) and the Quai aux Briques (Bricks Quay). The building that now houses the Koninklijke Vlaamse Schouwburg (Royal Flemish Theatre), on the Rue de Laeken, was the customs house for the port. The Rue de Flandre, which was the main road to Ghent, still has the atmosphere of a commercial *quartier,* even if most of the businesses have moved out.

In one of the classic Brussels comic novels, *Les Fiançailles de Joseph Kaekebroeck* (1902), by Léopold Courouble, Joseph Kaekebroeck remembers meeting his wife:

Suddenly, he arrived in the Place Sainte-Cathérine. He stopped pensively in front of the old belfry with its stones worn away by time, with its massive silhouette against the clear sky lit by the moon.

It was indeed here that he had seen her for the first time, on a rainy October morning, as she emerged without embarrassment, radiant and light, from the little hut at the foot of the tower. He had followed her into the picturesque market, where under the sodden marquees, she haggled over vegetables... He recalled the first words she had said to him, whose arbitrary syntax had charmed him...

The church of St. Cathérine stands in front of the Bassin St. Cathérine (filled in 1850). The original Romanesque church, first mentioned in 1201, was built up against the inside of the first city walls, and was the parish church for the *bateliers* or boatmen. This was replaced by a Gothic church that was itself entirely rebuilt in 1629. The tower (the only part remaining now) took some twenty years to construct. The area around the former St. Cathérine was one of the centres of the Irish community in Brussels during the Spanish period. After the accession of Elizabeth I of England, and maybe even before, an Irish regiment was set up with its headquarters in Brussels to serve in the Spanish Army of Flanders. Many of the Irish settled in Brussels and had children here; the Spanish regarded them as good soldiers, although they were cheated by their captains as most of them could not speak the local language.

The current church was begun in 1853 by Joseph Poelaert (architect of the Palais de Justice). For a while there was a debate as to whether it should become the new Bourse, but it was finally inaugurated as a church in 1874. Because of lack of money, cheap materials were used to construct St. Cathérine, and it will inevitably have to be demolished sooner or later. Yet in spite of its decrepit condition it is still in use. The Romanian Orthodox Church holds services there every Sunday morning in a part of the nave decorated with icons. There is a fifteenth-century Black Virgin and Child (visible behind glass), supposed to have been thrown into a canal by some Protestants in 1744. It was found floating on a piece of turf and fished out again. There is also the tombstone of the French priest Antoine Arnauld (1612-94), who spent the last fifteen years of his life in exile in Brussels. Arnauld was a follower of the Bishop of Ypres, Cornelius Jansenius, who inspired the Catholic sect of Jansenists, believers in predetermination and sworn enemies of the Jesuits. The conflict between the two is superbly satirized in Luis Buñuel's *The Milky Way* (1968). Blaise Pascal (1623-62), the French philosopher, wrote his *Lettres Provinciales* in defense of Arnauld.

Next to the Église St. Cathérine is one of the remaining towers of the first city walls dating from the twelfth century, absurdly stuck in the middle of a modern hotel, an egregious example of architectural philistinism. George Garnir gives this bitingly satirical description in his novel *Le Conservateur de la Tour Noire* (1908):

> The Tour Noire undoubtedly occupies one of the foremost places in the classification of Brussels monuments. The ruins of the Tour Noire were constructed around 1888. They constitute one of the most remarkable specimens of medieval architecture from the second half of the nineteenth century.
>
> They call it the Mustard Pot. That would be enough to consecrate it for the Belgian Baedeker; but the thing that gives it a value of the first order are the surroundings where it has been erected: a rectangular space within a building meant for a clothes shop... The juxtaposition in itself is an invention of genius: whoever thought of confronting like this, by the most striking and suggestive of contrasts, the architectural style of a

fashion shop with that of the citadels of our ancestors, the modern trade in jackets and trousers with military life in the twelfth century, certainly had some nerve...

The Tour Noire was originally destined for demolition, but Mayor Charles Buls insisted that it should be retained, so it was remodelled and surrounded by shops. The hotel is more recent.

The area around St. Cathérine is the place to go for Brussels cuisine at a reasonable price. The Pré Salé at 18 Rue de Flandre, is known as the place best for homely Brussels cooking. The Rue de Flandre and the surrounding area are generally becoming more Flemish, and much of the Rue Antoine Dansaert has been taken over by Flemish fashion designers. On the corner of the Rue Antoine Dansaert and the Rue du Vieux Marché aux Grains is the more up-market and highly rated La Villette. Almost next door is De Markten, a Flemish cultural centre offering space for any kind of exhibition or performance. There are helpful brochures on cheap courses in Dutch for foreigners and immigrants and a smart cafeteria.

The Antwerp-born writer Willem Elsschot (1882-1960), the best prose stylist in Dutch of recent times, situates his comic novel about a swindler (*Lijmen*, 1923) in the Rue de Flandre. The swindler, Boorman, persuades a gullible maker of kitchen lifts to advertise in a non-existent business journal. Elsschot drew on his experiences as a journalist in Brussels for this work, which has been translated as *Soft Soap* (1965). He also worked as a bookkeeper in a Vilvoorde gelatine factory for a while. Boorman's motto is "Payez comptant, soyez content" ("Pay cash and be happy").

INDUSTRIALIZATION IN ART AND LITERATURE

The immense changes that took place in nineteenth-century Belgian society could not be ignored by artists and writers. The first great work of Belgian French literature, *La Légende de Thyl Ulenspiegel*, by Charles de Coster, which came out in 1848, looked back to the period of the wars of religion and used Germanic myths in a Flemish setting. Hendrik Conscience's *Leeuw van Vlaanderen* (1838) marked a new phase in Belgian Dutch literature, similarly drawing on Flanders' medieval history. By looking back to the past, Conscience hoped to strengthen the feeling of Belgian national identity. As the Romantic Movement was coming to an end, Belgium began to feel the influence of a new naturalist school of writing coming from France, in particular Émile Zola's *Thérèse Raquin* (1867). There were those who believed that literature should deal with the lives of ordinary people, requiring a dispassionate and scientific observation of society. The most significant "naturalist" novel of the time was *Un Mâle* (1881) by Camille Lemonnier, which dealt with the sexual lusts of a Belgian peasant. In the same vein was Henri Nizet's *Bruxelles rigole* (Brussels Laughs, 1883), a novel of student life in the city.

Painters and sculptors also felt the necessity to respond to the harsh realities of life faced by the industrial underclass. The French painter Gustave Courbet (1819-77), who pioneered the realist style, had a considerable following in Belgium, in particular Louis Dubois (1830-80) and Charles de Groux (1825-70), whose works can be seen in the Musée des Beaux Arts. The outstanding realist artist in Brussels was Constantin Meunier (1831-1905), who after a long career as a classical artist discovered the world of blast furnaces and mining at the age of fifty, and from then on decided to devote himself to representing the toiling industrial workers. His works *Puddleur au repos* (Puddler at Rest, 1884), and *Le Grisou* (Gas Explosion in a Mine, 1887) are displayed in the Musée des Beaux Arts. More bronzes of toiling workers by Meunier (and contemporaries) can be seen around the Jardin Botanique, while his *atelier* has been preserved as the Musée Constantin Meunier, at 59 Rue de l'Abbaye, in Ixelles.

BRUSSELS THEATRE

Brussels has become a world centre for theatre and contemporary dance, largely thanks to generous subsidies from the Belgian regional governments. In the Rue de Flandre stands the Maison La Bellone, a centre for the study of performing arts with a well-preserved indoor pavilion from around 1700, now covered with a glass roof. The Théâtre National on the Boulevard Jacqmain makes use of "surtitling" to cater for both language communities (but not English), even though it is run by the French-speaking community. Ignoring the language barrier is now seen as a way to annoy far-right Flemish extremists. The most successful example is the annual Kunstenfestival des Arts.

Apart from the Koninklijke Vlaamse Schouwburg in the Rue de Laeken, which concentrates on bringing in foreign performers, Dutch-speaking theatres include the Kaaitheater near Place de Sainctelette, started in 1930, with the Vlaams Theater Instituut study centre next door. There are numerous other theatres in Brussels, all supported by regional subsidies.

Chapter Eleven

THE MAROLLES: WORKING-CLASS BRUSSELS

"Here lies the Developer with his faithful spouse Bureaucracy."
Sign on the Rue de Montserrat

A down-at-heel remnant of a once vibrant working-class area. This is one way to describe the archetypal *quartier* of the Marolles. But trying to define the actual area covered by what is called Marolles is the stuff of endless arguments. In its broadest use, the neighbourhood covers the whole southern tip of the *commune* of Brussels from Notre Dame du Sablon onwards, except for the area between the Rue aux Laines and the Toison d'Or. These days the locals will say that only the area between the Rue Haute and the Rue Blaes counts as the Marolles; strictly speaking, it is the area between the last hundred yards of the Rue Haute and the Rue aux Laines which is the real Marolles (some even exclude the Rue Blaes). Whatever the case, the whole area was devastated by huge building programmes in the nineteenth and early twentieth centuries, and the local culture and language have largely been consigned to history.

Even so, the Marolles still retains some characteristics of a "popular" quarter. It is still the poorest part of Brussels, with a high concentration of immigrants, first Polish Jews in the 1930s, followed by Spaniards and Italians after the Second World War, and then a new influx of Turks and Moroccans from the 1960s onwards. Most interesting is the local dialect *Marollien*, which mixes Flemish and French with a smattering of Spanish, incomprehensible even to other *Bruxellois*. Sadly, this has now more or less died out.

The name Marolles derives from the order of Apostolline nuns who moved here from France in 1686, Marolles being a contraction of Mariam Colentes (devotees of Mary), via Maricoles. The other explanation, that Marolles derives from the Spanish *marullerros*, meaning wily or cunning, can be discounted. The convent of the Sœurs Marolles was located on the

corner of the Rue de Montserrat and the Rue des Prêtres, behind the Hôpital St. Pierre. There is a statue of the Virgin Mary attached to the wall on the corner of the nearby Rue de la Prévoyance to recall the nuns' former presence. To some purists, only those who come from the Rue de Montserrat are real *Marolliens*; the immediate area is called La Marolle. The Rue de Montserrat owes its name to the fact that the Marolles sisters possessed a statue of the Black Virgin of Montserrat, the patron saint of Catalonia. In the nineteenth century the street was known as Rue des Marolles. These days there is no longer any street with that name.

The original twelfth-century inhabitants of the Marolles (which was originally called Bovendael or "higher valley") were those excluded from living within the city walls through poverty or because they were likely to cause trouble. There was a large influx of labourers from Wallonia around 1321, which strongly influenced the speech of the area. The clearance of the River Senne area, followed by the large-scale destruction of poor housing to make way for the Palais de Justice (1860-80), concentrated more people into a crowded area. Alcoholism was a serious problem in the late nineteenth century, as there were no controls on the number of drinking dens. The scale of destitution was such that three-quarters of the prisoners in the nearby Amigo prison were there at their own request. The main political issue was universal suffrage, which only arrived after 1918. These days the Comité Général d'Action des Marolles fights for the interests of the inhabitants. In 1998 it published *Les Marolles: 800 ans de résistance* (The Marolles: 800 Years of Resistance).

There is a plaque next to the Madonna on the Rue de la Prévoyance, which can be roughly translated as:

Bataille de La Marolle
13-9-1969
Here lies the Developer with his faithful spouse Bureaucracy. This tomb is permanent.

The term "Battle of the Marolles" is somewhat misleading, for the fight was not a violent one. This rather relates to a campaign to close the remaining *impasses* in the area and move the locals out. The programme started in 1952 with a visit by King Baudouin, who was shocked by the living conditions of the inhabitants. This was a period when it was deemed necessary to clear the slums, regardless of what came in their place. Matters came to a head in 1969, when news came out of a plan to extend the hated Palais de Justice still further to house its archives. A Comité d'Action des Marolles was formed and protests were organized. A programme was then presented that envisaged the gradual restoration of the area, with the emphasis on cheap housing for the people who wanted to stay in their *quartier*. For once the ordinary people got their way, but the area is a lot less lively than it was in the past.

After a large-scale clearance of the insalubrious *impasses* several blocks of flats were built for the locals, the most visible being the Cité Hellemans, from 1908. What are now called *les vieux blocs* were constructed with the French utopian sociologist Charles Fourier's theory of *phalanstères* in mind, namely that people should live in community groups of 810. Each of the streets between the blocks has been named after some traditional occupation, such as goldsmiths, chair makers, etc.

In times gone by the typical *Marollien* was known for his fierce pride, readiness for a fight (usually with the *Molenbeekers*), and love of jokes (the *zwanze* again). A *ketje* (from the Dutch *kereltje*), or young *Marollien*, could be recognized by his outlandish appearance, according to Louis Quiévreux in the *Dictionnaire du dialecte bruxellois* (1971):

The get-up of a Marollien is most unusual: tight trousers, a very short jacket, small shoes, sometimes varnished, if you please! A brightly coloured cravat. His hairstyle consists of one massive kiss-curl, which he glues down to his forehead, while the rest of his hair is scraped back over his ears, richly saturated with pommade about the choice of which he is extremely fussy. Finally, as his favourite headgear, he balances over his ear, with startling style, a black-and-white checked flat cap, which gives him that air of an ill-tempered brawler which he wants to affect above all else.

You would have to look quite hard to find someone answering to this description nowadays; the Toone puppet figure, Woltje, comes closest.

The *Marollien* in the past was both feared and respected. Thus Jacques van Melkebeke in his *Imageries bruxelloises*:

The Marollien loves, admires and respects physical force... You just have to look at the continuing vogue for the "sports tent" at the Foire du Midi. There is always someone in the crowd of amateurs who will take up the challenge. And, contrary to what you might think, it isn't always a sham. The custom is that a worthy amateur makes a collection amongst the audience, so more than one *kadeie* [lad] regularly comes and takes off his jacket. Then under the cynical but attentive eye of Frank, the patron, with his bashed-in face, remodelled with punches, known to the whole of old Brussels, the fight takes place.

The locals also had a softer side. They would always be ready to take in orphaned children, or to help anyone in trouble.

RUE HAUTE: HIGH AND LOW LIFE

Since Roman times and probably earlier there has been a road along the ridge of the hill between the Sablon and what is now St.-Gilles. The starting point of the present-day Rue Haute was the Steenpoort, one of the gates in the first city walls; in the twelfth century it was the main road leading towards Opbrussel or Obbrussel (now St.-Gilles). The first to move here were the weavers, dyers, and fullers who needed to be close to water for their work. With the building of the second set of city walls (1359-79) wealthier citizens started to move into the area, which offered more space to build large houses with gardens.

On the corner of the Ruelle de la Porte-Rouge, 132 Rue Haute, stands a step-gabled house that was probably the home of Pieter Brueghel the

Elder. It is certain that he was married at the Notre Dame de la Chapelle nearby in 1562 and that he was also buried there. His wife Mayken bore him two sons, Jan "Velvet" and Pieter "the Younger" before his death (see p.103). Anna Brueghel seems to have inherited the house from her father Jan, and lived there with the painter David Teniers the Younger (1610-90). On the corner of the Rue Haute and the Rue de l'Epée is the Square Breughel l'Ancien.

One of the legends of the jazz world, Jean "Toots" Thielemans, was born in 1922 at 241 Rue Haute, where his parents ran a *staminee* or café, the Trapkenaf, for the local *pottepei* (drinkers); he went to school in the same street. They noticed his interest in music and gave him an accordion at the age of three. He later took up the guitar before eventually turning to the harmonica, and started his career after the war entertaining US troops. He joined up with George Shearing in 1951 and gained US citizenship in 1952. Thielemans went on to play with many jazz greats, including Charlie Parker, Benny Goodman, and Ella Fitzgerald. He is well known for playing in the film *Midnight Cowboy* and for the theme tune of *Sesame Street*. There is a plaque on his old house with a harmonica embedded in it.

At the southern end of the Rue Haute, the Hôpital St. Pierre stands on the site of a medieval leper-house (St. Pierre-aux-Lépreux), which dated back to the twelfth century. The second set of city walls was extended to the Porte de Hal in order to enclose it. The extension of the hospital in the 1960s meant the destruction of a large part of the old Marolles, and these days the hospital is taking over more and more of the area. The Rue Haute near the hospital has sprouted several undertakers and flower shops, adding to the impression of decline.

The *Guide des plaisirs de Bruxelles*, published in Paris around 1900, gives the following suggestions:

> An hour spent in the area of the Rue Haute is enough to evoke the whole of the past of old Brussels and to procure a very pleasant experience for the lover of the picturesque... See the young apaches and their faithful ladyfriends, whose bright red and yellow dresses oddly complement the green trousers of their lords and masters. The high chignons of these Brussels beauties of the pavements do not lack a certain elegance, but it is as well to remember to be tactful in one's appreciation, for the com-

panions of these ladies will be keen to box with those who admire them
to excess—outside working hours.

The (anonymous) author has some advice on what to expect from the
women here:

> It would be an error to think that you will only find replicas of the
> "copious" Rubens woman in Brussels. Certainly, here, more than else-
> where, the amateurs (and they are legion) of ruddy complexions, prom-
> ising chests and aggressive behinds, will exult at every step, for one
> should remember that this fortunate land has seen the most unexpected
> mixing of races.
>
> One will find [with the demi-mondaine] something of that spirit of
> order, that love of comfort, that methodicalness which reigns everywhere
> in Belgium and which have made this small country into a great
> nation... The demi-mondaine is a bit of a homebody, which proves to
> us that the devil does not always wait until he is old before becoming a
> hermit.

VESALIUS AND THE RUE DES MINIMES

During the sixteenth and seventeenth centuries the top end of the Rue
Haute became popular with the French-speaking élite, as it was conveniently close to the Coudenberg and the Sablon. The great anatomist,
Andreas Vesalius (the latinized name of André Van Wesele), was born
nearby in the Helle Straetken (Hell Alley) close to the Rue aux Laines, in
1514. The alleyway can be roughly located between the Rue J. Dupont and
the Conservatoire.

Vesalius came from a medical family, his great-grandfather having
been the city physician in the 1430s, and his father an imperial pharma-
cist, whose work often took him abroad. The location of the Van Weseles'
house no doubt had a good deal to do with Vesalius' later expertise. The
family house was just a stone's throw from the Galgenberg (Gallows Hill),
where the cadavers of criminals swung in the wind as the birds pecked the
flesh off their bones. At the time the hill was still woods and fields; ap-
propriately enough it became the site of the present-day Palais de Justice.

According to a friend of the Vesalius family, the young André had
rather strange hobbies. At night he would go up to the Galgenberg, collect

bones and skulls, and try to classify them by types. In his spare time he practiced dissection on small animals, such as rats, cats, mice, and moles. Vesalius himself has left a graphic account of how he stole a cadaver from a gibbet in Louvain as a student. He went on to revolutionize Western medicine by making anatomy the foundation of scientific diagnosis at a time when the Catholic Church still strongly disapproved of any tampering with dead bodies. Before Vesalius there were no accu-

rate anatomical charts; much of the description of the body was based on animal dissection or pure fantasy.

Vesalius became professor of surgery at the University of Padua, and doctor to the King of Spain. Although he spent little time in Brussels, he was able to build a palatial house on the Rue des Minimes. Vesalius did not live to enjoy his retirement. In 1564 he became seriously ill while returning on a ship from a pilgrimage to Jerusalem and died on the Greek island of Zante. The story goes that, being of a miserly disposition, he had taken the cheapest passage available. The ship could not make land for a month, the food had run out, and the passengers were thrown overboard as they succumbed to the appalling conditions on board. Vesalius managed to hang on just long enough to be buried on dry land.

The Rue des Minimes, which begins at the Place du Grand Sablon, dates back to early medieval times; its original name was Blaerstraet or Rue des Feuilles (Leaves Street). The section between this street and the Rue aux Laines was then known as the Bovendael. In the sixteenth century it was a haunt of paupers and prostitutes. The Convent of the Minimes (or Minorites), an order of mendicants, was built on the site of André Vesalius' house. By an odd twist of fate, the chemist Jean-Baptiste Van Helmont was taken there to be questioned in 1634 when he was being persecuted by the Inquisition. It was taken over by the French in 1796 and used as a warehouse. The church of the Minimes reopened in 1819.

Rue des Brigittines and Georges Eekhoud

With the completion of the Jonction Nord-Midi in 1952, the original Rue des Brigittines, which ran more or less at right angles across the railway line, virtually ceased to exist; for this reason the church of the Brigittines has found itself transposed into the Rue des Visitandines. The railway runs behind what was the back garden of the convent of the Brigittines. The convent opened in 1652, while the church was built in 1672. In 1695 the tower was destroyed during the bombardment by the French. The shell of the church is used for exhibitions and concerts. The railway station stands over the Place des Wallons, named after a large influx of Walloon building workers who moved here in 1321. The present-day street can boast a railway station (Chapelle) and an unconvincing-looking park, but not one house. From the early Middle Ages it was part of a working-class area on the edge of the Marolles.

The gay writer Georges Eekhoud (1854-1927) loved this colourful locality and moved into a semi-derelict house here for a time. The Antwerp-born Eekhoud lived with his wife in the Rue du Progrès in Schaerbeek for most of his Brussels career, but found the area of the Marolles irresistible. Much of his work concerns the journey from the bourgeois to the "anti-bourgeois". In the ordinary people of the area he found the genuineness and life force that he thought was missing in the educated circles he came from. His earlier novels deal with the lives of dockers in Antwerp (*La Nouvelle Carthage*), and the farmers of the Campine region of Limburg (*Kees Doorik, Kermesses*). He eventually became a professor at the Université Libre de Bruxelles, but was forced out in 1918 because of his pacifist statements during the war. Much of his time was taken up with translating English Elizabethan dramas into French. He liked to write his diaries in English, perhaps in the hope that his wife would not be able to read them: "Half a dozen splendid roughs did play yesterday at the foot of the Palais de Justice, as I went down from the Place Poelaert, towards the High Street and that little street Our Lady of Grace… I love roughs."

His wife tore up or rewrote his diaries to make it appear that her husband was only interested in women. His erotic fantasies revolved around workmen's bottoms peeping out of mud-stained velvet trousers. At the same time, Eekhoud had a genuine sympathy for the downtrodden workers of the Marolles. The novel *Voyous de velours* (Velvet Scoundrels,

1904) takes place in a baroque fantasy version of the Marolles:

> How many times, at the sight of the little Mémène, haven't I said to myself: Have a good look at him, engrave his line and tone in your memory; you will never find him again in such an advantageous attitude, the scamp with big black eyes, rounded cheeks, tempting enough to eat, smart, precocious; worth ten thousand rich children, even though he often wears trousers that are so torn that you can see half his thighs with the rags hanging around them. Look at his rumpled mug, a bit mocking, creased by a sonorous laugh. The profound young scoundrel's jokes chime; he has made his judgement of social misery, and he knows that the best thing is to make fun of it by resigning oneself to it.

On a good day Eekhoud's fantasies would come true. Thus in his diaries for 1902: "I had him yesterday. It was long since I had got him in his velvet britches. We had a splendid sixty-nine." While his work appears preposterously camp these days, Eekhoud was a pioneer in his use of an intensely individualistic and hard-hitting language, which won him the admiration of the French literary establishment. His writings often appeared in two versions: the watered down one in Belgium and the stronger one in France. In 1900 he was prosecuted for disseminating pornography, along with another controversial writer, Camille Lemonnier, the charge revolving around a homosexual kiss in his novel *Escal Vigor*, an improbable tale of a Swedish nobleman who prefers a young man to his wife. The entire French literary establishment came out to support him and he was let off.

PLACE DU JEU DE BALLE AND THE OLD MARKET

The square was constructed on the site of a locomotive factory called Le Renard (The Fox) that existed here from 1835 to 1843. It took its name from the Rue des Renards, which itself was named after a tavern, In den Vos. The square was created on the initiative of M. Blaes, a local councillor, in order to give the inhabitants of the area some open space. For some years a ball game resembling *pelota* was played here, hence the name Place du Jeu de Balle. It is usually referred to as Vossenplein in Dutch, although officially it should be Kaatsspelplein, *kaatsspel* being the ball game in question. The Rue des Renards has itself had a checkered history. It started out as the Rue du Loup (Wolf Street), then became Rue des Rats Morts (Dead

Rats Street), then Rue des Rats, and finally Rue des Renards.

The Aâ Met (Marollien for Oude Markt in Dutch, or Vieux Marché in French) is now the site of a daily market, brought here from the Place Anneessens in 1873. During the week it is a chaotic collection of amateur junk dealers' stalls. Many of the goods are unsaleable and the whole thing seems to be more of a social event, especially for the immigrants who make up most of the sellers. Weekends and public holidays are something entirely different, for on these days there are some genuine antique items on sale next to the hopelessly outdated or damaged. To find a bargain it is best to come early in the morning.

Most of the action in Jean-Baptiste Baronian's novel, *Place du Jeu de Balle* (1980), is located around the square and its summer fair. The annual *kermesse* takes place from 20 July (its date commemorates the so-called Miracle of the Rue des Sols—see p.52). The novel mostly centres around the *brocanteurs* or antiques dealers who are part of the gentrification of the Rue Haute area. One has the slogan: "Chez Martial tout est banal. Le banal c'est pour Martial" ("Everything is banal at Martial's; anything banal is for Martial"). The novel even has the compulsory architect as one of the characters:

> Outside, there's the Rue de l'Hectolitre, at most thirty houses, almost all derelict; you can't call them ruins, a ruin is something else—an insult to memory, the trace of time which spans the centuries. Even so, just recently, some houses were restored, one of them quite massive, inhabited by an architect and his wife, a decorator who has painted big blue and red flowers around the door, the other smaller and lower, where Julien, a bearded antiques dealer, has opened his shop. Thirty houses survive, while so many others have been destroyed by the demolition men, in fact all those that used to run from the corner of the Rue du Radis to the Rue Sainte-Thérèse.

Baronian (the name is Armenian) is one of the most active writers in Brussels. He publishes his *romans noirs* under the name Alexander Lous; his real name is Joseph Lous Baronian.

Jacques De Decker's collection of twelve inter-linked short stories about Brussels people, *La Grande roue* (1985), also takes its name from the Ferris wheel at the summer fair. The anarchic young taxpayer Patrick persuades his tax inspector to go to the fair and throw his tax papers from the top of the big wheel, an arche- typal Belgian fantasy.

Rue Pieremans nearby was origi- nally Piermontstraet, named after some landowners in the area; Piere- mans (or Piermans) was an invention of the locals. There is now a street sign with Rue des Vers (Worms Street), as *pier* is Flemish for worm. The cartoon on the wall on the corner is of Petit Jojo, by André Geerts. The street is the backdrop for a short story by the Flemish author Herman Teirlinck, *Salomons erfgenamen* (Salomon's Inheritors, 1923):

> The old Jew was called Salomon. He lived with his wife in a narrow little house in the Pieremanstraat, with a dirty little kitchen on the fourth floor and just above a dirty bedroom under the roof. The Jew was old and poor. He sold pencils, shoe polish, keyrings and writing paper on the street. From noon until the early hours of the morning, by going round all the cafés of the high and low city, Salomon barely managed to keep himself alive. He lived on a piece of bread, three pounds of potatoes and a little vinegar a day. Everyone in the area thought he was wealthy and tight-fisted.

The Palais de Justice

Belgium's main courthouse is an indescribable mixture of different archi- tectural styles. The site covers some 26,000 square metres and was the final, and perhaps fatal, project of Joseph Poelaert (1817-79), King Leopold II's favorite architect. Some 3,000 houses had to be demolished to make way for this mammoth folly, and the purpose of locating it here, on the old Galgenberg, was no doubt to intimidate the rebellious residents of the Marolles. At the time, the Palais de Justice was the world's largest building project, costing 20 million francs to build, around $1 billion at modern prices. The architect went mad before the project could be fin- ished, supposedly cursed by a witch from the Marolles. The term *architek* or *schieven architek* (twisted architect) became a serious term of abuse in the Marolles thereafter (there is a café called De Skieven Architek on the Place du Jeu de Balle).

Octave Mirbeau describes the building in *La 628-E8* (1905):

I went to the Palais de Justice, where they have piled up, higgledy-piggledy, as far as they have been able to, souvenirs of monuments on souvenirs of monuments, only to end up with a monument of improbable ugliness. They have piled up the Assyrian on the Gothic, the Gothic on the Tibetan, Tibetan on Louis XVI, Louis XVI on Papuan... It's so ugly, that it becomes beautiful...

Verlaine was a little more flattering in his *Croquis de Belgique* (1895):

Externally it's a colossus, within a monster. It tries to be immense and succeeds. It wants to be as terrible as the Law, severe and sumptuously naked, and it is or comes close to it. In particular there is the Cour d'Assises where I would not like to be condemned to death whatever the reason might be. It's so black with marble and velvet (at least so it seems), that with the absence of daylight, it would be harder to hear one's sentence pronounced here than somewhere else.

The Dutch art critic, Conrad Busken Huet, thought the place "embodies the Indian tendencies of our somewhat mentally diseased century;

it fills a void in the history of European architecture, it vindicates the originality of Belgian art" (*Guide to Belgium and Northern France*, 1888). Another Dutchman, the poet Eddy Du Perron, declared: "The smallest canal in Amsterdam can easily swallow up the monstrous Palais de Justice, as far as its worth goes." The writer Franz Weyergans called it "pride made stone." Sigmund Freud said: "It reminds one of a print by Gustave Doré."

The authorities made the mistake of throwing the place open to the public the day after its inauguration on October 18, 1883. The *Marolliens* had their revenge by urinating on the carpets, tearing up the seats and carving chunks out of the columns before order could be restored. The building shows Poelaert's mania for symmetry to full effect. The style is officially Assyro-Babylonian, borrowing heavily from the palaces of Nineveh. Visitors can go into the main hall, the so-called Salle des Pas Perdus (Hall of Lost Steps).

For the revolutionary writer Victor Serge (1890-1947), who was born at 199 Rue du Trône, this was a childhood playground. He recalled in *Mémoires d'un révolutionnaire* (1947):

> The roofs of the Palais de Justice became our favourite haunt. We slipped through darkened staircases barred with No Entry notices. We left behind us, full of joyous contempt, the courtrooms, the empty, dusty labyrinths of the various floors, and emerged into the open air, in the light, in a world of iron, zinc and stone, geometrically irregular, with dangerous slopes, from where you saw the whole city and the whole sky. Below, in the square with tiny flagstones, some Lilliputian carriage brought some minute lawyer full of his own importance, carrying a minuscule folder full of papers that signified laws and crimes. We burst out laughing, thinking of him: "What a miserable existence..."

The current dome is not original and is somewhat more elongated vertically than the first one. The Germans used the original for wireless communications during the Second World War and set fire to it in September 1944 as the Allies approached. The steps of the Palais de Justice are a convenient place for demonstrations. The Place Poelart was the setting for a meeting in 1996 at the height of the political crisis surrounding the prosecution of the paedophile and child-murderer Marc Dutroux.

BRUSSELS DIALECTS

As we have seen, the original language of Brussels was a form of Flemish, known as Brabants, quite similar to the Flemish of East Flanders and Antwerp province. The use of French words was also evident in writings from medieval times, for example the expression *allez, allez*. In addition, the speech of the Marolles had a strong Walloon component. The period of Spanish rule provided a further source of new words. During the period of widespread "bilingualism" from about 1860 to 1930 a hybrid form of French with a Dutch basis also came into being. Dutch-speakers who were trying to make the change to French would use Dutch words where they did not know the French, or for humorous effect. Speakers of Dutch also resorted to using French words where they simply did not know the standard Dutch term, or where perhaps no such term had every existed.

In the modern-day situation, hybridized speech is not much used, except in humorous writing. The classic example is *Les Fables de Pitje Schramouille*, tales in a literary version of mixed French-Dutch dreamed up by the Ghent aristocrat Roger Kervijn de Marcke ten Driessche in the 1930s. The memoirs of Jef Kazak by Jean d'Osta are also immensely popular. The local dialect of the Marolles, in particular, was not the same as other dialects in the city. Marollien absorbed a certain amount of Walloon dialect because of the influx of Walloons from the early Middle Ages, which was added on to the confusing mix of French and Dutch, as well as Spanish. Maurice Mounesse, in *Bruxelles rive gauche* (1910), gives a good definition:

> Bruxellois should not be confused with Marollien, a sort of complicated, secret language, slangy, full of odd expressions some going back to the Spanish time. The inventiveness of the Marolliens made other Bruxellois imitate their dialect, or at least know some of their expressions.

The *Marolliens*, along with *Bruxellois* in general, are especially known for their creative insults. One may speculate on what purpose they serve; maybe they are used to compensate for a lack of articulacy. Some of the insults that are listed in Louis Quiévreux's *Dictionnaire du dialecte bruxellois* include *afkrabsel van mettekouwskluûte* (scrapings of a monkey's testicles), *spekscheeter* (bacon-shitter, i.e. a pretentious character), and *loïesenderm* (bag of lice).

Different degrees of drunkenness are distinguished by George Garnir and other experts in the field: *zat, schijlzat* (fairly drunk; literally, squint-drunk), *duudzat* (dead drunk), *strontzat* (shit drunk), *crimineelzat* (criminally drunk), *strontcrimineelzat* (criminally shit drunk), *bordijlegzat* (whorehouse drunk). A drunkard could be labelled a *zattepuut* or *zattekul*, which seems to have been a euphemism for the more obscene *zattekut*.

Marolliens used to take great pride in their extraordinarily rich vocabulary of insults. The worst thing in Brussels is to be called a *stoeffer* (bullshitter), as anyone who thinks they are better than other people is no good in this basically egalitarian society. Words related to food often appear in Brussels expressions, thus *être chocolat* (to be at a loss); to turn someone into *kipkap* (to make mincemeat out of them); *calichesap* (vanished, literally liquorice juice). Hergé uses the latter expression in *The Land of Black Gold* for the ruler Ben Kalish Ezab.

The more purely Flemish Brussels dialect known as "Brussels" in Dutch is dying out and is only being preserved by a few enthusiasts. There are regular meetings at the café Warm Water in the Rue des Renards in the Marolles, where speakers of standard Dutch perform songs and poetry in Brussels dialect. The effect is rather incongruous, given that many of the pieces have been translated from French songwriters such as Brassens or Ferrat, which goes to show that Dutch-speakers are generally very objective about who has the best literature.

There is now an Academie van het Brussels Dialect (the Flemish cultural centre, De Markten, will tell you where to find it). There is also another for speakers of Bruxellois, i.e. those whose language is basically French. The original speakers of Brussels Flemish, who are mostly quite old, have adopted French as their main language. Dutch-speakers who have come from outside Brussels generally speak standard Dutch or something close to it. The Marolles dialect is preserved at the famed puppet-based Théâtre Toone of the Rue des Bouchers, where it is known as "Vloms."

Outsiders who may know some French will be struck by the Brussels accent, which has a harder and more guttural sound than standard French, due to long-standing Germanic influences. The grammar of Brussels French also shows the influence of Dutch. Word order may be just as in Dutch, e.g. putting adjectives before their nouns, while whole expressions may be translated word for word from Dutch, with hilarious effect. There is the habit of using *ça* (meaning "that") in the Flemish (or one might say English) way; thus "ça est sûr" ("that's certainly true") rather than the correct "ça c'est sûr." The Dutch habit of putting two or three infinitives together gives rise to the clichéd joke expression, "ça peut pas rester continuer durer" ("that can't continue to keep on going on"). The tendency to put the syllable *–tche* on the end of words is very typical: *voilatche* for *voilà*. Verbs ending in *–ez* end in *–eie*, thus *alleie* for *allez*. The verb infinitive ends in *–eire*, hence *toucheire*, to claim unemployment benefit. A man and a woman are a *pei* and a *mei* (from the French *père* and *mère*). Note Hergé's Syldavian *dzapeih*, from Brussels *da pei*, meaning "the guy."

The French subjunctive is used incorrectly, or simply not at all, by many speakers of French in Belgium. Someone with a Flemish background may speak fluent French and never dream of using a subjunctive. *Bruxellois* tend to use the verb *savoir* (to know) instead of *pouvoir* (to be able), thus giving inanimate objects the power to know things. The Brussels French speaker may use *tu* where a standard French speaker would use *vous*; the reverse may also apply.

Brussels Flemish differs in some marked respects from the dialects of East Flanders. It is interesting to note that the inhabitants of Ghent imitated the speech of Brussels in the Middle Ages, which makes Ghent dialect sound rather different from those surrounding it. The most striking difference is in the pronunciation of the *aa* sound. *Straat* (street) becomes *stroet* (roughly stroo-uht in English), whereas in Ghent it is *stroit*. The long *aa* sound replaces other sounds, on the other hand, so that *gij* (you) becoming *gaâ*. A manual of Brussels Flemish has appeared entitled *Kende gaâ ons moojertoel nie?* (Don't You Know Our Mother Tongue?)

Brussels French is not a specific language. It can range from nothing more than French spoken with an accent, to something which would be quite far removed from standard French. There are words that are part of Belgian French and are used throughout Belgium, such as the numbers *septante* and *nonante* (seventy and ninety), which are also used in Switzerland. A *tirette* is a zip fastener; in standard French it is a *fermeture éclair*. A telephone directory is a *bottin* and not an *annuaire*. An *annuaire* in Belgian French is a desk diary or yearbook. The Belgians have also come up with the wonderfully evocative *aubette* for a newspaper stand, a word that the Académie Française would like to be used for a bus shelter.

Specifically Brussels French dialect words mostly originate from

Dutch. The best-known expressions, which should be pronounced as in French, include:

Brol—junk, odds and ends, loose change.

Broubeleir—someone who talks nonsense (from Dutch *brabbelaar*).

Caberdouche—a cabaret, i.e. a café with entertainment.

Cavitche—a gin-cellar.

Choukelief—from French *chou* (cabbage) and the Dutch diminutive - *ke*, and *lief*—meaning "darling". The same as French *petit chou*.

Clachekop—bald, a "slaphead", from the Dutch *kletskop*.

Douf—muggy, close, from Dutch *dof* or maybe Spanish *tufo*.

Drache—a sudden downpour, from Dutch *dretsen*. More or less accepted as standard Belgian French. The *drache nationale* is the downpour that always seems to happen on national holidays.

Faire scampavie—to vamoose, or to cheat on your partner, from the Spanish *escampavia*, a small boat used to pursue smugglers.

Froucheler—to fiddle about with, to bodge, from Dutch *frutselen*. It also has connotations of fondling. The noun is *froucheleir*.

Schieve lavabo—a bent washstand, meaning someone who is not as attractive as they think, and, by extension, untrustworthy.

Sukkeleir—incapable or pitiful person, from the Dutch *sukkelaar;* feminine *sukkelesse*.

Zieverer—to talk nonsense, to dribble, from the Dutch *zeveren*. Noun *zievereir*.

Zwanzer—to joke, from the Yiddish for penis or tail, *schwanze*.

As far as Spanish words go, *ploete* or money may well be derived from the Spanish *plata* (*cens* is the usual word for money); *mokske* or girl is certainly from the Spanish *moza*. An admirable young woman is a *tof mokske* (from Yiddish *tov*). There is a café on the Rue Haute called Ma Moke Es Een Zwette: My Girl is Black. The Spanish for wolf, *lova*, has given rise to the word *loff* or *loubas,* meaning a large but innocuous dog, and also a big man.

Brussels Flemish has spread far and wide without anyone realizing it. The invented languages in the Tintin books are Brussels-inspired, a sort of linguistic practical joke on the rest of the world. The whole thing has been studied by Frédéric Soumois in *Dossier Tintin* (1987), although one might argue with some of his conclusions, and there are Internet sites dedicated to deciphering Syldavian and Arumbaya and other imaginary languages, which lead us back to the city in question. In the case of Arumbaya, this has been turned into Cockney in the English version. Hergé's grandmother spoke Brussels dialect, so he had a good knowledge of the language. In *The Land of Black Gold* (1951), names of characters and places are from Brussels: the city of Wadesdah means "What's that?"; the deadly enemy of the Sheikh Ben Kalish Ezab (liquorice juice in Marollien), is Bab El-ehr, Flemish for chatterer (*babbeler*).

While Brussels Flemish has not been the subject of a thorough scientific investigation, Brussels French has been exhaustively described by Hugo Baetens Beardsmore in *Le Français régional de Bruxelles* (1971). There is also Jeanine Treffers-Daller's *Mixing Two Languages: French-Dutch Contact in a Comparative Perspective* (1994), which deals with Brussels speech. There are several dictionaries of Brussels dialects to be found in public libraries in Brussels. Needless to say, without a good understanding of Dutch and French, the charm of these dialects is not easy to appreciate.

RUE BLAES AND RUE DES TANNEURS

The Rue Blaes was only created in 1854 when a large number of the disease-infested *impasses* were demolished. The whole project was forced through by the *échevin* or city magistrate, Auguste Blaes, hence the street's name. The area to the west towards the railway line was in medieval times the Blyckerye or bleachers, where cloth was hung up on racks.

The last brewery to manufacture *gueuze* (see p.143) within the Brussels *commune* was Vossen in the Rue des Capucins, running between the Rue des Tanneurs and the Rue Haute. Quick et Flupke, two Brussels street urchins in a cartoon series by Hergé, are painted on the corner of the Rue des Capucins and the Rue Haute. The stock figure of fun is the *champetter* or policeman (from the French *garde champêtre* or rural policeman). The dialect name for a policeman was *ajoen* (onion). The children of the Marolles took a malign pleasure in waiting for an onion-seller to appear so that they could yell "*ajoen!*" before running off. A policeman had a hard life in the old Rue Haute. Jacques van Melkebeke in *Imageries Bruxelloises* (1943) writes:

It isn't for nothing that the windows of the *bureau de police* on the main street have bars, because, in the past, when they managed to bring in a criminal, his friends would try to set him free. Sometimes matters became so heated that only a pistol shot in the air would clear the area.

The Rue des Tanneurs (Tanners' Street) still retains its working-class atmosphere. It was the second large street to be built outside the city walls, in 1330. To begin with, it reached only as far as the Rue du Chevreuil, but was extended to the Boulevard du Midi in 1850. The tanneries existed here until the eighteenth century. The Rue du Lavoir recalls the public baths opened in 1859: entrance twenty centimes for second class, forty centimes for first. Since the 1950s the street has housed a large Spanish community. There are some 20,000 Spaniards in Brussels, who are well integrated into the community. Some Belgians have Spanish blood going back to the sixteenth century.

The Marolles has always had its share of charity workers. The journalist Jean de Vincennes wrote *De la Rue des Vers au paradis* (From Worms Street to Paradise, 1933) to bring to the public's attention the good work of the Entr'Aide aux Travailleuses (Charity for Working Women):

Why did I go inside 169 Rue des Tanneurs? I don't know... The door was half-open. I can see a short staircase, a room full of kids, and over there, a white room, the dispensary. I see mothers, children, young girls, smiles. It's an ordinary street. There are slimy gutters, a few cafés, dark windows, unattractive shops selling *boules* (doughnuts), serious, grave faces; even unpleasant faces. It's raining or it's dusty; just as usual.

The centre offers ultra-violet treatments for rickety or infirm children, courses in dressmaking, medical consultations, scout meetings, clubs for young women, for girls, mentoring for boys...

A good lady arrives in tears, plunged in appalling desolation. Her husband suffers from rheumatism, in spite of all the remedies and consultations. At her wits' end, she has made a pilgrimage to Notre-Dame de Hal to deposit a "little leg made of wax" at the feet of the Virgin, which is supposed to bring about an instant cure, but the wished-for effect did not come about. The poor woman finally comes to the "Moiselles" at the Rue des Tanneurs...

The Marolles has in the past had a reputation for witchcraft and generally superstitious Catholic belief. One of the more interesting customs was the use of *paaschnoegels*, small replicas of nails of the Cross made from the wax used for the Easter candles, which were put above doorways to keep out evil spirits. Black magic was generally taken very seriously in the pre-Enlightenment era. The practice of putting up *préaux*, little shrines to the Virgin or other saints, at crossroads in Belgium was intended to discourage the Black Mass at such locations which were particularly favourable for Satanism.

PLAGUE AND MEDICINE
Various plagues struck Brussels from the fourteenth century. One of the most mysterious was *la suette anglaise* or "English sweat", a fever that could kill within a few days and was reputed to have come from England. The bubonic plague appeared in 1663 in the Dutch ports of Rotterdam and Amsterdam, no doubt imported from Asia. Soon every major city in Holland had to experience its horrifying progress. Antwerp and Brussels passed ordinances banning imports from the Netherlands and requiring travellers to carry certificates of good health. Nonetheless, economic interests made it impossible to quarantine entire cities, and by the autumn of 1667 it was Brussels' turn. The epidemic was slow to take hold. Those who could left the city. As usual, the poor took the brunt of the sickness, the worst-affected areas being the Marolles, the Sablon and the Béguinage. In the worst month, October 1668, 1,500 people lost their lives. By the end of 1669, 4,000 inhabitants, or five percent of the population, were dead. It was the last time that Brussels had to face the dreaded disease.

As the plague took hold, the city authorities arranged for books to be published giving advice on how to combat the epidemic. Doctors at the time believed that plague was spread by "bad air" or "wild spirits". The disease was known as the *haestighe sieckte* (hasty sickness); those who were not dead within five days stood some chance of recovery. Householders were advised to air their houses and fumigate them with sulphur, the only substance that could not be infected by plague. Medicines considered useful included opium, powdered antlers and pigeon droppings. Most effective of all were amulets made from toads; even the great doctor Jean-Baptiste Van Helmont (see p.46) believed in them. In practice, the city authorities appointed a *pestmeester*, whose job was to isolate victims in *pesthuyzen*, plague houses, built up against the city walls; the main ones were in between the Place Rogier and the Botanique.

Looking after victims of the plague was the job of the lowest orders of monks, the Bogards or Third Order of St. Francis. The sick could expect rough treatment in the seventeenth century. The physician Van Helmont recounts that he was called to treat a woman who was completely covered in syphilitic sores. She had been admitted to the Béguinage, where the resident doctor had applied antiseptic directly to her wounds, with the intention of making her die more quickly. The unfortunate was then ejected from the Béguinage and left on a dung heap to die. Van Helmont cured her in twenty-five days.

Chapter Twelve

AN EMPIRE OF ONE'S OWN: VICTOR HORTA AND ART NOUVEAU

"Let me tell you what I think: Brussels is the most, most, most city in the world."

William Cliff

For about two decades (1893-1914) Brussels led the world in modern architecture. During this brief period some 500 Art Nouveau buildings appeared on the city's streets, fewer than half of which still remain today. The term requires some explanation. When Victor Horta designed the first Art Nouveau house, the Maison Tassel, at 6 Rue Janson, off the Avenue Louise, he was not even aware that it would be termed Art Nouveau. Indeed, the term did not even exist, although the artistic currents that gave rise to this style had been around for fifty years.

The ideas behind Art Nouveau developed to a large degree in Great Britain, beginning with the forming of the pre-Raphaelite Brotherhood in 1848. The pre-Raphaelites started out by rejecting the prevailing accepted artistic modes, whether classical, Renaissance or baroque, instead looking back to the primitive art of the pre-Renaissance. Their ideologues, Dante Gabriel Rossetti and John Ruskin, elaborated the theory that capitalist mass-production dehumanized workers. In their ideal world the workers would make objects of aesthetic value by hand, bringing new spiritual value to their lives.

The visionary socialist William Morris set up workshops to produce wallpaper and other articles that drew much of their inspiration from the forms of trees and flowers. Arthur Liberty had greater success, since he was willing to use machines in his production processes. The works of Burne-Jones, Millais, Holman Hunt and others naturally had their influence in Belgium. In particular, Fernand Khnopff's (1858-1921) idealized portrayals of women recall Rossetti's work.

A further important contribution to the new arts movement came from Japan. From the 1860s onwards, Japanese porcelain, prints and carvings were eagerly sought after in the West, and the work of artists such as James Whistler, Aubrey Beardsley and Toulouse-Lautrec soon showed the influence of an entirely new approach to art. On the face of it, the aesthetic of the Japanese print was far removed from Western art, being mainly concerned with representing surface textures in a highly stylized manner lacking perspective or realism. Even so, the use of large blocks of strong colours and the refreshingly different use of asymmetry had an immense impact on Western artists of the time.

From 1883 the Arts and Crafts Movement in England took on a more organized form with the setting up of the Arts and Crafts Exhibition Society. The Belgian equivalent, La Libre Esthétique, was set up in 1894 and lasted until 1914. This was itself the successor to the Groupe des XX (Group of Twenty), a body started in 1883 to allow young artists to present their work to the public. Brussels in the 1880s and 1890s was a dynamic centre for new ideas and the place where the British pre-Raphaelite movement had its first major impact on the continent. The architectural styles then in vogue looked back to the past: the classical style favoured by Leopold II side-by-side with the neo-Gothic and Flemish Renaissance, none of them actually reflecting the age itself. There was also now a wealthy middle class open to new ideas in art, which provided the conditions for original architectural styles.

Victor Horta (1861-1947), the son of a Ghent shoemaker, was the embodiment of the idea of Art Nouveau. He was already attending a design college at the age of fifteen, and worked with his teacher Alphonse Balat on the gigantic greenhouses at the Royal Palace in Laeken. He had seen how iron and steel could be used in the Eiffel Tower and in London's Crystal Palace. The local *Bruxellois* called it *poelingk stijl* (eels style). The line he adopted, the arabesque, expresses both energy and grace. The use of steel girders was considered unacceptable in private dwellings, but nonetheless Horta took that risk. The internal structure of the house could now be "read". Unobstructed space where light could pour in—the open hallway that would stretch up to the top floor rather than a staircase— was a defining feature of his architecture. A house should reflect the person who lives in it, he believed. Such individualized design, of course, limited such buildings to those who could pay for them. It also made it difficult to convert the building to other uses. Horta favoured a "total" approach to house design. He would design the furniture, the interior decoration, everything down to the last detail. His methods were expensive and time-consuming; he had to design one museum three times before he was satisfied. Thus he did not become a rich man, his own house in the Rue Américaine being relatively small, although beautifully designed.

There were few architects who were able or willing to follow Horta's total design approach. Art Nouveau became associated with buildings for the wealthy, as the decorative aspect took over from an overall concept of art meant to promote social equality. By 1914 Art Nouveau had run its course. It gave way to a more severe Art Deco style, which also originated in Brussels. Horta's later work, such as the Gare Centrale and the Palais des Beaux Arts (see p.113), is far more modernist as well as being oriented towards classical models.

ART NOUVEAU IN THE CITY

Most of the private Art Nouveau houses are concentrated around the Avenue Louise in Ixelles and St.-Gilles. The most impressive is the Hôtel Solvay at 224 Avenue Louise, built between 1894 and 1898 by Horta for one of the wealthiest families in Belgium. By placing bow windows over two floors on either side of the central body of the building, Horta creates the effect of a wave. The wide, low balcony was for the family to watch the promenaders going past.

The most visible Art Nouveau building in the city is the Old England department store on the Rue Montagne de la Cour. This is an eclectic construction designed by Paul Saintenoy (1862-1962), a grandson of J.-P. Cluysenaar, the architect of the Galeries St.-Hubert. The bow window that extends over two floors is typically Art Nouveau. The steel and glass building has a popular tea room on the roof terrace. It now houses the Musée d'Instruments de Musique, part of what is probably the world's largest collection of musical instruments, belonging to the Brussels Conservatoire.

Two of Brussels' most popular cafés, the Falstaff (19 Rue Henri Maus, near the Bourse) and De Ultieme Hallucinatie at 316 Rue Royale are in Art Nouveau style. The Rue Defacqz, running off the Avenue Louise has three Art Nouveau houses at nos.48, 50, and 71, designed by Paul Hankar (1859-1901). It is also worth having a look at the Isabelle de Backer flower shop at 13 Rue Royale, another Hankar creation, where the sinuous mahogany window frames are a perfect setting for the flowers.

Anyone who spends some time in Brussels will want to visit Victor Horta's own house at 25 Rue Américaine. The St.-Gilles *commune* acquired the building in 1961, with most of the original contents intact, and turned it into a museum. One can see very clearly the attention to detail and the way that the ensemble reflects the personality of the man.

Art Nouveau design was expensive and elitist, intended to affirm the identity of the owners, who were generally wealthy, liberal bourgeois. After the First World War the lifestyle of the upper classes changed and such ostentation was no longer considered acceptable. The next phase, Art Deco, used more geometrical forms without entirely abandoning the decorative elements of Art Nouveau (hence the name). The best example in Brussels is the Hôtel Stoclet at 275 Avenue de Tervuren, built between 1905 and 1911 by the Austrian Josef Hoffmann (1870-1956), a leader of the Vienna Secession. The owner, Adolphe Stoclet, was hoping to have the Avenue de Tervuren named after him, so when the city authorities refused he had the building designed with the rear backing on to the street. The starkly rectangular design was well ahead of its time and is only softened by the four nude statues on the tower. The house is not open to visitors. The best house to see in completely Art Deco style is the Musée David et Alice van Buuren, at 41 Avenue Léo Errera in Uccle. Art Deco was, again, not exactly for the masses. The heavy emphasis on expensive materials such as silver and ebony eventually made it just as elitist as Art Nouveau.

ARCHITECTURAL CONSERVATION

Charles Buls, mayor of Brussels from 1881 to 1899, was greatly concerned with the preservation of the city's heritage and wrote on the subject in *Esthétique des villes*. His concern was such that he resigned from his post as mayor in 1899 rather than have to carry out Leopold II's orders to demolish historic buildings on the Mont des Arts. In an article in the journal *Tekhnê* from 1911 (translated by Pierre Puttemans in *Modern Architecture in Belgium*, 1976), he shows remarkable prescience:

> Councillor Gürlitt fears that to conserve by order the old bourgeois houses in what has always been the centre of traffic, can only result in the gradual replacement of their occupants by an inferior class who would not undertake the upkeep of these houses with the zeal of their previous inhabitants... M. Gürlitt considers that this danger would be largely averted by instituting severe measures of sanitary control. We would also like to see a strict limit on the height of buildings imposed in areas of historic importance, and on the encroachment on land which is now reserved for inner courtyards. To our mind, the municipal administration would be committing an error both of economy and hygiene if it favoured the construction of skyscrapers with a view to increasing the value of building land.
>
> It would be a black day indeed for Brussels if these tendencies came to pass: for it would be unable to extend its territory by annexing the suburbs. Indeed, many of its inhabitants have already moved out there and come to town only to shop or go to their offices; and that is why the population of the capital is diminishing.

Much of this has come to pass. The population of the capital fell between 1980 and 1996 from 1,008,000 to 949,000 but is increasing again. Many streets in the city centre are derelict and likely to be taken over by more cheaply designed office buildings. Better-off *Bruxellois* have always shown a distaste for living in the city centre. Like any other Belgian, they want as big a garden as possible and do not want to live in an apartment. For political reasons the city cannot expand any further into what is nominally Dutch-speaking majority territory.

The city has time and again sold or leased its land too cheaply out of a desire to keep the big institutions in the city centre, while not receiving any taxes from the people who work in these monstrous edifices. Since the nineteenth century it has been the practice to rent out houses to immigrants and then allow them to fall into disrepair. Eventually these buildings become uninhabitable and have to be pulled down, leaving space for

a lucrative new office block. Action on preserving buildings has also been hampered by the fact that until 1988 Brussels did not have its own assembly and regional status, leaving the fate of the city's architectural heritage in the hands of the Dutch- and French-speaking community bodies.

Leopold II: Lust for Empire

Facing the Boulevard de Waterloo is the equestrian statue of Leopold II (r.1865-1909), a hate figure to many people. When he came to the throne he vowed to make "Belgium greater and more beautiful". This he perhaps achieved, but at the expense of several million Africans. To get a sense of Leopold's impact on Brussels, one can look at the numerous building projects that he started or completed in his lifetime. The arch of the Parc du Cinquantenaire is a case in point. But to know more about his place in history, go to the Midden-Afrika Museum (or Musée de l'Afrique Centrale) in Tervuren, to the southeast of the city, which houses the world's most important collection of ethnographic objects from Africa. The building was once a palace belonging to the Austrian governor-general Charles of Lorraine, who died here in 1780. The museum itself is a little disappointing in spite of the wealth of remarkable exhibits, seemingly stuck in a time warp where nothing has been touched for fifty years. Some of the exhibits are falling apart; some cases have no explanations at all. There is no compromising with political correctness here. Everything is just as it was: the whites are the heroes and the blacks the benighted savages. One may feel queasy viewing Henry Morton Stanley's trunk and his patented solar hat when one considers that he sailed down the Congo River shooting any blacks who annoyed him.

Leopold II, the "Rubber King" (Roi Caoutchouc) has been airbrushed from the scene. The story of how Belgium managed to acquire a colony 81 times its own size has been told many times, perhaps best of all in *King Leopold's Ghost* by Adam Hochschild. Leopold II's obsession with finding a colony for Belgium started at an early age. His parents treated him coldly; he even had to apply for an audience if he wanted to speak to his father. From the age of twenty he went travelling and started to cook up far-fetched schemes to acquire foreign colonies, which he thought were absolutely necessary if Belgium was to become a rich country. He thought of buying up part of the Nile delta, or Ethiopia. After one trip to the East in 1864 he made inquiries about buying the Philippines from Spain, or taking over the island of Fiji.

Leopold's obsessions led him to spend a month in Seville studying the commercial records of the Spanish American Empire. The Belgian government had absolutely no interest in financing Leopold's wild schemes, so he was left to find another way of realizing his dreams. His chance came in 1878 when he met up with the explorer Henry Morton Stanley, a Welshman who had become a best-selling journalist in the American Civil War and who was only too delighted to be patronized by royalty. Leopold put him under contract and used a bogus organization, the International African Association, to drive forward his colonial projects. The Belgian monarch offered finance for more exploration of the Congo River by Stanley. Another organization, the International Association of the Congo, was set up with the hidden agenda of forcing local chiefs along the river to sign away their territory, and thus ultimately set up a new state under Leopold's control. The trick worked; the US recognized the Congo Free State in 1884, and the other Great Powers followed suit at the Conference of Berlin in 1885.

By 1890 Leopold controlled a large area of the Congo, but the king had serious financial difficulties and had many other projects to finance; worse, the amount of ivory coming from the Congo had fallen dramatically. The solution came in the form of the wild rubber that grew in abundance in the jungles. The villagers had to be forced by Leopold's agents to go into the jungle to tap the rubber plants. The usual stratagem was to kidnap their wives. Those who refused were likely to have their hands amputated or worse.

Leopold finally convinced the Belgian government that his new colony was worth investing in. At the same time, stories of atrocities committed by the Belgians multiplied in the press abroad. The Congo attracted all kinds of adventurers and freebooters, most of whom seemed to have a psychopathic hatred of the natives. At the same time there were missionaries and others who tried to bring the Belgian reign of terror to the attention of the world's media. Among the many who tried their luck there was Joseph Conrad, a Pole who had spent ten years in the British merchant marine. The six months he spent in the Congo from August 1890 gave him the material for his novel *The Heart of Darkness*, which later inspired the film *Apocalypse Now*. The character Kurtz was based on one or two Belgian officials he had met there.

There have been many estimates made of the number of natives who died during Leopold's reign of terror, and it has been said that the population of the Congo fell from 20,000,000 to 8,500,000. For some Leopold can be mentioned in the same breath as Hitler and Stalin. Whether he knew the full extent of the atrocities being carried on his name is a moot point, for he never set foot in his colony. Towards the end of his life there was a campaign in the British press against his rule, and he became an instantly recognizable figure in cartoons thanks to his huge beard and outsize nose. The Belgians have generally preferred to draw a veil of silence over their "Rubber King".

Belgium's prosperity was underwritten by the Congo; the country recovered far more quickly from the Second World War than did the Dutch thanks to its huge African colony, which became independent in 1960.

Belgium had also gained control over Rwanda and Burundi after they had been taken away from the Germans in 1919. This entire colonial episode is a huge embarrassment to Belgians. The bungled withdrawal, the assassination of Patrice Lumumba by the CIA with the connivance of the Belgian authorities, and more recent fiascoes in Rwanda are painful memories which no one likes to evoke.

The Congo was by no means Belgium's only colonial adventure. There was a small colony in Guatemala in the 1840s, as well as the disastrous intervention in 1860s Mexico, when Leopold II's sister Charlotte was briefly Empress of Mexico before she went mad and her husband was shot. Leopold also tried to acquire a part of China by starting up a railway company at the turn of the century to link Hankow with Peking, during the carve-up by the colonial powers. The Belgians achieved the extraordinary feat of building a 750-mile rail line through inhospitable and hostile country, but nothing came of Leopold's plans and the line was bought by the Chinese government shortly after it was completed. Under the Austrians there was also the Ostend East India Company, which had a trading post in Bengal at Bankibazar, but the venture was closed down at the insistence of the Dutch and British in 1727.

THE CURSE OF THE RUBBER KING

On the inner ring road is the Boulevard de Waterloo, extending down the hill towards the Porte de Hal. What is now a Louis Vuitton shop on the corner of the Rue du Grand Cerf is the site of one of the city's most improbable mysteries. On January 21, 1867, Maxime Weygand was born here, at what is now no.59. During the First World War he was chief-of-staff of the allied armies. He dictated the terms of surrender to the German in November 1918 and commanded the allied armies again in 1940. His parentage has always remained a secret; indeed one may wonder why the child was allowed to live at all. His birth certificate states "parents unknown". The child received annual payments from the Belgian state.

The most likely explanation is that the child was the illegitimate son of Leopold II's demented sister, Empress Charlotte of Mexico, and a Belgian officer in Mexico, General Van der Smissen. Charlotte was married off to Maximilian, the brother of the Habsburg Emperor Franz-Joseph II, at the age of sixteen in 1857. In 1864 the French occupied a large part of Mexico to try to recoup large loans that had been made to the Mexican government. A scheme was dreamt up whereby Maximilian and Charlotte would become emperor and empress, even though there was no monarchist party in Mexico. They landed in 1864 and found themselves fighting a hopeless war against Mexican revolutionaries. Charlotte, or Carlotta as she had become, set off for Europe to try to gain support from her supposed French backers. They showed no interest, and so she went to the Vatican to try to get help from the pope. At this point she started to suffer from paranoid delusions. She entered the pope's chambers while he was having breakfast and demanded that all her entourage should be arrested as they were trying to poison her. As she refused to leave, a bed was made up for her in the libraries, so that she had the distinction of being the first woman ever to stay overnight (officially) in the Vatican.

Charlotte's brother Prince Philippe was sent to deal with the situation, and from this time until her death in 1927, Charlotte was kept locked up in various castles. It is likely that she had experimented with hallucinogenic drugs in Mexico, which may well have triggered off her breakdown. As far as is known, she gave birth to Maxime Weygand in Brussels. Without a DNA test it would be difficult to establish the truth of the matter, but Weygand's remarkable resemblance to General Van der Smissen seems to put the matter beyond doubt.

The existence of the illegitimate child posed a serious problem for both the Habsburgs and the Belgian royal family, as neither monarch had a direct successor to the throne. Two of Charlotte's female attendants died in suspicious circumstances, quite probably murdered to stop them from talking. Weygand never met his mother; at the end of her life he received letters saying "your mother is dying."

The Place and Tunnel Stéphanie recall another of Leopold II's unfortunate daughters, Stéphanie (1864-1945). She was the second of three daughters; her parents wanted sons. Her brother Leopold died when he was nine years old after contracting pneumonia. At the age of fourteen it was already decided that she was to marry the heir to the Habsburg throne, Archduke Rudolph, the marriage taking place when she was sixteen. The prince was highly intelligent, but also mentally unstable and an inveterate womanizer. The marriage was not a success, and Rudolph continued with his numerous mistresses. On January 30, 1889, the crown-prince shot himself and his mistress, Mary Vetsera, at the hunting lodge of Mayerling. The reasons are not clear; most likely he was sinking into insanity and was convinced that the only option was to kill himself. Stéphanie was still young, and later remarried to the Hungarian Count Lonyay. They remained married for 45 years, and Stéphanie stayed in Hungary to the end of her days. Her own account is to be found in her autobiography, *Je devais être impératrice* (I Should Have Been Empress, 1937).

The Avenue Louise, which starts from Place Louise, was named after Stéphanie's sister, another tragic figure in the line of Charlotte. Louise was married to Prince Philip of Saxe-Coburg, another high-up figure at the Habsburg court who was present at Mayerling when the bodies of Rudolph and Mary Vetsera were found.

Louise's marriage was equally unsatisfactory; she fell in love with a Croatian officer, Count Mattachich Keglevitch, and ran away with him to the French Riviera. Her husband and her lover fought a duel, which her husband lost without being seriously hurt. Louise found herself in financial difficulties—in modern parlance, she was a shopaholic—and accordingly falsified her sister's signature on a warrant, though she denied the charge herself. As Louise embarked on a mad shopping spree, her father Leopold II published advertisements warning the shopkeepers of the Côte d'Azur not to give her any credit.

In the end, her husband undertook to pay off her debts, while Count Mattachich-Keglevitch was stripped of his rank and condemned to six years in prison. Louise was given the choice of returning to her husband or being confined to a sanitarium for the mentally ill. To her credit, she chose the latter.

After four years in prison Mattachich Keglevitch was finally freed and set off to find Louise, still locked up in the sanitarium. It took another two years for the two of them to be reunited after a whole series of adventures that would be worthy of a comic opera. Keglevitch published articles in the press, as well as a book, *Mad for Reasons of State*, to draw attention to the injustice of Louise's situation.

Even then, their troubles were not over, as Louise's creditors were still hot on her heels. Her mother Marie-Henriette had died, and it was assumed that she would inherit a large amount of money, namely her mother's dowry. Yet Leopold II's daughters received nothing. Louise's creditors, along with Princess Stéphanie, took Leopold to court, demanding that he pay off her debts. Leopold won the case under Belgian law, and his daughters were left empty-handed. Not only did he never speak to Louise and Stéphanie again, but he also did everything to ensure they would receive as little as possible when he died by selling many of his possessions or giving them away (including the Congo). After Leopold's death there were more legal arguments. Stéphanie remained happily married to her Hungarian count, while Louise was hard up for the rest of her days, unable to give up her extravagant lifestyle. She published her own version of events: *My Own Affairs*.

AVENUE LOUISE AND THE BOIS DE LA CAMBRE

The Bois de la Cambre is an extension of the Forêt de Soignes, part of an ancient charcoal forest. It formed part of the ducal hunting grounds from time immemorial (the name Cambre came about from an abbey known as Camera Beatae Mariae: the Chamber of the Blessed Mary). Two property speculators, J.-P. de Joncker and J.-B. Jourdan, started to develop the area of the Avenue Louise from 1838. They proposed building an avenue that would lead right up to the Bois de la Cambre, which would have the advantage of giving the city an extensive park near the city centre, and would also encourage more building in between. The project was approved and work started in 1859. The avenue was first called Avenue du Bois de la Cambre, but was then renamed after Leopold II's daughter, Louise. The Avenue Louise and the Bois de la Cambre were incorporated into the central Brussels *commune* in 1864. A plan to landscape the Cambre was also set in motion.

The job of landscaping the Bois de la Cambre fell to the German Edouard Keilig. In order to make the park easily accessible and to open up new alleys for carriages, he would have to cut down one-third of the ancient trees, mostly consisting of beech trees and some oaks. There were to be restaurants, kiosks, and a theatre-hippodrome. On the side of the Chaussée de Waterloo were two popular *guinguettes* (open-air taverns), Chez Moeder Lambic and Chez Moeder Kramiek. The two pavilions flanking the entrance were originally situated at the Porte de Namur. They were moved here when the *octroi* was abolished in 1860, to allow the Boulevard to be enlarged. To make it possible for the masses to reach the Bois de la Cambre easily, a horse-drawn tram on rails—the *hippomobile*—was instituted in 1869. Other services followed. The Avenue Louise was constructed with a central alley planted with trees, where the prosperous could exercise their horses. The trees have been removed to make space for modern-day traffic.

Unlike many French exiles, Léon Daudet (1867-1942) had only good things to say about Brussels. He wrote the following on the Bois de la Cambre (*Vingt-neuf mois d'exil*, 1929):

> I entered the forest and found myself before a stand of gigantic trees: elms, plane trees, lime trees and ash trees... The proud, impenetrable vegetation lifted to the sky, so tall, so hard, so straight, attached to the soil by roots as thick as knots in a boa constrictor, so that no storm could move them. Their crowns bent over, alone, were shaken a little... Gold leaves rained on two lovers with their gazes fixed on each other, as well as on a mythological couple, to remind them that the season was passing, that you should hasten when you are in love and you are two, to become one.

THREE BRUSSELS POETS

Odilon-Jean Périer (1901-28) spent most of his short life at 50 Rue Defacqz, a house designed in Art Nouveau style by Paul Hankar. Born into a wealthy family, Périer uses Brussels or his own house as a backdrop for much of his work. He is *the* Brussels poet. As he said: "He who loves me, loves my city, and follows me through her." He writes of his attachment to the city environment in *Notre mère la ville* (1922):

The city is in my room:
This armchair is a port.
Have you seen my lamps
My masts and my boats?

The tobacco and the singing
Waves of the black sky,
The play, the noise of seaweed
At the windows, my mirrors,

Everything pleases here, and agrees with me:
I breathe in the good air
As light as a lovely verse.

O ravaged city
Stay in my house
That has only one season.

Another collection, *Le Citadin* (The City-Dweller, 1924) celebrates the
capital:

Still we should sing of the smallest streets:
Of the sun abandoned to their pale stones,
And the sky around washed out.
The flower-sellers look for a smile
They have the colours of those things that we desire.

Café terraces under a vermilion ivy
From where I watch my industrial city in movement.

Henri Michaux (1899-1984) lived at 69 Rue Defacqz from the age of
one; although he called it the house of his birth, he was actually born in
Namur. He had an unhappy childhood after his mother committed suicide
and he suffered some miserable years at a boarding school near Antwerp.
After moving to Paris in 1923, he ceased to have any contact with his
native country. He spent some time travelling the world as a merchant
seaman trying hard to forget about his origins: he had to "travel it out of
him."

Michaux claimed not to write poetry at all, even though he received
numerous literary awards. His style of stream-of-consciousness, capture-
the-moment writing has some links with the Surrealists, although his
angry style speaks more of frustration and alienation from the rest of humanity. Like the Surrealists, he claimed the Comte de Lautréamont's
Chants de Maldoror (1868) as his main literary inspiration, and he in turn
strongly influenced Allen Ginsberg. Michaux uses invented words or
changes the regular French word order to jarring effect. From 1956 he experimented with mescaline, and wrote and painted under the influence
of the drug. He produced a rambling account of his mescaline trips in
L'Infini turbulent (1957), translated by Michael Fineberg as *Infinite Tur-
bulence* (1975):

THE EFFECTS OF MESCALINE

A shock-zone has been entered. Phenomenon of massed presences, but infinitesimal, infinitely tumultuous.

Inward visions appear before the closed eyes.

Thousands and thousands of flashing microscopic points, sparkling diamonds, fulgurations for microbes.

Palaces with countless turrets which shoot into the air as though weightless. Arabesques, festoons. Fairground proliferation. Light which explodes beyond its confines and impales your nerves; colours suddenly gone berserk which attack you and bite you and whose associations ruthlessly wound.

Lawrence Durrell observed in *Henri Michaux: The Poet of Supreme Solipsism* (1990): "He gave me the impression of having some deep psychotic wound, due to an unpardonable neglect during a critical stage of his mental development."

Another major poet of this era is Norge, pseudonym of Georges Mogin (1898-1990). Unlike the previous two, he was born in the industrial *commune* of Molenbeek-St.-Jean at 14 Rue Jennart. His family was of French ancestry and worked in the cloth trade. Norge started off as a sales representative, taking his bicycle with him onto the train to sell his company's wares. He felt embarrassed by his profession and published under the name of Géo Norge (Norway), because of his admiration for Scandinavia. He is often considered French rather than Belgian (during the First World War he was exempted from military service as he was considered to be of French nationality).

In common with many Belgian poets, much of Norge's work is concerned with a spiritual quest. He is equally a master of the lyric form. His main themes concern the absurdity of human life that must inevitably end in death, and the need to overcome death through joy and energy. The following extract from "Orgie" gives an idea of his thinking:

Eternity is tomorrow,
Tomorrow there is the church organ and its rage
My easy one.

But today, there is wine,
Which doesn't last, and there is your taste
Of ferns.

Just one day for our highlights
And so many centuries for the
Seraphim.

Let's praise all that is ephemeral
To fleeting wine and love that is
Temporal.

Beauty, vines, O this earth.
Praise for our stay here,
Temporary.

Michaux, Norge, and the playwright Michel de Ghelderode were condemned by the Brussels Surrealists as "false modernists". On one occasion in 1926 the Surrealists prevented a performance of an early Norge piece, *Tam-tam*, from going ahead by shouting and walking around. Norge was a far better poet than any of the Surrealists and was not much concerned with their opinions.

Chapter Thirteen

CAPITAL OF EUROPE

"Our aim is that Brussels should go with a big bang."
                    Charlie de Pauw, Sixties property developer

TWO GERMAN OCCUPATIONS
On the accession of Albert I in 1909, Belgium, and Brussels, had gained an unprecedented level of prosperity. The great European powers were arming for war, while the Belgians hoped that their neutrality would be respected. When the Germans invaded in August 1914, the king called on the country to resist to the best of its power, but it was only a matter of days before Brussels fell. The city was on the main road from Aachen to the Western Front. In 1914 it took two weeks for the German army to march through Brussels via the *petite ceinture* (inner ring road). The locals joked that it was the same detachment of soldiers marching round and round the city. One part of Belgium to the west of the River Yser was never occupied by the Germans throughout the entire war. Albert I remained as commander-in-chief of the Belgian army, earning the sobriquet "the soldier king".

On arriving in Brussels, the Germans demanded a war indemnity from the city of 50 million francs, a sum equivalent to about a billion dollars in modern currency. There were also demands for huge amounts of food to feed the German army that was passing through the city. Foodstuffs were in short supply, and there was a real threat of starvation for the less well-off. The situation was saved by US President Hoover, who set up the Commission for Relief in Belgium, which channelled food to charitable organizations in Belgium. The American Ambassador in Belgium, Brand Whitlock, became a popular hero—there is a boulevard named after him—and he published his memoirs, *Belgium under the German Occupation* in 1919. Another interesting American account is Julia Helen Twells' *In the Prison City* (1919). *The Rape of Belgium* (2004) by Larry Zuckerman is also essential reading.

The burgomaster Adolphe Max was deported to Germany early on in the war for refusing to carry out German orders. To the Belgians he stood out as a symbol of liberty and resistance to the *boches*, as the Germans were called. Apart from lack of food, the civilian population also had to suffer various petty restrictions on their freedom, such as not being allowed to sing the Belgian national anthem, or to wear the black, gold and red colours of the national flag. The official press fed disinformation to the public about the course of the war, but the underground *La Libre Belgique* did its best to tell the real story. The Germans employed numerous plain-clothes spies to arrest anyone trying to sell illegal newspapers. The *Brux-ellois* tried to combat their oppressors with their particular humour. The following was reported in *Pourquoi Pas*, a magazine that no longer exists, on November 1, 1914:

> About fifteen days ago, a dubious-looking German policeman in plain clothes tried to arrest a street-vendor, near the Bourse who was selling newspapers prohibited by the military authorities. The street-vendor pushed him away, passers-by rushed to help and separated them. The officer then got out his revolver and was aiming it at the crowd just as two Brussels policemen arrived. One of them, seeing a private citizen brandishing a revolver hit him on the wrist so that he dropped his weapon, the other punched the renegade, and together they took him off to the police station in the midst of a shouting and menacing crowd. At this point the German let on who he was and showed his ID. Every-one thought this bungler would be relieved of his duties by the Germans until a few weeks later, but today the following poster has appeared:
>
> The military tribunal assembled on 28 October 1914 has pro-nounced the following sentences:
>
> 1. Against the policeman de Ryckere for attacking an agent of the German authorities... for aiding and abetting the escape of a person under arrest, and for having attacked a German soldier: Five years in prison.
>
> The other Belgian policeman got three years. In addition the commune of Brussels is required to pay an additional contribution of 5 million francs for the attack on a German soldier.
>
> Reported 26 October: All dogs measuring more than 40 centimetres at the shoulder must be declared. They will be sent to a special estab-

lishment where their flesh will be made into sausages, and their skins into furs for the functionaries and covers for cannons.

Some jokers have put about the rumour that the German military government is going to seize all the chamber pots, because the soldiers in the trenches are in pressing need of them.

Some of the boulevards that had been built over the Senne were renamed in honour of those who had resisted the Germans. Adolphe Max returned from Germany and continued as burgomaster of Brussels for another twenty years. Maurice Lemonnier, after whom the Boulevard Lemonnier is named, was also deported to Germany. Émile Jacqmain was a city magistrate who was deported to Germany for refusing to close the city's schools.

Irène Hamoir's novel *Boulevard Jacqmain* (1953) turns the Surrealist group into petty criminals. On page one, a certain Paul Nouguier is murdered in a bar—none other than Paul Nougé, the not always popular publicist and self-appointed leader of the Surrealists, who gave titles to many of Magritte's paintings. The owner is Edouard Massens, in other words E.L.T. Mesens, promoter and patron of Surrealism. Magritte appears briefly as Gritto. Hamoir was herself married to Magritte's great friend Louis Scutenaire.

Universal suffrage for men (women had to wait until 1949) was introduced on the insistence of King Albert I to avert unrest from the demobilized soldiers. The economy recovered slowly, but in 1924 there was a serious crisis caused by overproduction. Draconian measures, including the devaluation of the franc, temporarily restored the situation. In 1931 an even worse crisis came about as a result of a global economic depression. These were the years when Surrealism was most active, when it appeared that a revolution was imminent. The result of economic instability was a polarization in politics, with the extreme right-wing Flemish parties increasingly agitating for a federal state. In order to head off a civil war, Dutch and French were put on an equal footing in 1935 throughout the country and the principle of "unilingualism" adopted: only one language could be used for administrative purposes in one area, with the exception of Brussels, which had been a bilingual city since 1932.

The Belgians could only resist the German invasion of May 1940 for eighteen days. Leopold stayed behind in his palace when the Germans invaded in 1940, while the Dutch Queen Wilhelmina went into exile in England. In 1941 he married his children's Flemish governess, Liliane Baels with the blessing of the cardinal, which gave the impression that he was enjoying life too much while everyone else was suffering under the German occupation. The charges made against Leopold III, for instance that he had surrendered to the Germans without warning the British and the French, were quite unreasonable, but his marriage was the final straw for the Belgians. In 1945 he was being held by the Germans in a castle in Austria, from where he went to Switzerland to await his fate. His brother Charles took over as regent. A referendum in 1950 went in Leopold's favour, but while he had a comfortable majority in support of his return in the Dutch-speaking area, he received less than half of the votes in the French-speaking parts of the country. This may seem strange, in that the Belgian royal family is basically French-speaking, but republican sentiment is far stronger in Wallonia than in Flanders, and to the French-speakers the king appeared to be a collaborator. Rioting started, three men were killed, and Leopold saw that he would have to withdraw. His twenty-year-old son Baudouin, who never wanted to be king, had to take on the job.

The Second World War saw large-scale collaboration, in particular by far-right Flemish groups, but also by French-speakers. Some naïve young Flemings went to the Russian front to fight the Bolsheviks. After the war there was a witch-hunt against all suspected *collabos*. Some 550,000 people were investigated and about 250 executed after being tried. Others were imprisoned and deprived of their civil rights. Demands for an amnesty for collaborators started soon after. The recriminations have poisoned Belgian politics to the present day, with the ultra-right Vlaams Belang and more sinister organizations continuing the tradition of the pre-war fascist parties.

THE ATOMIUM AND THE HEYSEL

Baudouin proved to be a modest, low-key monarch, whose sincere Catholic beliefs made him popular with the Flemish. Following the Second World War, there was massive inward investment from the US and other countries, and the Belgian economy boomed through the 1950s and 1960s until the first oil shock of 1974. When Brussels held a World Fair in 1958, the Atomium was built as a monument to the Belgian steel industry on the northern edge of the city. Over the years the aluminium skin of the balls corroded and there was talk of demolishing the structure. Eventually the

Atomium was renovated in 2005, with the original aluminium panels being replaced with stainless steel ones. The general opinion is that it represents a crystal of iron magnified some 160 billion times. To be precise it is a cube with nine atoms, turned on its end. The structure is about 300 feet tall, with each ball weighing 2,000 tons.

Next door is the miniature village Brupark, further away the Parc des Expositions, also built for the World Fair. Nearby, too, is the Roi Baudouin national football stadium (formerly the Heysel Stadium), the scene of a disaster in 1985, when 37 Italian football fans were crushed to death before the European Cup final. Liverpool supporters in one section attacked Italian fans in the neighbouring sections and drove them into a corner, where a wall collapsed. Others were crushed against the fencing. The disaster led to the exclusion of British football clubs from European competition for five years. The Belgian authorities received a great deal of the blame, as they were evidently not expecting any trouble inside the stadium, even though there had been fighting between fans in the city during the day. The wrangling over who was to blame eventually led to the resignation of the government and early elections.

THE EUROPEAN COMMUNITY

The drive towards European cooperation following the Second World War was led by some far-sighted politicians, most of them French, such as Robert Schuman and Jean Monnet, both ministers in the post-war French government. The overriding concern in the first instance was to bring about a process of reconciliation between France and Germany and to prevent future wars. The start of the Cold War made it even more urgent to unify western Europe militarily, if possible, or at least economically.

The first agreement to set up a supra-national body that would require some concession of national sovereignty by its member states was signed in 1950 by Germany and France, followed by Belgium, the Netherlands, Luxembourg, and then Italy. The agreement placed the iron and coal industries under a separate authority—the European Coal and Steel Community—which would determine steel and coal policy, set quotas and tariffs, and so on. The six members of the ECSC signed a more far-reaching agreement on the formation of the European Economic Community (EEC) with the Treaty of Rome, which came into effect in 1958.

Belgium had already been something of a pioneer in the creation of a free-trade area, when it entered into the Belgium Luxembourg Economic Union (BLEU) in 1921. This was a customs union that eliminated tariffs and other barriers to the movement of goods between the two countries. In 1944, the exiled governments of Belgium, the Netherlands, and Luxembourg signed the Benelux accord, creating a similar free-trade area. Among the moving spirits behind the formation of the EEC was Paul-Henri Spaak (1899-1972) who at various times in his career was mayor of St.-Gilles, Belgian foreign minister (1954-1957; 1961-1966), President of the General Assembly of the United Nations (1948), Secretary-General of NATO (1957-1961), and President of the Organization of European Economic Cooperation (1948-1950). Spaak incarnated the European ideal to such a degree that he received the nickname "Mr. Europe", while the new united Europe was for a while dubbed "Spaakistan". He was born in the Rue Jourdan in St.-Gilles; his father was director of the Théâtre de la Monnaie for a time, and his brothers Charles and Paul were both well-known writers.

The Treaty of Rome that created the EEC eliminated customs barriers to goods circulating within the area of the six member countries, while keeping tariffs on imports. The EEC was enlarged by the accession of Great Britain, Ireland and Denmark in 1973 (the accession treaty was signed in the Palais d'Egmont in the Rue aux Laines). In 1981 Greece joined, and in 1986 Spain and Portugal, making twelve member states, and in 1995 Austria, Finland, and Sweden joined what was now a European Union of fifteen members. By 2007 the number had grown to 27, and there are more countries waiting in the queue. The accession of more states poses considerable problems. It has been the practice to translate all documents and meetings into all the languages of the community, but the permutations are now becoming unworkable. The European Union employs about 40,000 functionaries, with 25,000 located in Brussels. With each new member state, at least 400 new functionaries are required in Brussels. The buildings housing the various institutions are already too small, thus there will inevitably have to be more construction in the city.

The European Union is a complex organization, that is not well understood by the average citizen. The three main decision-making bodies are the European Commission, the Council of Ministers (strictly speaking the Council of the European Union), and the European Parliament. The Parliament does not have the same legislative powers as parliaments in the member states. Rather, the Commission proposes and puts laws into effect. The Council of Ministers, which is made up of ministers of the member governments, passes laws by a complex voting system. The Council is a fluid body, since only the ministers who have responsibilities in the area of the law in question are required to vote on its adoption. The European Parliament has been directly elected since 1979 and has a consultative role; it can also propose amendments to laws. It shares decision-making with the Council of Ministers. In particular it decides on the annual budget of over $1.5 trillion.

Real power lies with the Council of Ministers, which includes British government ministers. To say that "Brussels" imposes legislation on member countries is misleading. The ministers from the member countries have agreed to pass a piece of legislation in consultation with the Commission and the European Parliament; if the legislation is unpopular then it is convenient to blame "Brussels".

The European Commission consists of the President of the Commission and twenty-seven Commissioners, who oversee thirty-six Directorates-General. These are by no means the only European bodies. There is the European Central Bank in Frankfurt, which decides monetary policy and which came into being after the Maastricht Treaty was signed in 1992, paving the way for the Single European Market and the Single Currency, the euro. There is also the European Court of Justice in Luxembourg, which deals with disputes or breaches of European law by member states. Laws passed in Brussels override British and other national laws, giving "Eurosceptics" reason to say that Britain is run from Brussels.

The members of the European Parliament decided in 1985 that they wished to have their sessions in Brussels, and the Belgian government provided a tailor-made building for them. France exerted strong pressure for the European Parliament to be officially based in Strasbourg, in an equally impressive building; the French gave all the deputies a free colour TV, a fax, and a pager. Reluctantly the deputies go to France once a month for four days of plenary sessions, which requires shipping trainloads of documents to Strasbourg at vast expense, but most of the work is still done in Brussels. The Secretariat of the Parliament is in Luxembourg.

The notorious Berlaymont building on the Rond-Point Schuman is the seat of the European Commission. The building is named after the convent of the Dames du Berlaymont which once stood on the site. In

1991 it was hastily closed down; not only was it riddled with asbestos, but there were also rumours that it was actually in danger of falling down. The "Berlaymonster", with its four unequal arms, is a symbol of the European Union and for this reason it was not demolished, but renovated at enormous expense to the Belgian state. It only reopened in 2004. The structure that once earned the accolade of "the most polluting building in Brussels" has received awards for its new environmentally friendly design. The frontage is covered in glass panels that can be moved by computer to allow the building to breathe. Even the toilets are fed with rainwater.

The Commission is partly housed in the Berlaymont building at 200 Rue de la Loi while the Council of Ministers is on the other side of the Rue de la Loi in the Justus Lipsius building at no.175. The Commission also occupies the Charlemagne Building at 170 Rue de la Loi and the Madou Tower on Place Madou. The European Parliament meets for three weeks out of four at Rue Wiertz 43 in a building that has come to be known by its jocular name Le Caprice des Dieux (The Whim of the Gods), after a small cheese with an identical oval shape. More buildings are being planned for the Quartier Léopold (the European quarter) to accommodate the new member states.

The location of the EU institutions in Brussels was less by design than by historical evolution. Certain embryonic pan-European institutions already existed in the city from after the Second World War. Belgium was the first country to hold the presidency of the original Common Market in 1958, so it was natural that the functionaries should meet in Brussels.

Thereafter the decision on where to house the institutions was put off for three years, by which time it was no longer feasible to move elsewhere. The convenience of the location, a multi-lingual workforce, and the Belgians' lack of nationalism, made Brussels the obvious locale. The city is now home to some 1,500 international organizations and holds some 16,000 international conferences every year (so it is said). Brussels is still a relatively cheap place to live, and the city administration has always been happy to accommodate the wishes of its foreign guests.

VDB AND CDP: THE "CROCODILE"

There is no figure quite as colourful in Belgian political history as Paul Vanden Boeynants (1919-2001), known as VDB or "The Crocodile". VDB started out as a butcher in Forest and launched his career as president of the federation of butchers. His power base was first a shadowy extreme right-wing group, the NEM, within the French-speaking Parti Social Chrétien (Christian Democrats). He won plaudits as manager of the Universal Exhibition in 1958, from where he embarked on his extraordinary career of mixing public office with private business interests. As the *échevin* responsible for public works, he was in a position to favour the projects of the notorious property developer Charlie De Pauw (CDP), who had made his fortune from building multistorey car parks around Brussels. He unveiled a project in 1965 to flatten the area around the Gare du Nord and put up eighty tower blocks for offices (fortunately, only eight were actually built). The general system was to make generous guarantees to property developers to reimburse them if they were unable to find tenants for their office blocks. The building land would be sold as leasehold for a fixed period at a derisory sum, while the city would have to pay for the expropriation of existing buildings. Speculators could resell land, or renovate buildings, and make excessive profits, while the city had to hope for increased tax revenues from the businesses that would move into the city.

In the case of the Quartier Nord, few private tenants could be found, so government offices had to move into the developments. VDB became prime minister between 1966 and 1968 and was able to expand the scale of his corruption. His electoral campaign in 1968 was widely assumed to have been financed with bribes from the French aircraft manufacturer Dassault. In 1974, while he was minister of defense, he was reprimanded for signing agreements with Dassault for the purchase of planes without mentioning anything in the state budget. VDB was more or less excluded from becoming prime minister again as he was under investigation for fraud, and involvement in so-called "ballets roses" (pink ballets), a euphemism for orgies. He kept up close relations with Arab arms dealers through the intermediary of a certain "Madame Tuna", who supplied high-class call girls to his business partners. VDB was finally found guilty on seven counts of fraud and tax evasion in 1986, and sentenced to three years in prison, suspended. He was still popular (he held the record for the number of votes gained by a Brussels politician), and was preparing to run for mayor in 1988 before he was dissuaded. In 1989, he was kidnapped by Belgium's most notorious gangster, Patrick Haemers, and had to pay the equivalent of $1,500,000 from his own fortune for his release. Since he could not run for public office, he became the editor of a satirical magazine; he died in 2001. VDB was, of course, by no means the only corrupt city official. At one time, the offices of Brussels mayor and magistrate for public works were seen as nothing more than an opportunity to make millions at the expense of the citizens.

VDB's close associate, Charlie De Pauw, the King of the Car Park, made this extraordinary statement about his building activities (quoted in Georges Timmerman, *Geld, macht en beton*—Money, Power and Concrete, 1991):

> As the standard of living rises, so people move out to the suburbs. The centres of the cities are taken over by people with less capital. This has a negative effect on business, which is particularly concentrated in the centre. So there has to be a revival of the city centre. I have found that car parks and administrative buildings are the best solution for this rescue operation.

De Pauw's "rescue operation" means that Brussels has more cars in its centre than other Belgian cities, with pedestrianization viewed as a last resort. De Pauw owned some twenty multistorey car parks and ran about thirty inter-linked property development companies. Foreigners sometimes ask whether Brussels was bombed in the last war. The answers lie with the city officials.

ANTOINE WIERTZ: EUROMEGALOMANIAC

In the shadow of the European Parliament, in the Rue Vautier, you can visit the *atelier* (workshop) of Antoine Wiertz (1806-65), a painter who has a special place in Brussels folklore. From an early age he decided that he would try to surpass the great artists of the past. Winning the Prix de Rome in 1832 convinced him that he was a genius, but he suffered a crushing setback at the Paris Salon in 1839, when his "Greeks and Trojans Fighting Over the Body of Patroclus" was completely ignored by the critics. Another project, a gigantic "Fall of the Angels", which received a subsidy from the Belgian government; measured 35 by 25 feet, and could only be displayed in a church. But Wiertz wanted to paint even bigger canvases.

In 1850 Wiertz proposed a deal to the government: if the authorities would pay for a large enough workshop to be built, he would leave his works to the state on his death. The government agreed. A number of well-known literary figures, including Hendrik Conscience, have had the undemanding task of acting as curators to the collection. Many of his paintings seem to be the work of a madman: there are violent scenes of suicide, people being guillotined or blowing their brains out. Wiertz also specialized in heavy-handed moral messages, and sometimes hit on quite outlandish subjects (one painting shows Napoleon in hell, with a crowd of accusing victims waving their severed limbs at him). Another one, "The Premature Burial", has a surprised-looking cholera victim opening the lid of his coffin in a burial vault. Not surprisingly, Baudelaire and Joris-Karl Huysmans both appreciated Wiertz.

The Rue Wiertz runs through the middle of the European Union's institutions, although his *atelier* is actually in the Rue Vautier. Wiertz had a particularly grandiose view of Brussels' status in Europe. In one of his writings, *Bruxelles capitale et Paris province*, he proposes building a super-city based on Brussels:

> Let us see: Brussels has 300,000 souls: it is a centre that attracts all of Belgium.
>
> Paris has one million souls: it is a centre of attraction for a part of Europe.
>
> Well! If Brussels wants to dominate Europe, it has to gather three or four million souls in its bosom...

Mechelen, Antwerp, Ghent are reference points, they are conglomerations that attract; these conglomerations are already linked with railways; these are roads already mapped out, what else do we have to do? Support the mysterious task of propagation; plan your palaces, your mansions; rich developers, build from Brussels to Mechelen, build from Mechelen to Antwerp, build from Antwerp to Ghent; spread out. What do you fear, you who are so wealthy!

Chapter Fourteen

A NEW KIND OF VISITOR:
IMMIGRANT BRUSSELS

"Let's face it... Brussels—now don't get angry—is not really a Belgian city."

Alain Berenboom, *L'Auberge Espagnole*

Brussels is very much a city of immigrants. There are very few people who can say that their ancestors did not come from somewhere else, even if it was only from the surrounding countryside. The population has been growing since the low point of 1996, thanks to high birth rates among immigrants, and an influx of East Europeans since 2004. At the same time, many of the native French-speaking inhabitants have moved out to the suburbs. Thus there were about 950,000 people in the *agglomération* of nineteen *communes* in 1996, but by 2006 the population had gone up to 1,018,000, a figure not seen since 1978.

The nature of immigration has changed drastically over the years. In the nineteenth century, almost all immigrants came from Holland, France, Germany or Britain. The French are still the largest group of European immigrants. Many of the Germans were forced to leave after the First World War, while after the Second World War it was Poles and Italians who came in great numbers looking for work. In 1947, some 21 percent of immigrants were Polish. These days there is a new influx of Polish immigrants, as well as from other Eastern European countries.

The economic boom of the 1950s led to a new influx of Spanish, Greek, and Portuguese immigrants, many of whom have remained around the Gare du Midi. Those who are successful move from the western side of the city to the east. Affluent foreigners, and in particular European Union functionaries, favour Woluwe St. Pierre and Woluwe St. Lambert in the east of Brussels, while the poorer ones remain congregated around the main railway stations in the centre.

In the 1960s Belgium concluded agreements with a number of countries, including former Yugoslavia, Morocco, and Turkey, that they would supply labour that was badly needed in a time of industrial expansion. These agreements remain in place, although the central *communes* have tried to pursue a policy of only registering European Union newcomers. With the large-scale influx of immigrants, there has been an unfortunate tendency towards ghettoization.

The Turkish community has congregated around the Chaussée de Haecht in Schaerbeek and in the poorer *commune* of St.-Josse-ten-Noode above the Gare du Nord. The area either side of the Chaussée de Haecht, including part of St. Josse-ten-Noode, is known locally as Petite Anatolie. The magnificent Halles de Schaerbeek at no.75 house the local Turkish associations under the umbrella of the non-profit organization, ASBL Eyad-Maison de Turquie. The Eyad promotes Turkish culture, and each spring there are Turkish *soirées*, open days at the mosque, storytelling, music, and art exhibitions related to the Turkish Spring Festival, the Ilkbahar, culminating with the celebration of Turkey's national day on April 21. Turkish writers and artists are invited to the city to run workshops. Performances by whirling dervishes have recently taken place in disused churches and the Palais des Beaux Arts.

The area around the Gare du Midi, in particular the Rue de Mérode and the Avenue de Stalingrad, is very much the Moroccan quarter. The Moroccans, who number about 70,000 in the capital, generally speak better French than the Turks, and many are well integrated.

The underlying cause of immigrant alienation stems from an uncertain status. The Moroccans, and many other immigrants, came to Brussels assuming that they would return to their countries of origin after they had earned enough money. Although acquiring Belgian nationality used to be more difficult than it is now, it is still impossible to keep Moroccan nationality when changing nationality. As a result, younger Moroccans are stranded between two cultures, with pressures to conform to their parents' culture while living in a Western society. A poor grasp of French, and consequently unsatisfactory education, are further obstacles.

The younger Moroccans' frustration boiled over in May 1991 when there was serious rioting on the border of Forest and St. Gilles. There were riots in 2007 in Schaerbeek and in 2008 in Anderlecht. Since then the government has started to address the problem of social exclusion in a number of ways. Firstly, it has become much easier for immigrants to

become Belgian citizens. Anyone who has lived in Belgium for seven years and not committed any serious crime can apply for citizenship. The language tests are not as severe as they once were, while money is being invested in training for young Moroccans, and "street educators" are being employed to promote integration. In Molenbeek the Moroccan community has set up the Dar-el-Amal, "The House of Hope", to help young people. One of their initiatives is to send young Moroccans to visit elderly Belgians in the *commune*. In 2002, two Moroccans, Mourad Boucif and Taylan Barman, brought out a film about their sense of cultural dislocation. *South of Gibraltar* (2002) was filmed entirely in Molenbeek, with local people taking the starring roles.

Another highly visible community is made up of Congolese, again concentrated in their ghetto at the Porte de Namur and along the Chaussée de Wavre. There are Congolese supermarkets, restaurants, and tailors and everything else, with unheard-of vegetables in the grocer's shops. The area is known as the Quartier Matongé, after a forest near the Congolese capital, Kinshasa. The Congolese first settled around the Maison des Colonies in the 1960s and spread out from there.

The area between the Porte de Namur and the Chaussée d'Ixelles was home to a large Russian community in the nineteenth century (there is still a Russian Orthodox Church on the Rue de la Tulipe). Lenin stayed here in 1910. Tolstoy came to Brussels in 1861 to order a bust of his brother from the sculptor Willem Geefs, and to research Belgian education methods. He went to visit the anarcho-syndicalist Pierre-Joseph Proudhon at the nearby 8 Rue du Conseil and noticed that he was working on a treatise entitled *War and Peace*.

At 15 Rue de Naples, a street running north from the Chaussée de Wavre, is a plaque to one Charles Woeste (1837-1922), a Catholic politician who gained notoriety for his merciless persecution of Adolf Daens, a Flemish priest and political activist. It was also the home of Stanislas-André Steeman, a writer of thrillers, and father of the humourist Stéphane Steeman. To advertise one novel he had a headline put into *La Gazette*: "Two Brutal Murders in the Porte de Namur!!!" His habit of situating murders in their area led to protests from some residents, who feared that property prices would go down. Steeman's *L'Assassin habite au 21* was voted the best crime novel ever written in French by readers of a detective magazine in 1966. The plot is similar to that of Agatha Christie's *Who Murdered Roger Ackroyd?*—a group of people staying in a house where any one of them could have carried out the killing. Steeman believed that he had the idea first and was annoyed when Christie published her version before he could.

Belgium's greatest crime writer, Georges Simenon (1903-89), had almost no connections with Brussels. He originated from Liège and spent much of his life in France. On just one occasion, in *Le Suspect* (1938), Simenon used Brussels as a background for one of his novels. The action takes place around the Rue Snieders, near Schaerbeek railway station, barely disguised as Rue Snieder. A Frenchman living with his wife at no.23 suddenly disappears and is suspected of plotting to bomb an aircraft factory in Paris.

Alexandra David-Néel

The future explorer of Tibet, Alexandra David-Néel (1868-1969), spent much of her early life in Ixelles. She first moved to 105 Rue Faider, which runs parallel to the Avenue Louise, in 1875 with her parents, Louis David, a left-wing French Protestant, and Alexandrine Borghmans, a Catholic of

Dutch, Norwegian, and Siberian ancestry. The Davids came here to escape the political troubles in Paris; Alexandra's mother had Belgian nationality and her family was living in Brussels. Alexandra showed an early interest in exploration, and spent her free time reading Jules Verne and poring over atlases.

Her first career was as an opera singer, winning first prize for soprano in 1889 at the Brussels Conservatoire. Between 1891 and 1894 she lived at 17 Rue de Dublin, between the Chaussée de Wavre and the Rue du Trône. After a moderately successful career as an opera singer, she married a well-off French businessman who was able to fund her need to explore far-off places. With remarkable determination she managed to become the first Western woman to reach Lhasa, in 1922. Her accounts of her voyages, such as *Magic and Mystery in Tibet*, made her internationally famous. Eventually she settled down in the south of France with a Tibetan companion whom she had acquired in the course of her travels.

She always retained fond memories of Brussels. In her autobiographical *Sous des nuées d'orage* (Under Storm Clouds, 1940), she reminisces:

Dear old Brussels of my childhood! Each of your modest buildings, every one of your peaceful streets, evoked, before my steps, the shadow of my youthful self which remains true to you in spite of all the years that have passed, and obstinately brings me back for moving pilgrimages.

MIGRANTS AND LITERATURE

The impact of immigration on Brussels is a sensitive subject for writers with a political conscience. Alain Berenboom, in *L'Auberge espagnole* (The Spanish Inn, 2002) situates a discussion of immigration around the comic theme of the disappearance of the central heating boiler from the Palais de Justice. Jacques Crickillon approaches the theme of self-hatred in the ultra-alienated character of *L'Indien du Gare du Nord* (The Indian of the Gare du Nord, 1985). Dissociation and alienation are central to the work of Pierre Mertens, Brussels most highly respected writer. Mertens, a sociologist by training, has worked in the field of human rights for many years, and has obtained the release of political prisoners in Chile and Yugoslavia. His novel, *Terre d'asile* (Land of Asylum, 1978) has as its main character a Chilean, Jaime Morales, who has escaped from the Pinochet regime in

1977 to gain asylum in Brussels. Mertens criticizes the local culture through Morales:

> He asked himself what he had retained of Belgium since he had arrived. He thought to himself that you met more old than young people in the streets and squares, and a lot of dogs, well-fed dogs. In the elevators, people didn't speak to each other and took on a serious air. If by some chance they did speak to each other, it was enough for someone new to intrude on another floor and they would withdraw back into their silence. He asked himself if the Belgians liked Belgium.

The reference to an aging population is relevant. The average Belgian in Brussels is forty-two years old, while the average Turk is about thirty (in 2006). In particular, the original Flemish speakers are now very old and dying out. Turks and Moroccans live in larger families (it is rare for them to live on their own), while Belgians are more and more likely to live on their own.

Many political exiles have appreciated Brussels, including the great Catalan poet, Josep Carner, who lived here for 28 years until his death in 1970. He gives his feelings on the city in the poem "Belgica":

> I would like to grow old in a city
> Where the soldiers don't look too real...
> Where the bystanders admire a hundred new houses with gardens.
> You would see a crowd of scholars
> And official ranks of umbrellas
> At the inauguration of a monument.
> Here, at the end of long avenues,
> The beech trees and a chain of ponds
> For love and for joy or for solitude.

JEWISH LIFE IN BRUSSELS

Where the Rue Émile Carpentier and the Rue des Goujons meet, not far from the back of the Gare du Midi, stands the National Monument to the Jewish Martyrs (Square des Martyrs Juifs). A total of 23,838 names belonging to deportees are inscribed on a wall.

The Jewish presence in Brussels goes back at least to the thirteenth century. All Jews were expelled from Belgium in 1370 after they were accused of stealing hosts from the Église St. Cathérine (which started the legend of the Miracle of the Rue des Sols; see chapter four). A small number of Jews lived in Brussels during the Spanish period, mainly as *marranos* or false converts to Christianity. With the advent of Austrian domination in 1714, more significant numbers returned. Napoleon emancipated all the Jews in 1795 in the French territories, but even in 1848 there were still only some 1,500 Jews in the whole of Belgium. Large numbers came from Eastern Europe between 1890 and 1930 (many were in transit to America), and the population rose to an estimated 85,000. In 1940, during the Nazi occupation, the Belgian authorities were obliged to draw up lists of Jews, who then totalled 65,000, with some 30,000 in Brussels. Around 25,000 were deported to Auschwitz alone, and a total of 40,000 died. Many Belgians took great risks to save Jews in their midst by hiding them in their houses, so that considerable numbers survived the war. Some took the attitude that "they may be Jews, but they're our Jews", while an instinctive desire to frustrate the Germans had something to do with it. From the statistics it seems that Belgians rescued more Jews from Nazi persecution than the rest of Europe put together.

There are now about 20,000 Jews in Brussels, with ten synagogues. Antwerp has a Jewish population of 15,000, almost all involved in the diamond trade, and thirty synagogues. About eighty percent of all Belgian Jews are of Polish descent. The Jewish community is well organized. There is a Centre Communautaire Laïc Juif, a Cercle Ben Gurion that runs its own radio station, as well as organizing concerts, plays and conferences, and a Maison de la Culture Juive. A new Belgian Jewish Museum opened in 2004 at 21 Rue des Minimes in a building that was formerly a German cultural centre. The Grande Synagogue is in the Rue de la Régence.

GARE DU MIDI

The Gare du Midi (South Station) is the point of arrival for most foreigners from the south and west. The southern side is undergoing large-scale expansion to accommodate new high-speed train services to Amsterdam and Cologne along with the Eurostar to London and the Thalys to Paris. The north side, on the Rue Fonsny, was allowed to run down for many years, and is now undergoing the inevitable *assainissement* or "purification" (construction of large office blocks).

The Gare du Midi has stood on this site since 1869, when the original station, known as the Gare des Bogards and built on the site of what is now the Place Rouppe between 1835 and 1840, quickly turned out to be too small. The 1869 Gare du Midi had a magnificent frontage with a neo-Corinthian portico topped by a chariot and three figures representing Progress, Science and Labour by the sculptor Du Caju, looking out over the Place de la Constitution. A huge Sunday market grew up around the station from 1900, the biggest in Belgium it was said, which still continues to this day. The old station was demolished in 1949 to make way for the Jonction Nord-Midi and was replaced by a modernist construction by the architects Blomme and Petit, which forms the main part of the present station.

Thomas William Newton, in his *How We Saw Belgium, the Rhine, the Meuse, and Paris, in Fifteen Days* (1860), gives a picturesque impression of the early days of the railways:

> Belgian railways are kept in the neatest and most precise order, and the stations are prettily ornamented; soldiers may be seen at every stopping-place, and the duties of clerks are often performed by females. The guards wear a military uniform, and give signals with bugles; and by means of an exterior platform they walk from carriage to carriage while the train is in motion, and collect the tickets. In all the carriages smoking is carried on with tremendous vigour; while the engines which draw them bear the names most memorable in the land, such as Rubens, Quentin Matsys [sic], and Van Dyck.

The Gare du Midi has captivated many writers, including John dos Passos (1896-1970), who lived in the nearby Chaussée de Charleroi (no.90) between 1898 and 1901. On his arrival in Brussels with his mother he wrote:

> I must often have visited Brussels as a child. I can still see the vaulted roof of a big station, and the engines puffing clouds of steam, whistling as they thunder through the night...
>
> I flatten my nose on the pane and watch an army of square chimneys which loom up like dragons breathing fire. They vanish—and now I can see houses with lighted yellow windows, and I am no longer afraid.

The train slows down. Mummy collects our parcels and we get down on the cold platform. A stout porter smelling of beer and sweat picks up our luggage. We shiver in the cold, dank air of the foreign city and follow him, stumbling wearily towards the frightening strangeness of unknown streets. Chaussée de Charleroi smells close and stale...

W.H. Auden, who was staying near the Square Ambiorix in December 1938, wrote his "Gare du Midi" with the expectation, or certainty, that war was just around the corner:

A nondescript express in from the south;
Crowds round the ticket barrier; a face
To welcome which the mayor has not contrived
Bugles or brass: something about the mouth
Disturbs the stray look with alarm and pity.
Snow is falling; clutching his little case,
He walks out briskly to infect a city
Whose terrible future may have just arrived.

GARE DU NORD

The hotels around the Gare du Nord have their own particular place in literature. The Hôtel de Liège in the Rue du Progrès was the first stopping-off point for Paul Verlaine on his ill-fated arrival in 1873. Much of the street seems to be on the verge of falling down, and it will no doubt be turned over to the skyscrapers quite soon. At the northern end, the gay anarchist writer Georges Eekhoud (see p.176) lived for forty years at no.431 with his long-suffering wife Cornélie (in his day it was no.407).

Dominique Rolin, in *The Garden of Delights* (1998), a more or less autobiographical account of her development as a writer, has just met an alcoholic Flemish poet in a seedy hotel:

I think this is what love must be. A sob of distressed bewilderment prolongs my laugh. Finally my life is beginning to unfold, to burst open. I inhale it so deeply that I'm short of breath. It's possible to forget who we are and where we are. We tramp through a mad, twirling universe. We think we're so happy that we end up being happy. That's what intrigues me when H.H. takes me to a dingy bed at the India Hotel near the Gare du Nord. Romantic India, naturally! God it's cold, gray and damp! Except inside us. Especially at the enchanted moment when, for the first time, the Great Owl topples his own skinny, smooth, pale body over mine, and, as they say in novels, takes me.

The two towers to the west of the Gare du Nord are rather ominously known as the World Trade Centre. Towards the city centre, the Place Rogier and the area around the Sheraton Hotel are traditionally associated with prostitution in the minds of *Bruxellois*. The Rue d'Aerschot, running along the edge of the Turkish quarter by the railway line, has become something like the Nieuwmarkt in Amsterdam, with scantily clad women sitting in shop windows waiting for customers. In the early 1980s, the middle-aged civil servant, Georges, in Jacques De Decker's collection of twelve inter-linked short stories, *La Grande roue* (The Big Wheel, 1985), wanders into the red light area:

> He almost banged into a big girl with hair drawn back, with tight jeans and top, and red boots: "Coming with me? It's two thousand francs." "No. I'm not interested." She was shocked. "What the hell are you doing here, then? Get lost, hypocrite."
>
> He dove into a side street as fast as he could, where the multicoloured signs were further apart, and landed in an area where undefined lots bordered giant tower blocks, which gave this district the name of the "poor man's Manhattan." Old buildings had been abandoned in the middle of demolition, the megalomaniac projects of the developers unfinished. You could see from the rain-washed wallpaper revealed by the half-destroyed houses, what uses the rooms had been put to. "This is the leprosy of the city," he thought to himself.

THE MONARCH IN QUESTION

King Albert II, who has ruled Belgium since 1993, is as different from his predecessor Baudouin as could be. While his brother ruled, he carried on the life of a playboy. His marriage to an Italian aristocrat, Paola Ruffo di Calabria, barely existed until he found himself on the throne. There was amusement when it emerged that Albert had an illegitimate daughter living in London, a sculptor by the name of Delphine Boël. It is generally assumed that she is paid to stay out of the country. There was also embarrassment at allegations by two French journalists in 2001 that the king used the services of prostitutes and had sexual relations with minors in the past. The king took the publishers (Flammarion) to court and had a paragraph inserted in the book stating that he objects to the affront to his reputation.

The king's wealth is a subject of considerable speculation. It emerged that Baudouin left about $300 million, mostly in American bank accounts, on his death. Albert claims to only have $11 million, which makes him virtually a pauper among royalty. His son and heir, Philippe, has led an apparently blameless life, and is married to the very popular Princess Mathilde, who has the added attraction of being from an old Flemish noble family. It is surprising to note that this is the first time since the Belgian state was founded in 1830 that an heir to the throne has married a Belgian. It might be added that none of the royal family (apart from Mathilde perhaps) has ever been able to speak anything but rather stilted Dutch. The children of the monarch always have training in Dutch, but do not care to use the language at home.

THE FUTURE OF BRUSSELS

Political change in Brussels has often been driven by the evolution of the language question. In 1962 the Front Démocratique des Francophones was formed, after massive demonstrations in the city by Dutch-speakers protesting at the dominance of French-speakers in Belgian business and culture. Some French-speakers held up placards with the message "No French, no money". The situation is rather different now. Dutch is the language of success, and French-speakers are learning Dutch out of economic necessity. Some Dutch-speaking schools accept French-speaking pupils, and the idea has become so popular that the number of French-speakers has had to be limited to sixty-five percent of pupils. Another explanation for the Dutch-language schools' popularity is that they have few immigrant pupils, as most immigrants still see French as the prestige language or already speak French or a related language to begin with.

Tensions are increasing in the six *communes à facilités* (Kraainem, Drogenbos, Linkebeek, Rhode-St.-Genèse, Wemmel, Wczembeek-Oppem) around Brussels where there are supposedly protected French-speaking "minorities" (even though the French-speakers are in the majority).

French-speakers have to ask for forms in French to be sent to them on every occasion they need them, whereas before they only had to make one request. The local functionaries reason that the French-speakers have lived in these *communes* for long enough to learn Dutch. Local council meetings are conducted in Dutch; if French-speaking councillors do not use French, then it is assumed that only Dutch will be used in the future.

French residents of the *communes à facilités* can vote for the Front Démocratique des Francophones. It appears that 68 per cent of residents voted for such French-speaking parties in 2006. French speakers who live outside these six communes in Flemish Brabant itself are now a growing minority and have their own party, the Union des Francophones. French-speaking councillors and those from the ultra-right Vlaams Belang cannot work together or even communicate with each other. The Flemish who have always lived on the edge of Brussels naturally resent the demands of newly-arrived Brussels French-speakers to attach their municipalities to Brussels. French-speakers claim that they are discriminated against as regards housing, schools, subsidies for cultural organizations, and so on. Buildings used by French-speakers have been vandalized by Flemish extremists, and bilingual notices defaced.

On the basis of local elections, one might assume that about 15 per cent of Brussels residents are Dutch-speakers by preference. More Dutch-speakers are being encouraged to live in the city by the Flemish regional government, which treats Brussels as its capital, while more French-speakers move out to the suburbs. Many Dutch-speakers only stay for a few years in Brussels for career reasons and then move back to Flanders. Research carried out annually by the sociologist Rudi Janssens paints a picture of linguistic change which shows an increasing variety of languages in Brussels. Janssens questioned 2500 *Bruxellois* in 2007 and found that 35 per cent claimed to speak good to fluent English, but only 28 per cent claimed the same for Dutch. In general French is gaining ground, with 57 per cent of respondents stating that they speak French exclusively at home. Only 15 per cent of respondents grew up in a household where Dutch was the sole language, against 75 per cent for French. Immigrants tend to opt for French, but more French-speakers are studying Dutch in the hope of finding work. Most unemployed people in Brussels, which has an unemployment rate of 20 per cent, only speak French. Brussels is a relatively poor region, and is heavily indebted. Many of its wealthier residents have moved out to the suburbs, while EU functionaries pay taxes to the European Union rather than to the Brussels Region.

The capital's future is more and more linked with big business and the international institutions that are based here, given that the wealthier residents are moving out to the suburbs. The Flemish regional government, on the other hand, is going to great lengths to bring more Dutch-speakers into the city centre. The city will become increasingly multicultural: a sort of Belgian New York, with immigrants concentrated in their own ghettoes.

The importance of Brussels as capital of Europe has made its residents take more pride in their city. The destruction of the city's architectural heritage has slowed. Old façades are preserved when new buildings go up. Brussels was a provincial city to start with, lacking a strong local cultural identity. It was Belgian with the international institutions tacked on. The city has become far more cosmopolitan since the 1950s and so a more interesting place to live for those who come to work at the EU and other organizations.

Further Reading

Alphabet des lettres belges de langue française. Brussels: Association pour la Promotion des Lettres belges de langue française, 1982.

Ameeuw, Patrick (ed), *Bruxelles, au fil des jours et des saisons.* Brussels: ARC, 2001.

Anon., *Paris-Bruxelles. L'Annexion.* Brussels: Le Cri, 1997.

Aron, Jacques, Burniat, Patrick, & Puttemans, Pierre, *Bruxelles et environs: guide d'architecture moderne.* Brussels: Didier Hatier, 1990.

Assouline, Pierre, *Hergé.* Paris: Plon, 1996.

Baetens-Beardsmore, Hugo, *Le Français régional de Bruxelles.* Brussels: Presses Universitaires de Bruxelles, 1971.

Baetens-Beardsmore, Hugo, *Linguistic Accommodation in Brussels.* Brussels: VUB, 1991.

Ballegeer, Joost, *Vlamingen in de Brusselse smeltkroes.* Kortrijk, Uitgeverij Groeninghe, 2002.

Bernaerts, Aimé, *Proscrits, exilés, écrivains étrangers en Belgique.* Brussels: Paul Legrain, 1980.

Bernaerts, Aimé, *Les noms de rues à Bruxelles.* [1951] Brussels: Paul Legrain, 1975.

Biebuyck, J. & D'Ydewalle, C. et al., *Bruxelles ville en forme de cœur.* Brussels: Editions Universitaires, 1957.

Billen, Claire & Duvosquel, Jean-Marie (eds), *Brussels* [in English]. Antwerp: Mercatorfonds: 2000.

Blyth, Derek, *Belgium: Blue Guide.* New York: Norton, 2000.

Blyth, Derek, *Brussels for Pleasure.* London: Pallas Athene, 2003.

Blyth, Derek, *Flemish Cities Explored.* [1990] London: Pallas Athene, 2003.

Blyth, Derek, *Live & Work in Brussels.* London: Crimson Publishing, 2008.

Bodart, Roger, Galle, Marc, & Stuiveling, Garmt, *Guide littéraire de la Belgique, de la Hollande, et du Luxembourg.* Paris: Hachette, 1972.

Bogaert-Damin, Anne-Marie, & Maréchal, Luc, *Bruxelles: développement de l'ensemble urbain, 1846-1961: analyse historique et statistique des recensements.* Namur: Presses Universitaires de Namur, 1978.

Carson, Patricia, *The Fair Face of Flanders.* Tielt: Lannoo, 1995.

Clough, S.B. *A History of the Flemish Movement.* New York: Richard R. Smith, 1930.

Cox, Marina *et al, Baraques à frites = Fritkot.* Louvain-la-Neuve: Octogone, 2002.

Danckaert, Lisette, *Bruxelles: cinq siècles de cartographie*. Tielt: Lannoo, 1989.

de Decker, Jacques, *Bruxelles autrement*. Paris: Autrement, 1987.

de Ghelderode, Michel, *The Siege of Ostend*. Austin TX: Host Publications, 1990.

de Ridder, Paul. *Brussels: History of a Brabant Town*. Ghent: Stichting Mens en Cultuur, 1990.

Dictionnaire de la peinture flamande et hollandaise. Paris: Larousse, 1989.

Dieckhoff, Alain (ed), *Belgique: la force de la désunion*. Brussels: Editions Complexe, 1996.

Diericx de ten Hamme, Joë, *Souvenirs du vieux Bruxelles*. Brussels: Libro-Sciences, 1979.

d'Osta, Jean, *Dictionnaire historique et anecdotique des rues de Bruxelles*. Brussels: Legrain, 1986.

d'Osta, Jean, *Mémoires de Jef Kazak*. Brussels: Éditions Racine, 2002.

Dumont, Georges-Henri, *Belgique, des maisons et des hommes*. Brussels: Nouvelles Editions Vokaer, 1980.

Dumont, Georges-Henri, *Histoire de Bruxelles: biographie d'une capitale*. Brussels: Le Cri, 1999.

Dumont, Georges-Henri, *Histoire de la Belgique*. Brussels: Le Cri, 1999.

Fitzmaurice, John, *The Politics of Belgium*. London: Hurst, 1995.

Fox, Renée C., *In the Belgian Château*. Chicago: Ivan R. Dee, 1994.

Goffin, Joël, *Sur les pas des écrivains à Bruxelles*. Brussels: Les Éditions de l'Octogone, 1998.

Govaert, Serge, *Bruxelles en capitales, 1958-2000*. Brussels: De Boeck: 2000.

Gubin, Eliane, *Bruxelles au XIXe siècle: berceau d'un flamingantisme démocratique (1840-1873)*. Brussels: Crédit communal de Belgique, 1979.

Guicciardini, Lodovico, *Description of the Low Countreys*. [1593] Norwood NJ: Walter J. Johnson, 1976.

Haulot, A., *et al. Les Belles heures de Bruxelles*. Brussels: Elsevier, 1952.

Henne, Alexandre & Wauters, Alphonse, *Histoire de la ville de Bruxelles*. [1845] 5 vols, Brussels: Flatau, 1958-1959.

Hochschild, Adam, *King Leopold's Ghost: a story of greed, terror and heroism in Central Africa*. Boston: Houghton Mifflin, 1998.

Hooghe, Liesbet, *A Leap in the Dark: Nationalist conflict and federal reform in Belgium*. Ithaca, NY: Cornell University Press, 1991.

Ide, Paul & Gillet, Anne-Marie, *Je me souviens, Bruxelles...* Le Mans: Ed. Cénomane, 1999.

Kervyn de Marcke ten Driessche, Roger, *Les Fables de Pitje Schramouille*. Brussels:

Labor, 1999.

Lannoy, Corijn de (ed), *Crossing Brussels. La qualité de la différence*. Brussels: VUB Press: 2000.

Lebouc, Georges, *Le bruxellois en septante leçons*. Brussels: Labor, 1999.

Longcheval, Andrée & Honorez, Luc, *Toone et les marionettes traditionnelles de Bruxelles*, Brussels: Legrain:1984.

Mallinson, Vernon, *Modern Belgian Literature, 1830 to 1960*. London: Heinemann, 1966.

Mallinson, Vernon, *Power and Politics in Belgian Education, 1815 to 1961*. London: Heinemann, 1963.

Mann, Théodore-Auguste, *Abrégé de l'histoire ecclésiastique, civile et naturelle de la ville de Bruxelles, et de ses environs*. Brussels, 1785.

Martens, Mina (ed), *Histoire de Bruxelles*. Toulouse: Privat, 1976.

Martiny, Victor-Gaston, *Bruxelles: architecture civile et militaire avant 1900*. Braine l'Alleud: J. M. Collet, 1992.

Mason, Antony, *Brussels: Bruges, Ghent, Antwerp*. London: Cadogan Guides, 1995.

Meers, Louis, *Promenades Art Nouveau Bruxelles*. Brussels: Éditions Racine, 1995.

Mols, R., *Bruxelles et les Bruxellois*, Louvain-Brussels: Éditions de la Société d'Études Morales, Sociales et Juridiques, 1961.

Monteyne, André, *Le monde flamand de Bruxelles*. Brussels: Vander, 1982.

Monteyne, André, *Les Bruxellois, un passé peu ordinaire*. Brussels: Centre de recherche et d'information socio-politiques, 1977.

Neirinckx, Hugo, *Literaire gids voor Brabant en Brussel*. Schoten: Hadewijch, 1986.

O'Malley, C. D., *Andreas Vesalius of Brussels*. Berkeley: University of California Press, 1964.

Pavy, Didier, *Les Belges*. Paris: Grasset, 1999.

Preszow, Gérard, *Bruxelles, lieu commun*. Brussels: Ercée, 1989.

Przybylski, Eddy, *Brel à Bruxelles*. Brussels: Le Roseau Vert, 2001.

Puttemans, Pierre & Hervé, Lucien, *Modern Architecture in Belgium*. Brussels: Vokaer, 1976.

Quaghebeur, Marc, *Balises pour l'histoire des lettres belges*. Brussels: Labor, 1998.

Quiévreux, Louis, *Dictionnaire du dialecte bruxellois*. [1951] Brussels: Libro-Sciences, 1985 (5th ed.).

Renieu, Lionel, *Histoire des théâtres de Bruxelles*. Paris: Duchartre & Van Buggenhout, 1928.

Robert, Yves, *et al, Bruxelles et sa région*. Tournai: Le Guide, La Renaissance du Livre: 2000.

Roberts-Jones, Philippe (ed), *Brussels: fin de siècle*. Cologne: Evergreen, 1999.

Séjournet, Donatienne & Halleux, Vincent, *Secluded Gardens and Nooks of Brussels*. Liège: Editions du Perron, 1996.

Sion, Georges, *Regards venus d'ailleurs sur Bruxelles et la Wallonie*. Brussels: Trois Arches, 1980.

Siraut, Marcel, *Bruxelles littéraire*. Brussels: Pré aux Sources, 1987.

Starck, O., *Gauloiseries Marolliennes*. Brussels: Lojipe, 1989.

Starck, O. & Claessens, L., *Dictionnaire Marollien-Français, Français-Marollien*. Brussels: SGDL, 1988.

Stengers, Jean (ed), *Bruxelles, croissance d'une capitale*, Antwerp: Fonds Mercator, 1979.

Swing, Elizabeth Sherman, *Bilingualism and Linguistic Separation in the Schools of Brussels*. Québec: International Center for Research on Bilingualism, 1980.

The Low Countries (series). Rekkem: Stichting Ons Erfdeel, 1993-.

Todd, Olivier, *Jacques Brel: une vie*. Paris: Laffont, 1984.

Treffers-Daller, Jeanine, *Mixing Two Languages: French-Dutch Contact in a Comparative Perspective*. Berlin: De Gruyter, 1994.

Uyttendaele, Marc (ed), *De la Belgique unitaire à l'Etat fédéral*. Brussels: Bruylant, 1996.

Vandeputte, O., Vincent, P., & Hermans, T., *Dutch* [1981]. Rekkem: Flemish-Netherlands Foundation, 1994.

Vanhamme, Marcel, *Bruxelles: de bourg rural à cité mondiale*. Brussels: Mercurius, 1968.

Van Istendael, Geert, *Arm Brussel*. Amsterdam/Antwerp: Uitgeverij Atlas, 1992.

Van Istendael, Geert, *Het Belgisch labyrint: wakker worden in een ander land*. Amsterdam, Antwerp: Arbeiderspers, 2001.

Van Nieuwenborgh, Marcel, *A Bruxelles: guide pratique et littéraire des itinéraires poétiques*. Brussels: Didier Hatier, 1990.

Van Waerebeek, Ruth, *Everybody Eats Well in Belgium Cookbook*. New York: Workman Publishing Company, 1996.

Verhavert, Cypriaan, *Van ketjes en kiekefretters: uit Brussels verleden*. Brussels: Office de Publicité: n.d.

Verhoeyen, Etienne, *La Belgique occupée*. Brussels: De Boeck Université, 1994.

Verniers, Louis, *Les transformations de Bruxelles et l'urbanisation de sa banlieue depuis 1795*, in *Annales de la société royale d'archéologie de Bruxelles*, tome 37, 1934, p.84-220.

Wauters, Alphonse, *Histoire des environs de Bruxelles*. 3 vols, Brussels:

Vanderauwera, 1850-1857.

Willinger, David, *Theatrical Gestures from the Belgian Avant-garde*. New York, New York Literary Forum, 1987.

Witte, Els & Baetens-Beardsmore, Hugo, *The Interdisciplinary Study of Urban Bilingualism in Brussels*. Clevedon (U.K.): Multilingual Matters, 1987.

Witte, Els; Craeybeekx, Jan; Meynen, Alain (eds), *The Political History of Belgium from 1830 onwards*. Brussels: VUB Press: 2000.

Witte, Els & Van Velthoven, Harry (eds), *Language and Politics: The Belgian case study in a historical perspective*. Brussels: VUB Press, 1999.

Zuckerman, Larry, *The Rape of Belgium*. New York: New York University Press, 2004.

Index of Literary & Historical Names

Index of Literary & Historical Names

Jacobs, Edgar P. 58-9, 95
Jacqmain, Émile 209
Jaquet, Joseph 22
Jeanne, Duchess of Brabant 12, 64, 161
Jeanne the Mad 67
John I, Duke of Brabant 12, 63, 64, 111
John II, Duke of Brabant 12
John III, Duke of Brabant 12, 57
John IV, Duke of Burgundy 65
John of Ruysbroeck 82-4
Jorn, Asger 109
Joseph II, Emperor of Austria 73, 120
Josephine, Empress 122
Joyce, James 132

Keersmaeker, Anne Teresa de 137
Kervijn De Marcke ten Driessche, Roger 182
Khnopff, Fernand 191
Kuyper, Eric de 80

Lafosse, Joachim 117
Lambert I, Count of Louvain 3
Lambert II, Duke of Brabant 3, 49, 63
Lambert le Bègue 5
Lanoo, Vincent 117
Lemmonier, Camille 26, 96, 140, 167, 177
Lemmonier, Maurice 209
Leopold I, King of the Belgians 25, 151
Leopold II, King of the Belgians 22, 55, 98, 152, 179, 196-200, 201
Leopold II, Emperor of Austria 120
Leopold III, King of the Belgians 210
Licas, Antoine 34
Ligne, Charles Joseph, Prince de 120
Louis XIV, King of France 102
Louis XVIII, King of France 122, 123, 124, 127
Louis de Male, Count of Flanders 12
Louise, Princess 201, 202
Louvain, Jean de 52
Lumumba, Patrice 199
Luther, Martin 84, 86

Maeterlinck, Maurice 139
Magritte, René 6, 45, 96, 105, 106-8

Malibran, La 136-7
Marguerite of Parma 88
Maria Theresa, Empress of Austria 71, 119, 120
Marie-Louise Bonaparte, Empress 122
Marlborough, John, Duke of 102
Marx, Karl 22, 37, 38, 109, 141
Mathilde, Princess 228
Max, Adolphe 32, 208-9
Maximilian, Emperor of Mexico 200
Melkebeke, Jacques van 53, 172, 186
Merckx, Édouard "Eddy" 99
Mertens, Pierre 223
Mesens, E. L. T. 7, 209
Metternich, Count 73
Meunier, Constantin 167
Michaux, Henri 204-5, 206
Mirbeau, Octave 9, 25, 26, 180
Mols, Roger 49
Mont, Pol de 140
Morgan, Lady Sydney 4, 6
Motley, John Lothrop 8
Mounesse, Maurice 182
Moustaki, Georges 29
Multatuli 149

Nerval, Gérard de 25
Newton, Thomas William 225
Ney, Marshal 124
Nijlen, Jan van 92, 93
Nizet, Henri 167
Noiret, Joseph 109
Norge, Geo 26, 141, 107, 209
Nothomb, Amélie 100
Nougé, Paul 6, 106, 107, 209
Nys, Jef 58

Offenbach, Jacques 142
Oistrakh, David 114
Orley, Bernard van 20

Pansaers, Clément 105-6, 140
Pascal, Blaise 165
Pastorana, Antoine 104
Périer, Odilon-Jean 203-4
Peter the Great 73
Philip II, King of Spain 20, 68-9, 87-8,

241

Index of Places & Landmarks

BRUSSELS